COMIDA CASERA

More Than 100 Vegan Recipes, from Traditional to Modern Mexican Dishes

Dora Ramírez

balance

New York Boston

Copyright © 2025 by Dora Ramírez
Cover design by Terri Sirma
Cover copyright © 2025 by Hachette Book Group, Inc.
Book design by Shubhani Sarkar, sarkardesignstudio.com
Food Photographs copyright © 2025 Dora Ramírez,
lifestyle photographs copyright © 2025 Andres Ibanez, and
copyright © 2025 Brandi Morgan Photography

Balance
Hachette Book Group
1290 Avenue of the Americas
New York, NY 10104
GCP-Balance.com
@GCPBalance

First Edition: March 2025

Balance is an imprint of Grand Central Publishing. The Balance name and logo are registered trademarks of Hachette Book Group, Inc.

The publisher is not responsible for websites (or their content) that are not owned by the publisher.

The Hachette Speakers Bureau provides a wide range of authors for speaking events. To find out more, go to hachettespeakersbureau.com or email HachetteSpeakers@hbgusa.com.

Balance books may be purchased in bulk for business, educational, or promotional use. For information, please contact your local bookseller or the Hachette Book Group Special Markets Department at special .markets@hbgusa.com.

Library of Congress Cataloging-in-Publication Data has been applied for.

ISBNs: 978-0-306-83281-9 (hardcover), 978-0-306-83282-6 (ebook)

Printed in China

APS

10 9 8 7 6 5 4 3 2 1

A mis padres, Dora y Noe, gracias por siempre ayudarme a cumplir mis sueños, sin ustedes ninguno hubiera sido posible.

To my three beautiful children, Tomasito, Karina, y Pio.
I love you more than you could ever imagine.
Ser su mamá es mi mayor logro.

CONTENTS

4

A FONDA BREAKFAST

5

STREET FOOD

6

MOLE FROM THE MARKET

7

COMIDA CASERA

LA TAMALERÍA

9

MODERN MEXICO

10

¡SALUD!

11

LA PANADERÍA AND LA PALETERÍA

INTRODUCTION

"Can't you make this more Mexican?!"

I watched in horror as my mom spit out a piece of tofu. She looked at me with betrayal in her eyes: How could I do this to her? I had left a block of tofu on the table in preparation for the meal I was going to make in my quest to convince her to go vegan. I walked away from the kitchen for only a second, a second in which my mom thought this glistening white block looked like a very fresh panela cheese. Yet it was her words of frustration that changed everything. She looked at me, as only a mother can, and uttered those words of frustration.

And that changed everything.

I was born in Acuña, Coahuila, a small town on the border of Texas and Mexico, where my family has operated a restaurant, Los Tacos Grill, for the last thirty-five years. I guess you could say I grew up in the business—the business of eating, that is—because up until it was time to go to college, I was not the least interested in cooking. By the time I was six, my mother stopped cooking at home and we ate all our family meals at the restaurant. I did my homework there after school, as a teenager I worked the cash register as punishment for my misdeeds, and as a family we all helped out at big catering events, dishing out food at company picnics and serving weddings.

After high school I was on a spiritual quest to discern my vocation in life (I almost became a nun!) and spent a year in Mexico City as a missionary. There I experienced Mexican cuisine in a way I never had before. For the first time I tried tortillas made with blue corn nixtamal, quesadillas filled with zucchini blossoms cooked with epazote, earthy huitlacoche, and chiles in nogada. I got to experience firsthand the gorditas de la villa and the antojitos of the floating trajineras of Xochimilco. One of my responsibilities was to help out in the kitchen, and this is what opened my eyes to the magic of cooking. And it did seem like magic to me, because I marveled constantly at the ease with which the house cook took the scarce ingredients available and turned them into chilaquiles smothered in a spicy tomato sauce, sopa de fideo topped with crema, and enfrijoladas bursting with stewed calabacitas.

I returned home and enrolled in the Culinary Institute of America in New York. I graduated in 2006, ready to conquer the food world.

Fast-forward to that fateful day in my kitchen. I had made it my life's mission to veganize all of my family recipes, and between the daily tasks of raising three wonderful children, I spent every minute I could doing just that on my recipe site, Dora's Table.

WHY VEGAN?

I know if you picked up this book it's because you are at least veg curious or are trying to incorporate more vegetables into your diet, but maybe you're not quite ready to make the full jump to veganism. I get it, believe me. I was the last person in the world you would think would go vegan. After culinary school I fell in love with cheese—stinky, oozing French cheeses and semisoft aged sheep's milk Spanish cheese. I also took pride in the fact that I would eat everything from menudo (cow stomach soup) to grasshoppers. Going vegan was not a choice I made lightly.

My main motivation was a health problem that had plagued me for years. With each passing year my pain and discomfort grew, and doctors prescribed me more and more medications. After a friend hounded me for weeks to watch the documentary *Forks Over Knives*, which goes into detail about the health benefits of living a plant-based lifestyle, I decided to give it a try. I failed miserably. I simply couldn't do it, I felt the sacrifice was too great, and I saw no improvement in my health. It wasn't until I was able to do it for forty days straight one Lent that I began to see a cloud lift. My pain diminished and eventually disappeared. I never looked back.

Even though health was what brought me to veganism, there are many more reasons to stop eating meat, and I discovered those as well along the way. Before going vegan, I already knew about the unspeakable cruelty that takes place at factory farms, to both the animals and the workers who process them, but I had convinced myself that buying organic or grass-fed meat was enough. But something happened after months of not eating meat that I didn't expect: I began to see those foods for what they really are: animals, intelligent creatures who deserve our compassion. Later I learned about the severe ecological costs of that same factory farming and its contribution to the precipitation of climate change. All of this reinforced my decision to stay vegan, and I can now say with certainty that I made the right choice. I hope you will consider it too.

DECOLONIZING YOUR DIET

I paced around the room more times than I can count. I was panicking. A video recipe post I had made for a vegan cream cheese brand was going viral and not in a good way. The video was a step-by-step tutorial on how to make a blackberry and cream cheese tamal, a contemporary flavor combination very popular in Mexico City. Initially the video was shown to my audience and all the comments were positive, but then the video became popular with the Mexican American community, who was deeply insulted by my video. They saw it as an attack on Mexican culture, our food, and our traditions. Some of them didn't know sweet tamales are actually a thing in Mexico, and were horrified at the thought of a sweet version of their beloved tamales. Others were adamant that Mexican food without animal products was not Mexican food. I didn't know how to respond to or handle all that negativity so I had to take a two-week break from social media, but during that time I was able to reflect on the impact of colonization on our community. How is it that in only one or two generations our culture has become diluted to the point of not recognizing something as ancestral as sweet tamales?

Decolonizing your diet simply means a return to our ancestral foodways. It is recognizing that the loss of that knowledge has caused us harm, and that we need to provide ways for our community to access those foodways by addressing issues like food deserts that are prevalent in low-income communities of color. Before the arrival of the Spanish in 1519, the basis of Mexican cuisine was an agricultural practice called la milpa. The milpa was the intercropping of corn (the main crop) along with beans, chiles, squash, and tomatoes. The herbs and greens that grew around the crops were called quelites and were also consumed along with insects and even the fungus (huitlacoche) that grew on the corn. It was and still is an ecologically sustainable system that is nutritionally complementary. Additionally, the diet was complemented by wild animals like fish, turkey, rabbit, armadillo, and iguana, and insects like grasshoppers and ant eggs. When the Spanish arrived, they brought

My goal has always been to shout from the rooftops that it is possible to be vegan and Mexican. That it is possible to live a compassionate life while honoring and celebrating your culture. Every day I receive messages from people who for health reasons can no longer eat meat, and from others who are passionate about animal rights or the health of our planet and who thought that by giving up meat they had to give up their abuelita's pozole, their mom's sopa fideo, or tamales at Christmas. Food is such an important part of Mexican culture. It is an expression of our traditions, a catalyst for family unity, and the centerpiece of all our celebrations. We are deeply rooted in it; it defines who we are. At the heart of this is our comida casera (home cooking). Every family brings to the table their own traditions and their own way of preparing the meals that nourish us, and this book is a reflection of mine. It honors traditional Mexican flavors and techniques but relies on the immense world of plants to do so.

It is structured as a journey through key culinary landmarks that highlight the regionality and diversity of the cuisine. We start at home with the vegan Mexican pantry, a walk-through of the most important ingredients and tools we will be using. This is followed by the Indigenous kitchen, the basis of Mexican cuisine, with a Thickened Squash Vine Soup. Then we pay a visit to la fonda (the mom-and-pop restaurant) for Red Chilaquiles, the street vendor for Al Pastor Tacos, and the mercado (the market) for Mole Poblano. We continue with a visit to try Mom's comida casera for Swiss Enchiladas, the tamalería (tamales store) for Sonoran Red Chile Tamales, and then to modern Mexican restaurants for Huitlacoche Crepes. We toast with a glass of Cantaloupe Seed Horchata from the ¡Salud! (cheers) chapter before ending at the panadería (the bakery) and paletería (ice cream parlor) for a dessert of Tres Leches Cake and Strawberries and Cream Paletas. Some of the recipes are very traditional, some are veganized versions of meaty classics, and some are a reflection of my time working in professional kitchens. I hope this book brings you joy and inspires in you a desire to cook and learn more about Mexican cuisine.

not only the destruction of thousands of lives but also the suppression of the Indigenous religions, customs, medicinal knowledge, and cuisine. Corn was seen as inferior to wheat, and the wild animals were replaced by domesticated pigs and cows brought from Spain. The effects of this colonialism transformed the Mexican diet from one based on the plants from the milpa to a meat-centered cuisine. This, and the introduction of highly processed food, has plagued our community with diabetes, heart disease, and a deep ignorance of our ancestral foods like the necuhtamalli, a tamal sweetened with agave honey eaten by the Nahuas of Mesoamerica and still prepared to this day in Quitupan, Jalisco.

There's a much longer discussion about this that goes beyond this book, so I encourage you to continue your own education. If you want to learn more about how you can decolonize your diet, I recommend the book *Decolonize Your Diet* by Luz Calvo and Catriona Rueda Esquibel.

THE VEGAN MEXICAN PANTRY

My pantry is always on the verge of overflowing, yet it is a beautiful reflection of our family's cultural background where dried chiles and achiote paste sit next to a jar of gochujang and a 15-pound bag of medium-grain rice from Korea.

It brings me so much joy that popular knowledge of Mexican cuisine and its ingredients has grown so much in the last ten years, but there are still some ingredients that you might not be so familiar with and that could be difficult to find depending on where you live. So let me walk you through the essentials of the vegan Mexican pantry and all the ingredients you will need to make the recipes in this book, as well as basic cooking techniques and equipment.

In the Resources section of this book (page 309), I have listed where you can source some of these unique ingredients. While those ingredients are important to the recipes, I have also included suggestions for substitutions in the recipe and in the ingredient glossary that follows to help you delve fully into the complexity and beauty of Mexican cuisine.

INGREDIENTS

Achiote paste is a brick-red paste made from ground dried annatto seeds. It is a very important ingredient in the cuisines of southeast Mexico, specifically Yucatán, where it is used to make soups, marinades, tamales, and even chorizo. The paste is known as recado rojo there, but it differs from the paste in other states because it is spiced with black pepper, oregano, and cloves. You can find it at your local Mexican and Central American market or online.

Agar-agar is a plant-based gelatin used to make jellies and puddings and to thicken sauces in vegan cooking. It comes in powdered and flake form. I use the powdered form. You can find it at Asian grocery stores or online.

Amaranth (amaranto), also known as alegría (joy), is an herbaceous plant endemic to Mexico that has been cultivated since pre-Hispanic times. The small, cream-colored seeds are used to make breads and atoles and, when puffed, to make a candy also called alegría. The leaves are called quintoniles and are used to make soups, quesadillas, and stews. I usually puff my own amaranth seeds, but you can purchase them already puffed. You can find them at Mexican candy stores (dulcerías), where they usually sell them in bulk, or online.

Anise seed is a small greenish-brown seed of the anise plant with a characteristic sweet, aromatic, and licorice-like flavor. It is used to flavor pan dulce, mole, and syrups for buñuelos. You can find it at most grocery stores.

Aquafaba is a fancy name for the liquid in a can of chickpeas. It is as simple as it sounds. Drain the chickpeas and reserve the liquid, which is what you will be using for the recipe. Aquafaba is used as a substitute for egg whites, since it acts as a binder, but you can also whip it to create a foam that when added to baked goods gives them structure and leavening. Be sure to buy low-sodium or no-salt chickpeas when you are using aquafaba for dessert purposes.

Avocado leaf (hoja de aguacate) is an army-green color and has a strong anise-like flavor. These leaves can be used fresh or dried to make stews, beans, moles, and soups from the states of Chiapas, Oaxaca, and Veracruz. You can find them at Mexican markets or online.

Avocado oil is extracted from the pulp of avocados. It is the oil I prefer when cooking because I like the mild flavor and the high smoke point. It is a little pricey, so if you are looking for a more budget-friendly oil, I suggest canola oil.

Ayocote morado bean is the biggest variety of bean in Mexico. Although it has a thick, bright purple skin, the bean becomes extremely creamy when cooked, while maintaining its structure and bite, giving it a hearty texture that makes it a great meat substitute. The purple variety is used in soups and stews in the central states of Hidalgo, Tlaxcala, and Estado de México and in Mexico City. There is also a black variety that is used in Oaxaca in mole coloradito. These beans are difficult to find outside of Mexico, but you can purchase them online.

Banana leaf is the large green leaf of the banana plant. In the central and southern Mexican states, it is used to wrap tamales, and to bake meat or vegetables in an underground oven (pib). You can find them fresh at your local Mexican market or frozen in the freezer section of your grocery store.

Ceylon cinnamon, also known as true cinnamon, comes from the bark of the *Cinnamomum verum* tree, which grows in Sri Lanka. It is less potent than cassia cinnamon and has a thin, papery texture that easily crumbles. This is particularly important, because some recipes call for blending the cinnamon stick with the sauce, and that's not possible with cassia cinnamon. You can find it at your local Mexican market or in the Mexican section of your grocery store.

Chamoy is a spicy and sweet sauce made from pickled dried apricots and dried chiles. It is most commonly used in desserts—drizzled on fruit, raspados, and even potato chips. You can find it at Mexican candy stores or the Mexican section of your grocery store.

Chaya

Chaya, also known as tree spinach, is a big leafy shrub native to the state of Yucatán and parts of Central America. The leaves are large, maple-shaped, and bright green and have a mild spinach-like flavor. Chaya was domesticated by the Mayans and is used to this day in the states of Yucatán, Chiapas, Tabasco, and Veracruz to make soups, stews, tamales, and aguas frescas, and for medicinal purposes. It is hard to find outside Mexico, but check your local Mexican market, or you can substitute spinach.

Chayote is a green, pear-shaped squash with white flesh, a thin skin, a crisp texture, and a mild flavor similar to a cross between cucumber and apple. It can be eaten raw or cooked and is used throughout Mexico to make soups and stews, or it is stuffed and baked. It is easily found in your local grocery store or Mexican market.

Chepil (chipilín), a leguminous plant, is native to the southern states of Oaxaca, Chiapas, and Tabasco. Its leaves and shoots are used as quelites (wild greens) to make soups, tamales, and stews. The flavor is reminiscent of a cross between spinach and purslane. It is difficult to find outside of Mexico, but you can substitute pea shoots, watercress, or purslane.

Chickpea flour, made by grinding dried chickpeas into a fine powder, is used as a thickener, binder, or flour substitute in gluten-free baking. I like to use it as a binder, but also because it adds an eggy flavor to dishes. It is often found in the gluten-free section of the grocery store.

Chiles are an irreplaceable component of Mexican cuisine. They were cultivated along with corn, tomatoes, and beans by the Indigenous civilizations of Mexico approximately 8,000 years ago. In Mexico, chiles equal flavor, and what better way to express this than the popular saying "¡Sin chile no sabe!" (Without chile there is no flavor), and that certainly holds true for many Mexicans. Chiles not only add heat to dishes, but each one has a characteristic flavor and aroma that defines certain dishes like Beluga Lentil Chiles en Nogada (page 253).

I realize not everyone has the same tolerance for chile, so if you are looking to decrease or increase the spice in the recipes, here are a few things you can do. If you want to reduce the heat, the easiest way to do it is to reduce the number of chiles. If you are working with dried chiles, you can omit the very spicy ones like chile de árbol. If you want to keep the flavor of the chile but with less heat, you can remove all the seeds and ribs from the chiles. If that is still too hot, soak the fresh chiles in cold water for ten minutes, then rinse and use as directed.

To increase the heat with fresh chiles, the best way is to leave in the seeds and ribs and increase the number of chiles in the recipe. When working with dried chiles, adding a couple of spicier chiles, such as chile de árbol or chile piquín, increases the heat and doesn't affect the flavor too much.

I also recommend that if you are working with very spicy chiles or are not used to working with chiles, you wear gloves and wash your hands very well. Rubbing your eyes after working with chiles is the worst!

TYPES OF CHILES

FRESH CHILES	DRIED VERSION
Poblano chile: Large green chile that is stuffed or cut into strips. It needs to be roasted and peeled before use. It has a mild to medium heat and a smoky flavor.	**Ancho chile:** Large chile with a brick-red color, mild heat, and a rich, almost plumlike flavor. **Mulato chile:** Large chile with an intense dark red color, mild heat, and a smoky, chocolaty flavor.
Jalapeño chile: Small to medium-size green or red chile with medium to high heat and a fresh bell pepper flavor.	**Chipotle meco:** Small to medium-size chile with a light brown color, medium-high heat, and a grassy flavor. **Morita chile:** Small to medium-size chile with a dark red color, medium heat, and a smoky, berrylike flavor.
Serrano chile: Small, bright green pepper with medium-high heat and an intense bell pepper flavor.	**Dried serrano:** Small chile with a deep maroon color, medium-high heat, and a fruity, mildly smoky flavor.
Chile de árbol: Small, elongated, bright red chile with high heat and a fruity taste with smoky undertones.	**Dried chile de árbol:** Small, elongated, bright red chile with high heat and a smoky, nutty flavor.
Mirasol chile: Medium-size, conical chile with a bright red color, mild heat, and a fresh, fruity flavor.	**Guajillo chile:** Medium-size, elongated chile with a reddish-brown color, mild heat, and a sweet, fruity flavor.
Chilaca chile: Medium-size, elongated, dark green chile with mild heat and an earthy flavor.	**Pasilla chile:** Thin, elongated chile with a dark red, almost black color, mild to medium heat, and a smoky, fruity, and raisin-like flavor.
Piquín chile: Tiny oval chile with very high heat.	**Dried chile piquín:** Tiny, bright red chile with very high heat and a nutty, earthy flavor.
Chile tuxta (tusta): Small chile that can be green, red, or orange, with medium to high heat and a smoky but sweet flavor. This is a rare chile native to Oaxaca.	**Dried chile tuxta:** Small, elongated chile with a deep red color, medium to high heat, and a smoky but sweet flavor. Can substitute chipotle meco.
Chile güero (Hungarian wax pepper): Medium-size light yellow chile with mild to medium heat and sweet bell pepper flavor.	**Dried chile güero:** Medium-size, elongated chile with a deep red color, low to high heat, and a smoky but sweet flavor.
Habanero chile: Small orange or green chile, with extremely high heat and a fruity flavor. It is used extensively in Yucatecan cuisine.	**Dried habanero chile:** Small reddish chile with extremely high heat and a fruity, citrusy flavor.
Anaheim chile: Medium-long green pepper with mild heat and a sweet bell pepper flavor.	**California chile:** Medium-long maroon chile with mild heat and a sweet flavor. Can be used as a substitute for guajillo chile.
Chile chilhuacle negro: Medium-size, bell pepper–shaped chile with a dark brown color, medium heat, and a sweet and fruity flavor.	**Chile chilhuacle negro:** Small, pear-shaped chile with medium heat and a chocolaty, smoky, dried-fruit flavor. Native to Oaxaca, it is a famous ingredient in mole negro.

Jalapeño Chile

Poblano Chile

Habanero Chile

Güero Chile

Serrano Chile

Anaheim Chile

Chile Chilhuacle Negro

Guajillo Chile

Pasilla Chile

Morita Chile

Mulato Chile

Chipotle Meco

Ancho Chile

Arbol Chile

Chipotles en adobo are dried chipotle chiles marinated in a paste of dried chiles, piloncillo, vinegar, cloves, pepper, garlic, salt, and marjoram. They are sold canned at Mexican markets or the Mexican section of your grocery store.

00 ("double zero") flour is a very finely ground Italian flour made from the endosperm of the wheat kernel. It is so fine it resembles cornstarch in texture. It is commonly used in Italy to make pizza dough and softer pasta shapes like ravioli because it provides elasticity to the dough and results in delicate pasta. You can find it at specialty food stores.

Dried corn husks are one of the many tamal wrappers available. They are sold in bags at Mexican markets or in the Mexican section of your local grocery store. Sometimes they have dirt or dried corn silk on them, so it is very important to rinse them. Be sure to check for mold; if a corn husk has black spots, discard it.

Dried dent corn/native corn (maíz criollo) is dried field corn that has been cultivated and bred selectively by small groups of farmers in Mexico for generations. This corn is a reflection of its environment, so each variety has its own characteristics and identity. Outside of Mexico it is known as heirloom corn and can be purchased online to make masa for tortillas or tamales.

Epazote, an aromatic herb native to Mexico and Central America, has been used since pre-Hispanic times. It has 2- to 3-inch-long (5 to 7.5 cm) flat green leaves with serrated edges, a strong medicinal aroma, and a distinct flavor reminiscent of oregano, thyme, pine, and citrus. It is used to flavor stews, salsas, soups, and moles. It is well known for its gas-relief properties, so it is most often used to cook beans. You can find fresh epazote at Mexican markets or in dried form online. You can substitute a combination of cilantro and oregano.

Fava beans (habas), also known as broad beans, are usually available in the spring and early summer. They are light green and oval shaped, with long green pods. Fresh pods are sold at farmers' markets, specialty food stores, Mexican markets, or online. Dried beans are sold at Mexican markets or your local grocery store. They are very popular in Mexico City, where they are used to make tlacoyos, salads, and soups.

Fresh corn is quite different across countries, which will affect some recipes. American sweet corn, which is what is widely available in US grocery stores, is lower in starch and higher in sugar than Mexican corn. Mexican corn, sometimes known as field corn, has a higher starch content and is denser than American corn. Mexican corn takes longer to cook, so if you live in Mexico, you will need to adjust the cooking times according to the recipe notes.

Hibiscus (jamaica), a flowering plant native to Africa but cultivated in Mexico and Central America, is known for its large, colorful flowers. The flower's calyxes are dried and used to make teas, aguas frescas, margaritas, ponche, and tacos. Hibiscus has an acidic, cranberry-like tart flavor with floral notes. You can find it at your local Mexican market or online.

Huitlacoche, also known as cuitlacoche or corn smut, is a fungus that grows on young corn. It looks like a conglomeration of swollen, grayish-black bulbs and has an earthy mushroom taste with a sour undertone. It is considered a delicacy in central Mexico, where it is used to make quesadillas, mole, and soups and to fill crepes. You can find it canned at Mexican markets.

Huitlacoche

Ibes is a small white bean cultivated on the peninsula of Yucatán and used in soups, stews, and pipián. Ibe soup is often eaten during funerals because it is thought that the white of the beans helps the departed soul find its purity. They are hard to find outside of Yucatán, but you can substitute other small white beans, such as alubia blanca, caballero, or navy beans.

Jackfruit (yaca) is a very large, green, spiky tropical tree fruit native to Southeast Asia. When it is unripe, its stringy meat-like flesh is used as a meat substitute. You can find it canned in brine or fresh at your local grocery store or Asian grocery store. I like to use the canned version because cutting and prepping it when fresh is time-consuming and messy.

Jalapeños en escabeche are jalapeño chiles pickled in a brine of vinegar, oil, oregano, thyme, bay leaf, garlic, and onion. They are sold canned at Mexican markets or the Mexican section of your grocery store.

Jicama is a tuberous root vegetable with a thick, brown outer skin and crisp flesh. Jicama is native to Mexico and has been eaten since pre-Hispanic times. It tastes like a cross between a pear and a potato—a little bit sweet, but hearty. It is mostly eaten raw in salads, with chile powder and lime, but it can also be cooked. It is usually available in the tropical fruit section of the grocery store.

Kala namak, also known as Himalayan black salt, is a sulfurous mineral salt mined in the areas surrounding the Himalayas. It is used in Indian cooking but is also popular for vegan recipes as it adds an eggy flavor to dishes such as tofu scramble.

Kappa carrageenan powder is a food additive derived from red seaweed that is used as a thickener and emulsifier in vegan cooking. Food-grade carrageenan comes in powdered form and can be found online or at health food stores.

Masa is dough made from nixtamalized corn. Nixtamalization is the process of soaking dried field corn in an alkaline solution, made by mixing slaked lime and water; it is then drained, rinsed, and ground. This process improves the flavor, makes it easier to grind, and draws out essential nutrients. The dough that results is called masa, but in Mexico it is simply known as nixtamal. This masa is used to make tortillas, tamales, gorditas, and many other corn-based appetizers. You can purchase fresh masa at your local tortillería or Mexican market, or you can make it at home. If you can't find it, you can substitute masa harina.

Masa harina is nixtamalized corn flour or, in other words, dehydrated masa. The corn goes through the same process as for fresh masa, but it is dried first, then ground. Alternatively, the fresh masa is made and dried, then ground into a fine powder. Masa harina is widely available at grocery stores and Mexican markets. If you are looking for high quality non-GMO masa harina, see the Resources section (page 309).

Mexican hot chocolate tablillas are chocolate disks made by drying and toasting cacao beans, then grinding them with sugar, spices, or nuts. Tablillas are mainly used to make hot chocolate by dissolving them in water or milk or to sweeten mole. You can find commercial varieties at Mexican markets, but I recommend you use artisanal brands without additives (see Resources, page 309).

Mexican pepperleaf (hoja santa) is an aromatic herb native to Mexico, Central America, and South America with large (up to 9 inches/23 cm), thin, heart-shaped green leaves. It has a flavor reminiscent of anise, black pepper, and basil. Pepperleaf is used to make soups, tamales, stews, and moles. You can find it at Mexican markets or dried online. You can substitute a combination of chopped fennel leaves and basil.

Mushrooms have been an integral part of the Indigenous diet in Mexico since before the Spanish conquest. They were used for daily meals, medicinal purposes, and celebrations and rituals for their hallucinogenic properties. In Náhuatl (the language of the Mexica and Toltec civilizations), mushrooms were called nanácatl, which means "meat," and it is precisely because of that meaty texture that mushrooms make a great substitute in vegan cooking. Today, mushrooms still hold an important place in the local cuisine, and it is estimated that there are almost 200,000 different species in Mexico, of which 320 have been documented as being used for cooking. Mushrooms are my favorite meat substitute, so I use several varieties of them in the recipes that follow. Some are easier to find than others, but you can substitute any mushroom that is available to you.

Amanita basii/bas' Caesar are brown to reddish mushrooms with yellow flesh and are native to the pine and oak forests of Estado de México and Oaxaca. Their common name is enbeyupe or red mushroom. They are one of the most appreciated mushrooms in Oaxaca for their meaty flavor, aroma, and characteristic color and are eaten grilled, in soups, and in quesadillas. They are difficult to find outside of Mexico, but you can substitute fresh or dried lobster mushrooms.

Cremini, or brown button mushrooms, are commonly found at US grocery stores. They are the more mature version of white button mushrooms, which means they have a richer flavor. These are my go-to mushrooms because they are the most widely available.

Dried snow fungus, also known as white fungus, is a white wood ear mushroom that grows on the bark of dead tree branches and is used in Asian cuisine and traditional Chinese medicine. When rehydrated, it has a jellylike texture similar to tripe. You can find it at Asian grocery stores or online.

King oyster, also known as king trumpet mushrooms, are large mushrooms (2 inches/5 cm in diameter and up to 8 inches/20 cm long) with a brown cap and a white stalk. They are very versatile, as you can shred them to make shredded "meat" or cut them into rounds to make vegan scallops. You can find them at Asian grocery stores or specialty food markets.

Oyster mushrooms are named after their oyster-shaped caps and short stems, and are available year-round at farmers' markets or Asian grocery stores. They are a great shredded meat substitute because you can pull the caps into strands that crisp up when cooked.

Yellowfoot are trumpet-shaped, yellow-brown mushrooms native to the pine and oak forests of Oaxaca and Chiapas. They are commonly known as patitas de pollo and have a deep, smoky, rich flavor. They start sprouting in August but are more abundant in September. They are traditionally used in soups, yellow mole, and empanadas. You can substitute fresh or dried chanterelles.

Nopal is the common name used to refer to several varieties of the *Opuntia* cactus. The cacti have flat, tender paddles that are covered in spines and release a slime when cut and cooked. The flavor is a cross between okra and asparagus, with a citrusy undertone. You can find the paddles sold whole with the spines, whole without the spines, or already cut with the spines removed at Mexican markets. I like to buy the paddles whole without the spines so I can cut them to the shape I prefer. If you can't find fresh nopales, you can use jarred nopales in brine; just make sure to drain and rinse them before use.

Nopal de castilla/nopal grueso is a very large cactus with paddles that can grow as big as 23 inches (58 cm) long and 1 inch (2.5 cm) thick. They are native to Oaxaca and consumed primarily grilled or in soup. They are hard to find outside of Mexico, but you can substitute the regular nopales found at your local Mexican grocery store.

Nutritional yeast is a deactivated form of baker's yeast commonly used in vegan cooking to mimic the flavor of cheese. It tastes nutty and savory and is a rich source of vitamin B_{12}. It is available in powdered and flake form. You can find it at health food stores and the gluten-free section of the grocery store.

Pepita menuda

Pipitza (pipicha) is a quelite (edible wild plant) with long, thin, blue-green leaves that are similar to dill. Pipitza has a strong flavor of dill, marjoram, cilantro, and mint and is mainly used in Oaxacan cuisine to make white rice and sopa de guías. It is hard to find outside of Mexico, but you can substitute a mixture of cilantro, marjoram, and mint.

Porcini mushroom powder has the meaty, rich, pungent flavor of fresh porcini mushrooms. I use this powder when I'm trying to infuse a dish with a "porky" taste or add umami. If you can't find it, you can use any mushroom powder.

Pumpkin seeds (pepitas de calabaza) are the seeds of several varieties of pumpkin that are extracted, dried, and used to make candy, mole, soups, and stews. They are of vital importance to Mexican cuisine, especially in the central and southern states of Yucatán, Veracruz, and Oaxaca. In the US you usually find them already hulled, at Mexican markets or your local grocery store, labeled as raw pumpkin seeds. They are small and a dark army green.

Pepita menuda (chinchilla) is a small seed from the *Cucurbita moschata* (small native squash known as k'uum) used in Yucatecan cuisine. It is most often sold ground at Mexican markets. You can substitute regular hulled pumpkin seeds (pepitas).

Piloncillo, also known as panela, is an unrefined whole cane sugar, usually sold in cone form. It has a flavor reminiscent of molasses and is used to make pan dulce, desserts, and drinks. You can find it at Mexican markets or the Mexican section of the grocery store. Piloncillo is very hard and takes a while to melt if added to a sauce whole, so I prefer to break it up into pieces. To do this I whack it with a hammer or a heavy skillet (please be careful when doing this!).

Pink pine nuts are native to north-central Mexico, specifically the state of Hidalgo, from the *Pinus cembroides* tree. These rose-colored pine nuts have a sweet, aromatic flavor and a firm texture, and are used to make candy, cakes, salads, desserts, and mole rosa. They are hard to find outside of Mexico, but you can substitute regular pine nuts.

Quelites (edible wild plants) is a blanket term for edible wild plants eaten throughout Mexico. This includes but is not limited to quintoniles (typically amaranth), verdolagas (purslane), chaya (tree spinach), squash vines, radish greens, huazontle (lamb's quarters), and the garbanzo plant. Currently over 350 different plants are considered quelites in Mexico. They are consumed for their nutritional value and taste, and have been an integral part of the Mexican diet since before the Spanish conquest. The earliest recorded mention of quelites is in *Historia General de la Cosas de la Nueva España* written by Fray Bernardino de Sahagún in 1577, where he mentions more than 60 wild greens consumed by the Nahua civilization. In the US, purslane, radish greens, Swiss chard, and watercress are easy to find and can be used in this book whenever quelites are called for.

Quintoniles is a term given to several species of quelites eaten mostly in central Mexico. The most common one is amaranth, whose leaves and stems are consumed raw or in tacos, stews, soups, empanadas, or quesadillas. Swiss chard makes a great quintonil substitute.

Salt when called for in the recipes in this book should be iodized table salt. If you use sea salt, Himalayan pink salt, or kosher salt, you will need to adjust the salt measurements in the recipes. These measurements are a starting place, as everyone's salt tolerance is different, and I know some of you may have to limit your salt intake for health reasons. Please remember to always season according to your preference, and taste the food during the cooking process.

Semolina flour is a coarse, light yellow durum wheat flour that is high in protein and gluten, which makes it ideal for making pasta. The high gluten makes the dough more elastic and helps it keep its shape during cooking. Semolina is also used to make bread and pizza dough. You can find it in specialty food stores or online.

Slaked lime (calcium hydroxide) is a key ingredient in the nixtamalization process for corn. You can find it in powdered form online, but make sure it's food-grade.

Soy curls are an all-natural alternative to meat made from minimally processed whole soybeans. They are non-GMO, which means that they are as close to a whole food as you can get for a meat substitute. They are a great alternative to chicken, beef, and pork. The most popular brand is Butler, which you can find at natural food stores or online.

Tamarind is the fruit of a leguminous tree native to Africa. It is a brown, elongated bean pod with a hard exterior and a soft flesh that contains seeds. Tart and sweet with caramel undertones, it is very common throughout Mexico, where it is used to make chile-covered candy, aguas frescas, and cocktails. You can find it in Mexican or Asian markets.

Tapioca flour, also known as tapioca starch, is a fine white flour made from the starch of the cassava plant. It is used in gluten-free baking to add crispness to baked goods and as a thickener in savory applications. You can find it in the gluten-free section of the grocery store.

Tequesquite is a mineral salt collected from lagoons and lakes from the Valley of Mexico. It has been used as a leavener, a seasoning salt, and an aid in the process of nixtamalization and fermentation since pre-Hispanic times. It is commonly used to make the masa for tamales light and tender. You can find it at your local Mexican grocery.

Tofu is my second-favorite meat substitute, after mushrooms. It is also known as soybean curd and is made by curdling fresh soy milk, then pressing it into blocks. There are silken (soft), firm, and extra-firm varieties available at your local grocery store or Asian market. Tofu is packaged in water to keep it fresh, so I recommend you press the tofu, either in a tofu press or between two plates with a heavy object on top, to squeeze out the excess water. This allows the tofu to better absorb the sauce it is marinated or cooked in.

Tomatillos are small, bright green tomatoes covered in a papery husk. Native to Mexico, they are highly acidic with sweet undertones, and can be eaten raw or cooked. Tomatillos are most commonly used to make salsa verde or as a flavor component in stews and soups. You can find them fresh at your local Mexican market or grocery store. They are also sold canned.

TVP (textured vegetable protein) is a processed form of soybeans (the protein is separated from the whole soybeans) used as a meat substitute. TVP has the texture of ground beef but no real flavor itself. This is actually a good thing because it means that it absorbs the flavor of whatever marinade or seasoning you are using.

THE VEGAN MEXICAN PANTRY

Vegan bouillon comes in powdered, paste, or cube form. It is a great substitute for Knorr Suiza, a common chicken or beef bouillon used in Mexican home cooking. I like to use it when trying to mimic meaty flavor. You can find it at many grocery stores, specialty food stores, and online.

White miso, also known as yellow miso, is a soybean paste fermented with koji (rice cultivated by fungus). It is commonly used in Japanese cuisine, but in vegan cooking it is used to add umami to dishes. It is mild and sweet, and a yellowish-brown color. You can find it at Asian markets or specialty food stores.

Xoconostle is a sour prickly pear native to Mexico that is famous for its use in mole de olla. It is also used in salsas, stews, salads, and candies. It is green when unripe and turns light orange-pink as it matures. You can find it fresh or dried at your local Mexican market or you can purchase it dried online.

Young squash vines are the young, tender vines of the squash or chayote plant. The leaves are tender and used as greens, and the stems are cut and used as a vegetable. In Mexico they are sold in markets in bunches and are used to make soups and stews or served in mole. In the US, you will have to grow your own, or talk to the vendors at your local farmers' market. You can substitute Swiss chard, using both the leaves and the stems.

Yuba, also known as tofu skin or bean curd skin, is the thin skin that forms on the top of soy milk when it boils. It is often used as a meat substitute in Chinese and Japanese cuisine because of its chewy texture. You can find it fresh, dried, or frozen in Asian markets, specialty food stores, or online.

Zucchini blossom (flor de calabaza) is the edible flower of the Cucurbitaceae family of plants, which includes squash, pumpkin, zucchini, and gourds. It is eaten raw in salads, cooked in soups and quesadillas, or stuffed and fried. You can find zucchini blossoms during the rainy months of June to October at farmers' markets. You can also find them canned, but I prefer to use them fresh.

EQUIPMENT

There are traditional cooking tools used in Mexican cuisine, like the molcajete and the tortilla press, but they are not absolutely necessary. Modern appliances go a long way in making cooking easier and faster, and I certainly take advantage of that, but there is a sort of magic in using the same tools that have been used for thousands of years to grind corn and make tortillas.

Circulator, also known as a sous-vide machine, is a small immersion cooker that heats and circulates water to a specific temperature. It is used in sous-vide cooking, which is a cooking technique that involves vacuum sealing food, then placing it in a water bath at a precise temperature. If you don't have a circulator for sous-vide cooking, I suggest an alternative cooking method in the recipe notes.

Comal is a flat, circular griddle used to cook tortillas or toast chiles and seeds. The Indigenous civilizations of pre-Columbian Mexico used clay comales, which were called comalli in Náhuatl and xamach in Mayan, to cook their tortillas. Today the comal remains an important part of Mexican cuisine, but clay comales are not as common because they are fragile and difficult to transport. Instead, cast iron and aluminum have replaced the more traditional clay comal. If you don't have a comal, you can use a heavy-bottomed skillet instead.

Metate is a rectangular stone with three legs paired with a cylindrical stone called a metlapil; it is used to grind chiles, corn, mole, and chocolate. It has been used by the Indigenous civilizations of Mexico since before the Spanish conquest. It is not so common in modern kitchens, where it has been replaced by a blender or electric grinder, but is still so vital in Indigenous cooking that it is often given as a wedding present or is a very precious family heirloom.

Molcajete is a mortar made from basalt (volcanic rock). It is a tool that has been used in Mexico since before the Spanish conquest and is still used to this day to grind ingredients, but mostly to make salsa. A salsa made in the molcajete is called salsa molcajeteada. The pestle is called a tejolote. If you don't have a molcajete, you can use a blender instead.

Pasta machine is a manual or automatic kitchen tool used to roll out pasta into thin sheets. It consists of two stainless steel rollers with adjustable settings. If you don't have a pasta machine, you can use a rolling pin instead.

Tamal steamer (vaporera) is a large steamer pot used to cook tamales. The most common ones are made from aluminum and have a metal grate with holes that serve as the steamer rack, lid, and handles. It makes cooking a large quantity of tamales easier, but any pot with a steamer insert will work.

Tortilla press is a tool used to flatten the dough for tortillas. It can be made of cast iron, wood, stainless steel, or aluminum. To use it, a thin piece of plastic is placed on each side of the press and the dough is set in the middle. Then the top part of the press is closed, and the lever is pushed to apply pressure. The tortilla should be about 1/16 inch (1.5 mm) thick. If you don't have a tortilla press, you can use two heavy books lined with thin plastic to achieve the same effect.

HOW TO ROAST POBLANO CHILES

If a recipe calls for poblano chiles, you will need to roast them and remove their skin. Roasting the chiles brings out their smoky flavor and makes removing the tough skin easier.

1. Place one or two poblano chiles right on the burner of your gas stove and let the flame char the pepper on all sides. (If you don't have a gas stove, preheat the broiler to high. Place the chiles on a rimmed baking sheet lined with aluminum foil and broil for 1 to 2 minutes, until the skin is black and charred. Flip the chiles and broil for 1 to 2 minutes on the other side.)

2. Place the chiles in a heatproof container and cover with a lid. Let them sit for 5 minutes. This will trap the steam and soften the chiles' skin, making it easier to peel.

3. With a paring knife, scrape the skin off the chiles.

4. If you are making chiles rellenos, cut a 2- to 3-inch (5 to 7.5 cm) slit lengthwise down each chile and remove the seeds. Your chiles are now ready to stuff.

5. If you are making rajas, cut the stem off the chiles, remove the seeds, and cut them into strips.

Note: You might be tempted to run the chiles under water to make the peeling easier, which it would, but you risk washing away the veins of the chile, which would dilute some of the heat.

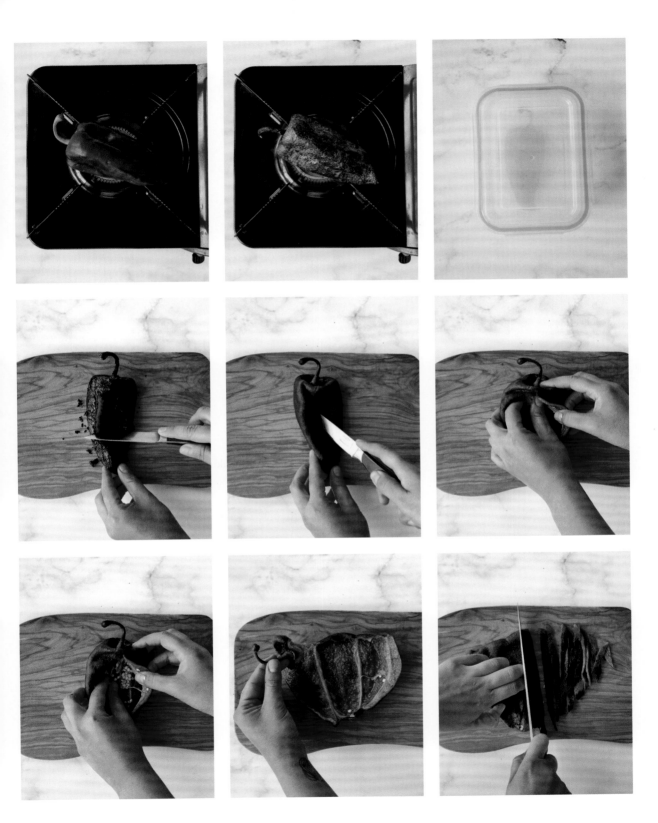

HOW TO TOAST AND SOAK DRIED CHILES

If a recipe calls for dried chiles, you will need to rehydrate them. This helps soften them, making them easier to blend, chop, and use in cooking. Some of the recipes call for toasting the chiles first to intensify the flavor, but be careful because if you burn them they will become bitter.

1. Wipe the chiles clean with a damp towel to remove any dust.

2. Using kitchen shears, cut off the stems, then make a slit lengthwise from top to bottom. Remove the seeds.

3. Heat a large, heavy-bottomed skillet over medium-high heat. Add the chiles and toast on each side until they turn a deep red color, are browned in spots, and become fragrant. (The time the chiles need to be toasted will vary according to the recipe.)

4. Transfer the chiles to a heatproof bowl.

5. Pour boiling water over the chiles and let them soak for 15 minutes.

6. Drain. Your chiles are now ready to be added to salsas or sauces.

HOW TO CLEAN NOPALES

Nopal paddles are usually sold with their spines still on, but you can sometimes find them already prepared and cut. I recommend you buy the paddles and clean them yourself, to minimize the amount of slime they produce when you cut them.

1. Use a towel to hold down the base of the nopal paddle flat on a cutting board. Be very careful as nopales have large prickly spines but also tiny, almost invisible spines that will get stuck in your fingers.

2. Use a knife to cut ¼ inch (5 mm) around the edge of the nopal, then cut off the thick base.

3. Use the same knife or a vegetable peeler to cut away the bumps or nodules where the spines grow on both sides of the paddle. You don't want to peel off all the dark green skin, only the nodules.

4. Give the paddles a rinse, then cut into the desired shape.

2

THE BASICS

I want you to think of the recipes in this chapter as those elements that are always present on the Mexican table: rice, beans, salsas, tortillas. They have a role in every meal, and sometimes they are the ones that take the most practice to get right. God knows it took me forever to get Mexican rice right, even after culinary school. The beauty of these basic dishes is that more often than not you can make a meal out of them, just as many Mexican families do and have done for hundreds of years when they can't afford to buy meat.

When I began the process of veganizing my family recipes, I quickly realized that I needed a substitute for crema and cheese. I have never been a fan of processed vegan cheese, so it was not an option for me. After many years of experimentation, I came up with substitutes that I am very proud of: a crema made from almonds that has its roots in a Mexican colonial sauce called nogada; a queso fresco made from almonds, which is inspired by a Mexican candy called queso de almendra; and a melty cheese made with cashews that I'm still amazed turned out so good. Once you get the basics down, we'll go back to our Indigenous roots in the next chapter.

OAXACAN REFRIED BLACK BEANS
Frijoles Refritos Oaxaqueños

There is no comida casera without beans. Beans are such an essential element of Mexican home cooking that I always have a pot on the stove. I have purposely made this a recipe that yields a large quantity because you will need these in your life every day after discovering the fragrant taste of anise that the avocado leaves add. The good news is that they freeze wonderfully! Eat them alongside the Spicy Machaca Tofu Scramble (page 82), spread them on crusty bread to make Mexican Bean and Cheese Toast (page 94), or sprinkle some Almond Queso Fresco (page 31) on top and dig in with some chips.

MAKES: **6 to 8 servings**

TOTAL TIME: **10 hours 20 minutes**

1 pound (453 g) dried black beans, rinsed and cleaned

5 garlic cloves (15 g), peeled and smashed

1 large white onion (232 g), cut in half, divided

1 tablespoon + ¾ teaspoon salt, divided

1 dried árbol chile, stem and seeds removed

2 small dried avocado leaves

1 tablespoon avocado oil

1. To cook the beans, place the beans, garlic, half the onion, and 1 tablespoon of the salt in a large slow cooker and fill with enough water to cover the beans by 3 inches (7.5 cm). Cover and cook on low for 10 hours. Discard the onion and garlic.

2. Set a comal or heavy-bottomed skillet over medium-high heat and toast the chile de árbol and avocado leaves for 30 seconds on each side, or until they are slightly darker in color and become fragrant. Transfer them to a blender.

3. Drain the beans, but reserve 1¾ cups of the broth. Add the beans, broth, and remaining

¾ teaspoon salt to the blender and puree until smooth. You might have to do this in batches. The beans will be thick but runny.

4. Finely chop the remaining half onion. Heat the oil in a large skillet over medium-low heat, add the onion, and cook for 4 to 5 minutes, stirring often, until the onion begins to brown.

5. Reduce the heat to low and pour in the pureed black beans while stirring continuously. Be careful as there might be some splashing if the skillet is still very hot. The beans will begin to bubble; let them cook for 7 to 8 minutes, stirring occasionally, until they have reached the consistency of a thick puree.

6. Serve immediately or store in an airtight container in the fridge for up to 3 days or in the freezer for up to 3 months.

VARIATIONS

Stovetop instructions: Place the beans in a large pot with enough water to cover by 2 inches (5 cm). Add the garlic, half the onion, and 1 tablespoon salt. Bring the beans to a boil over high heat, reduce the heat to low, and let the beans cook at a slow simmer until almost tender, approximately 1½ hours. Discard the onion and garlic and continue to step 2.

Refried pinto beans: Substitute pinto beans for the black beans and omit the avocado leaves.

Oil-free: Sauté the onion in ¼ cup broth or water, then add the beans.

Canned beans: To make this with canned beans, start with step 2, but use 3 (15-ounce/425 g) cans black beans, drained, and ¾ cup warm broth or water to puree the beans, and decrease the salt to ½ teaspoon.

Pasta de frijol: To make this runny bean puree used in Oaxaca to spread on tlayudas, molletes, or memelas, use 2¼ cups bean broth to puree the beans.

MEXICAN COWBOY BEANS

Frijoles Charros

Charro (cowboy) beans are a northern Mexico specialty. Traditionally, the beans are slowly simmered with chorizo, bacon, and sometimes even sausage along with a sauté of onion, tomato, and serrano chiles. This recipe is an adaptation of the charro beans served in our family restaurant, which I happily grew up eating every day. For this vegan version, I use my homemade Mushroom Chorizo (page 93), but you can substitute store-bought vegan sausage or bacon. Serve them as a side to the Mushroom Carnitas (page 114), or if you are a bean lover like me, you can enjoy them all on their own with some warm corn tortillas.

MAKES: 4 servings

TOTAL TIME: 2 hours + soaking time

8 ounces (227 g) dried pinto beans, soaked in water overnight and drained

1 large white onion (232 g), cut in half, divided

3 garlic cloves (9 g), peeled and crushed

2½ teaspoons salt, divided

1 tablespoon avocado oil

1 or 2 serrano chiles (43 g), finely chopped

2 medium Roma tomatoes (148 g), chopped (about 1 cup)

1 cup (172 g) Mushroom Chorizo (page 93)

2 cilantro sprigs

⅛ teaspoon freshly ground black pepper

1. Place the beans in a large pot and fill with enough water to cover by 2 inches (5 cm). Add half the onion, the garlic, and 1½ teaspoons of the salt. Bring to a boil over high heat, reduce the heat to low, and let the beans cook at a slow simmer until almost tender, approximately 1½ hours.

2. Finely chop the remaining half onion. Heat the oil in a large skillet over medium-low heat. Add the onion and serranos and cook, stirring often, until the onion is tender and translucent, for 4 to 5 minutes. Add the tomatoes and cook until they have begun to soften and release some of their juices, about 7 minutes. Add the chorizo and cook until slightly browned, stirring occasionally, for about 4 minutes.

3. Transfer the chorizo mixture to the pot of beans, add the cilantro sprigs, and simmer for 20 minutes, or until the beans are completely tender. The beans should be soft and creamy. Add the remaining 1 teaspoon salt and the pepper and stir. Before serving, remove the half onion and cilantro sprigs. I like to leave the garlic cloves in, but you can remove them if you prefer.

4. Serve hot or store in an airtight container in the fridge for up to 3 days or in the freezer for up to 3 months.

VARIATIONS

Oil-free: Omit the oil and cook the chorizo in a nonstick skillet. Add ¼ cup broth if it sticks to the pan.

Canned beans: Start step 2 in a large pot. After cooking the vegetables and chorizo, add 2½ (15-ounce/425 g) cans pinto beans, drained, the cilantro sprigs, 4 cups broth, and ½ teaspoon salt to the pot and simmer for 20 minutes.

MEXICAN RED RICE

Arroz a la Mexicana

I know my mom will deny this because I didn't get into cooking until I was much older, but this is the first thing I learned how to cook. I remember asking her to show me how she made this fluffy tomato- and cilantro-scented rice. I must have been around six years old. She explained that the tomato puree is called recaudo, and I remember asking her to give me some of the toasted rice to snack on. One of the ingredients in my mom's original recipe is chicken bouillon, so to replicate that flavor I am using a chicken-flavored vegan bouillon instead. Serve this alongside Mole Poblano (page 141) or Meatless Meatballs in Chipotle Peanut Sauce (page 178).

MAKES: **4 servings**

TOTAL TIME: **30 minutes**

3 large Roma tomatoes (326 g), roughly chopped (about 2 cups)

¼ large white onion (65 g), roughly chopped (about ⅓ cup)

2 garlic cloves (6 g), peeled

2 teaspoons no-chicken bouillon

1 teaspoon salt

1 tablespoon avocado oil

1½ cups (288 g) long-grain rice

2¼ cups (530 mL) vegetable broth

1 small carrot (88 g), chopped (about ½ cup)

2 cilantro sprigs

1 jalapeño chile (25 g)

1. Place the tomatoes, onion, garlic, bouillon, and salt in a blender and puree until smooth. Pass through a fine-mesh sieve. You should have a little less than 2 cups (473 mL) of puree.

2. Heat the oil in a medium saucepot over medium heat. Add the rice and toast until golden brown, stirring constantly, for 3 to 4 minutes. Reduce the heat to low and pour in the tomato puree while stirring constantly. Be careful as there might be some splashing if the pot is still very hot. Simmer for 2 to 3 minutes, until the puree changes to a deep red color.

3. Add the vegetable broth, carrot, and cilantro sprigs. Using a paring knife, score an *X* on the tip of the jalapeño and add it to the pot. Bring to a simmer over high heat, reduce the heat to low, cover, and cook for 16 to 18 minutes, until all the liquid is absorbed and the rice is tender. Remove from the heat and let sit for 10 minutes. Uncover and fluff with a fork.

4. Serve hot or store in an airtight container in the fridge for up to 4 days or in the freezer for up to 3 months.

VARIATIONS

Canned tomatoes: Replace the fresh tomatoes with 1 (14.5-ounce/411 g) can diced tomatoes (about 1½ cups).

With peas: Add ½ cup (66 g) frozen peas instead of the carrot.

Oil-free: Dry-toast the rice instead of using oil, then add the tomato puree.

MEXICAN GREEN RICE

Arroz Verde

Anytime I make green food for my kids, I try to come up with a fun name to get them excited about eating it. Unofficially, this bright green rice studded with corn is called green monster rice! The combination of smoky poblano chiles and fresh cilantro infuses the rice with an irresistible quality that will have you making it over and over again. Enjoy it with Miner's Enchiladas (page 184) or Lentil Picadillo (page 162).

MAKES: **4 servings**

TOTAL TIME: **30 minutes**

2 large poblano chiles (240 g), seeded and roughly chopped (about 1⅔ cups)
½ cup (25 g) packed fresh cilantro, roughly chopped
¼ large white onion (65 g), roughly chopped (about ⅓ cup)
1 garlic clove (3 g), roughly chopped

2⅓ cups (552 mL) vegetable broth
2½ teaspoons salt
1 tablespoon avocado oil
1½ cups (298 g) long-grain white rice
¾ cup (103 g) fresh or frozen corn kernels

1. Place the poblanos, cilantro, onion, garlic, broth, and salt in a blender and puree until smooth. Pass through a fine-mesh sieve.

2. Heat the oil in a medium saucepot over medium heat. Add the rice and toast until golden brown, stirring constantly, for 3 to 4 minutes. Reduce the heat to low and pour in the poblano puree, stirring constantly; be careful as there might be some splashing. Add the corn and stir. Bring to a simmer over high heat, reduce the heat to low, cover, and cook for 16 to 18 minutes, until all the liquid is absorbed and the rice is tender. Remove from the heat and let sit for 10 minutes covered.

3. Uncover and fluff with a fork. Serve hot or store in an airtight container in the fridge for up to 4 days or in the freezer for up to 4 months.

VARIATION

Oil-free: Dry-toast the rice instead of using oil, then add the poblano puree.

ALMOND CREMA
Crema de Almendras

This sauce continues to surprise me every time I make it. It is amazing that a bunch of almonds can make such a creamy and versatile sauce. In Mexico, this is known as a nogada sauce (a sauce made from nuts). Cooks have employed it since the sixteenth century to make dishes like chiles en nogada (see my vegan version on page 253). Although you may have used cashew crema before, I prefer almonds because they are not as sweet and thus complement the flavors of Mexican cuisine better. You will have to soak the almonds overnight and then peel them, but I promise the extra time this takes is worth it. We will be using this crema many times in this book, but it truly shines in the Creamy Poblano and Corn Tacos (page 97).

MAKES: 4 servings (1½ cups/354 mL)

TOTAL TIME: 15 minutes + soaking time

¾ cup (103 g) whole raw almonds
1 garlic clove (3 g), peeled
¼ cup (59 mL) unsweetened almond milk

1 tablespoon fresh lemon juice
½ teaspoon salt

1. Place the almonds in a heatproof container and pour in enough boiling water to cover them by 2 inches (5 cm). Let them soak overnight at room temperature. Drain the almonds. To peel them, place each almond between your thumb and forefinger and press slightly. The skin should pop right off.

2. Transfer the peeled almonds to a blender, add the garlic, ½ cup (118 mL) water, the almond milk, lemon juice, and salt and blend for about 2 minutes, stopping halfway through to scrape down the sides of the blender. It will start out looking grainy and may be too thin, but as you blend it will become smooth and thicken up. If it is too thick, add an additional ¼ to ½ cup (59 to 118 mL) water. It should be the consistency of a heavy cream. Keep in mind that it will thicken as it chills in the fridge.

3. If the sauce is not as smooth as you would like, you can pass it through a fine-mesh sieve. Use immediately or store in an airtight container in the fridge for up to 2 days.

TIME-SAVING TIP

Use ¾ cup (90 g) blanched slivered almonds instead (no need to soak or peel them) and blend for an extra 2 minutes. If you don't have a high-powered blender, pass the crema through a fine-mesh sieve.

VARIATION

Cashew crema: Use 1 cup (140 g) cashews, soaked overnight in hot water.

ALMOND QUESO FRESCO

Queso Fresco de Almendras

Vegan cheese has come a long way, but sometimes I still struggle with fully enjoying it. So I made my own version. While it is not dairy cheese, this much simpler version ticks all the boxes and adds just the right amount of fat, texture, and flavor to my favorite dishes. It can be the filling for Chiles Rellenos (page 175), or you can bake it and crumble it on top of Green Chilaquiles (page 87) or Bean and Nopal Tostadas (page 117).

MAKES: 4 servings (about 1 cup/117 g)

TOTAL TIME: 15 minutes + soaking and chilling time

---

1 cup (147 g) whole raw almonds

1 garlic clove (3 g), peeled

1 teaspoon fresh lemon juice

2 tablespoons avocado oil

2 teaspoons nutritional yeast

¾ teaspoon salt

1. Place the almonds in a heatproof container and pour in enough boiling water to cover them by 2 inches (5 cm). Let them soak overnight at room temperature. Drain the almonds. To peel them, place each almond between your thumb and forefinger and press slightly. The skin should pop right off.

2. Transfer the peeled almonds to a food processor and add the garlic, lemon juice, oil, 1 tablespoon water, the nutritional yeast, and salt. Process for 1 minute, or until the almonds turn into a powder. Stop and scrape the sides of the bowl. Process for another minute, or until the nuts turn into a paste that resembles ricotta cheese. If your paste is too grainy or thick, add an additional tablespoon of water and process for 1 more minute.

3. Moisten a large piece of cheesecloth, approximately 12 × 12 inches (30 × 30 cm), and wring out any excess liquid. Place the almond paste in the center and form it into a ball by gathering the edges of the cheesecloth around the cheese.

4. Twist the top edges of the cheesecloth to tighten and give it a rounded shape. Some oil and maybe a little bit of liquid will seep through the cheesecloth. Place the cheese bundle on a plate and let it sit overnight in the refrigerator. The next day, unwrap your cheese and serve.

5. If you want the cheese to crumble, put the ball of cheese on a rimmed baking sheet lined with a silicone mat or parchment paper and bake at 325°F (160°C) for 7 minutes, flip the cheese, and bake for 8 more minutes. Serve on your favorite dishes, sliced or crumbled, or store in an airtight container in the fridge for up to 5 days.

VARIATION

Oil-free: Replace the oil with 2 tablespoons unsweetened almond milk.

CASHEW QUESO ASADERO

Queso Asadero de Nuez de la India

Finally, a beautiful melty cheese I can get behind! Giving up dairy was one of the hardest things about going vegan for me. I really liked cheese, all kinds of cheese, especially the fancy stinky kinds. Over time I have come to accept that commercial vegan cheese is just not for me, so I have had to come up with my own versions. This one uses an ingredient that might be new to some of you, kappa carrageenan, but don't let that intimidate you as it is pretty easy to use. I can finally have quesadillas again, and that is certainly a beautiful thing! You can use this to make Poisoned Tacos (page 98) or Swiss Enchiladas (page 187).

MAKES: **4 servings (about 3 cups/283 g)**

TOTAL TIME: **15 minutes + soaking time**

½ cup (70 g) raw cashews
⅓ cup (60 g) refined coconut oil, melted
¼ cup (32 g) tapioca flour
1 tablespoon (7 g) kappa carrageenan powder

3 tablespoons (40 g) unsweetened almond yogurt
2 teaspoons (12 g) yellow miso paste
1 teaspoon fresh lemon juice
1½ teaspoons salt

1. Place the cashews in a heatproof container and pour in enough boiling water to cover them by 2 inches (5 cm). Let them soak overnight at room temperature. Drain the cashews.

2. To make the cheese base, place the cashews and 1½ cups (354 mL) water in a blender and puree until completely smooth, about 1 minute. Add the coconut oil, tapioca flour, kappa carrageenan, almond yogurt, miso paste, lemon juice, and salt and puree for 1 more minute, or until smooth.

3. Transfer the cheese base to a small saucepot and bring to a simmer over medium heat, stirring constantly, for about 2 minutes. It will thicken and look lumpy. As soon as it starts to bubble, reduce the heat to low and start beating the puree vigorously with a spatula. Keep beating for 3 to 4 minutes, until the cheese base thickens, becomes glossy, and begins to pull away from the sides of the pot. When you lift the spatula, the cheese should stretch and pull.

4. Pour the cheese into a heatproof 3-cup (710 mL) glass container or two 1½-cup (355 mL) glass containers. Let cool in the fridge for at least 3 hours. Unmold the cheese and grate, slice, or melt to your heart's content. Store in an airtight container in the fridge for up to 5 days.

CASHEW REQUESÓN
Requesón de Nuez de la India

Requesón is a fresh cheese resembling ricotta. It is used in Mexico to fill quesadillas, enchiladas, tlacoyos, and gorditas. It can be used in any recipe in this book that calls for cheese. It is also great in lasagna, or you can add fresh herbs to it and use it as a dip. The cashews give it a creamy texture and the tofu a lightness that makes this an excellent alternative to dairy cheese.

MAKES: 4 servings (about 2 cups)

TOTAL TIME: 20 minutes + soaking time

- 1 cup (140 g) raw cashews
- ½ block (7 ounces/ 198 g) extra-firm tofu, pressed
- 2 garlic cloves (6 g), chopped
- 1 tablespoon nutritional yeast
- ½ teaspoon grated lemon zest
- 1½ tablespoons fresh lemon juice
- ½ teaspoon + ⅛ teaspoon salt
- ⅛ teaspoon freshly ground black pepper

1. Place the cashews in a heatproof container and pour in enough boiling water to cover them by 2 inches (5 cm). Let them soak overnight at room temperature. Drain the cashews.

2. Place the cashews in a food processor and process for about 1 minute, stopping halfway to scrape down the sides of the bowl, until the cashews become a thick paste. Add the pressed tofu, garlic, nutritional yeast, lemon zest and juice, salt, and pepper and process until you have a smooth paste resembling ricotta cheese, for about 1 minute.

3. Transfer to a bowl and serve as a dip with crackers or use in quesadillas. Store in an airtight container in the fridge for up to 5 days.

MOLCAJETE SALSA

Salsa Molcajeteada

Every time I use a molcajete something awakens within me. The repetitive motion, the sound of the stone grinding, and the smell of the chiles roasting on the comal transport me to another time. I feel connected to the thousands of women before me, across generations, who have also participated in this ritual that seems almost sacred. A molcajete is a mortar and pestle, made from volcanic rock, that has been used in Mexico to make salsa since before the Spanish conquest. They can be purchased online, but if you don't have one you can make this salsa with a blender or food processor. This salsa is spicy! Don't say I didn't warn you. That being said, if you want it to be less spicy, you can reduce the number of serrano chiles or eliminate them completely. Eat with chips or serve it on top of Fava Bean and Mushroom Stuffed Blue Corn Cakes (page 123).

MAKES: **4 servings (2 cups/473 mL)**

TOTAL TIME: **20 minutes**

- 3 medium Roma tomatoes (223 g), cored
- 1 beefsteak tomato (196 g), cored
- ¼ large white onion (65 g)
- 3 garlic cloves (9 g), unpeeled
- 1 poblano chile (120 g), stem removed
- 1 güero chile (50 g), stem removed
- 1 jalapeño chile (25 g), stem removed
- 2 serrano chiles (43 g), stems removed
- 1 teaspoon salt
- ¼ cup (12 g) chopped fresh cilantro

1. Heat a comal or heavy-bottomed skillet over medium-high heat. Place the tomatoes, onion, garlic, and all the chiles on the hot comal. Let the vegetables char until they become soft and have black spots all over, flipping them frequently, for 8 to 9 minutes. The garlic will be done about 2 minutes in; remove and peel it.

2. Transfer the vegetables from the skillet to a bowl. Here you have the choice to remove the charred skin or to keep it. I like to remove some of the tomato skin because they are harder to grind down in the molcajete, but I keep the skin on the chiles.

3. To make the salsa, place the salt and garlic in a molcajete and grind down in a circular motion until a thick paste forms, about 1 minute. Add the chiles one by one and grind down until they incorporate into the garlic paste, in 2 to 3 minutes. Continue by adding the tomatoes one at a time and keep grinding, for 2 to 3 minutes.

4. Finely chop the charred onion and add it to the molcajete, along with the cilantro, and stir. You can serve the salsa right in the molcajete or store it in an airtight container in the fridge for up to 3 days or in the freezer for up to 3 months.

VARIATIONS

Oven instructions: Preheat the broiler to high. Place the tomatoes, onion, garlic, and chiles on a rimmed baking sheet lined with aluminum foil and place under the broiler for 5 to 6 minutes, flipping the vegetables halfway through, until the tomatoes and chiles are charred and have black spots all over. The garlic will be done 2 minutes in; remove it from the oven and peel it. Continue to step 2.

Blender or food processor instructions: After step 2, transfer the charred vegetables to a blender or food processor, add the salt, and blend or pulse until you have a thick and chunky salsa. Add the cilantro and stir.

NOTE

If you can't find güero chiles, you can substitute Anaheim or Hatch chiles.

ROASTED TOMATILLO SALSA

Salsa Verde de Tomatillo

A good tomatillo salsa is an essential part of Mexican cuisine, especially if you love enchiladas. This is another salsa recipe from the family restaurant, where it is served on every table with a basket of crisp tortilla chips. It is also one of the first recipes that a young cook learns when they start working there, just as I did at the ripe age of eighteen. This version is one of the best I know and is very adaptable. When you add avocado to it, it becomes a creamy avocado salsa, or you can add toasted chile de árbol to make a fiery salsa roja. I like to char the tomatillos, but you can boil the tomatillos and chiles instead if you prefer. Your Green Chilaquiles (page 87) will be forever transformed with this salsa.

MAKES: 4 servings (2 cups/473 mL)

TOTAL TIME: 20 minutes

7 medium tomatillos (453 g), husks removed, rinsed
¼ large white onion (65 g), peeled
2 garlic cloves (6 g), unpeeled

1 or 2 serrano chiles (27 g), stems removed
⅓ cup (16 g) packed fresh cilantro, roughly chopped
1 teaspoon salt

1. Heat a comal or heavy-bottomed skillet over medium-high heat. Place the tomatillos, onion, garlic, and serranos on the comal. Let the vegetables char until they become soft and have black spots all over, and the tomatillos change from bright green to a dull green, in 8 to 9 minutes. Flip the vegetables halfway through. The garlic will be done about 2 minutes in; remove and peel it.

2. Transfer all the charred vegetables to a blender and add the cilantro and salt. Blend until the vegetables are pureed to your desired salsa consistency, either chunky or smooth. Serve hot or cold or store in an airtight container in the fridge for up to 3 days or in the freezer for up to 3 months.

VARIATIONS

Creamy avocado salsa: Add the flesh of ½ avocado (84 g) and blend until completely smooth.

Oven instructions: Preheat the broiler to high. Place the tomatillos, onion, garlic, and chiles on a rimmed baking sheet lined with aluminum foil and place under the broiler for 5 to 6 minutes, flipping the vegetables halfway through, until the tomatillos are soft and the chiles are charred and have black spots all over. The garlic will be done 2 minutes in; remove it from the oven and peel it. Continue to step 2.

CHILE MORITA SALSA

Salsa de Chile Morita

This is a tangy and smoky salsa that is good with just about anything, but especially tacos! It is also known as a salsa taquera, which means you can find it as a complement to your tacos on street carts all over Mexico. Serve it with Black Bean Zucchini Tamales (page 217) or Requesón and Carrot Crispy Tacos (page 111).

MAKES: 4 servings (about 2 cups/473 mL)

TOTAL TIME: 20 minutes

4 to 6 dried morita chiles (20 g), stems removed
7 medium tomatillos (453 g), husks removed, rinsed
¼ large white onion (80 g)
2 garlic cloves (6 g), unpeeled
1 teaspoon salt
⅛ teaspoon freshly ground black pepper

1. Heat a comal, cast-iron, or heavy-bottomed skillet over medium-high heat. Toast the chiles for 30 seconds on each side, or until the color changes to a brighter red and they are lightly toasted. Transfer to a heatproof bowl and pour boiling water over them. Let them sit for 15 minutes.

2. Meanwhile, place the tomatillos, onion, and garlic on the same comal and let the vegetables char until they become soft and have black spots all over, flipping them frequently, in 8 to 9 minutes. The garlic will be done about 2 minutes in; remove and peel it. The onion will be done about 6 minutes in. The tomatillos are done when they go from bright green to dull green with black spots all over.

3. Drain the chiles, but reserve ½ cup of the soaking liquid. Transfer the chiles and reserved soaking liquid to a blender and puree until smooth. Add the charred tomatillos, onion, and garlic, along with the salt and pepper, and blend until the vegetables are coarsely pureed. Serve hot or cold or store in an airtight container in the fridge for up to 3 days or in the freezer for up to 3 months.

VARIATION

Oven instructions: Toast and soak the chiles as described above. Preheat the broiler to high. Place the tomatillos, onion, and garlic on a rimmed baking sheet lined with aluminum foil and broil for 5 to 6 minutes, flipping the vegetables halfway through. The garlic will be done 2 minutes in; remove it from the oven and peel it.

CHILE DE ÁRBOL SALSA

Salsa de Chile de Árbol

This is another great salsa taquera (taco salsa). You can find it in plastic squeeze bottles on taco stands throughout Mexico. It is spicy, smoky, and a little bit tangy. The addition of toasted sesame seeds gives it a touch of creaminess that is the perfect finishing touch to any taco. I like to leave the seeds in the chiles for this one to make it extra spicy, but you can remove them for a milder salsa. It is excellent on top of Hibiscus Flower Barbacoa (page 108).

MAKES: 4 servings (1½ cups/354 mL)

TOTAL TIME: 20 minutes

10 dried árbol chiles (8 g), stems removed
2 teaspoons avocado oil
½ large white onion (152 g), roughly chopped (about 1 cup)
2 garlic cloves (6 g), peeled
2 small tomatillos (115 g), husks removed, cut into quarters
3 medium Roma tomatoes (330 g), cut into quarters
1 tablespoon toasted sesame seeds
1 teaspoon salt
⅛ teaspoon freshly ground black pepper

1. Heat a large, heavy-bottomed skillet over medium-high heat. Add the chiles and toast for 30 to 40 seconds on each side, until they brown in spots and become fragrant. Transfer the chiles to a blender.

2. Heat the oil in the same skillet over medium heat. Add the onion and cook for 3 to 4 minutes, stirring often, until it begins to brown. Add the garlic and cook for 1 more minute.

3. Reduce the heat to medium-low, add the tomatillos, and cook, stirring occasionally, for about 4 minutes, or until they begin to change to a dull green color. Add the tomatoes and continue to cook for 5 more minutes, or until both the tomatoes and the tomatillos are soft. Transfer everything to the blender.

4. Add ¼ cup (59 mL) water, the sesame seeds, salt, and pepper and puree until completely smooth. You can serve this salsa hot or cold with your favorite tacos. Store in an airtight container in the fridge for up to 5 days or in the freezer for up to 6 months.

VARIATION

Oil-free: Omit the oil when cooking the onion and use ¼ cup (59 mL) vegetable broth or water instead.

BLISTERED SERRANOS

Chiles Toreados

Our family restaurant is, ironically, a steak house—I know, sometimes I can't believe it either. All the tacos made in the restaurant are served with a side of chiles toreados, which translates to "blistered chiles." They are of course very spicy, so if you love spicy food, you will love these. For a less spicy version, you could use milder jalapeño or shishito chiles. I always make these when we have Poisoned Tacos (page 98) for breakfast.

MAKES: **4 servings**

TOTAL TIME: **10 minutes**

2 teaspoons avocado oil
6 serrano chiles (111 g)
½ large white onion
    (152 g), sliced (about
    1 cup)

2 teaspoons soy sauce
1 tablespoon fresh lime
    juice

1. Heat the oil in a small skillet over medium heat. Add the serranos and cook for 6 to 7 minutes, stirring occasionally, until they are blistered and covered in black spots and are a dull green color.

2. Reduce the heat to medium-low, add the onion, and continue to cook until it begins to soften and brown, in 4 to 5 minutes. The onion should still have some crunch to it. Remove the skillet from the heat, add the soy sauce and lime, and stir. Transfer to a plate and serve hot or cold. Store in an airtight container in the fridge for up to 4 days.

VARIATION

Oil-free: Preheat the broiler to high. Place the chiles on a rimmed baking sheet lined with aluminum foil and broil for about 2 minutes on each side. Transfer them to a skillet, add the onion and ¼ cup (59 mL) broth or water, and cook as above.

CACTUS SALAD

Ensalada de Nopales

As a child, I was very grossed out by the gooey slime that comes off nopales. I didn't particularly mind the flavor; it was the slime! Come to find out your nopales will only be excessively slimy if you don't cook them correctly. This means they need to be cooked at really high heat, so pan searing in a really hot pan or grilling is a good option. The easiest option, though, is boiling them in water, but you must add them when the water is already boiling or you will end up with a slimy mess on your hands. This is a classic nopales salad and one of the best ways of trying nopales for the first time. They have a tart, almost citrusy taste with a texture similar to that of okra, and when mixed with tomato, onion, cilantro, jalapeño, and lime juice they make the perfect topping for Fava Bean and Mushroom Stuffed Blue Corn Cakes (page 123) or Bean and Nopal Tostadas (page 117).

MAKES: 4 servings (about 4 cups)

TOTAL TIME: 20 minutes

NOPALES
1 large white onion (232 g), cut in half, divided
1 dried bay leaf
1 tablespoon salt
1 pound (455 g) nopales, cleaned (see page 17) and diced (about 3½ cups)

SALAD
4 Roma tomatoes (338 g), chopped (about 2 cups)
1 jalapeño chile (39 g), finely chopped
⅓ cup (12 g) packed fresh cilantro, chopped
2 to 3 tablespoons freshly squeezed lime juice
½ teaspoon salt

1. Bring a large pot of water to a boil over high heat. Add half the onion, the bay leaf, salt, and nopales. Reduce the heat to medium, cover, and let simmer for 10 minutes. Drain, discarding the onion and bay leaf, and rinse the nopales very well to remove any excess slime.

2. Finely chop the remaining half onion and transfer to a large bowl. Add the cooked nopales, tomatoes, jalapeño, cilantro, lime juice, and salt and stir. Let the flavors marinate for about 30 minutes, then serve. The salad will keep in an airtight container in the refrigerator for up to 1 day. After this the nopales will begin to release slime again.

VARIATION

Jarred nopales: If you can't find fresh nopales, you can use 1 (30-ounce/850 g) jar of nopales in brine, drained and rinsed, then continue to step 2.

BLUE CORN TORTILLAS

Tortillas de Maíz Azul

The first time I tried blue corn tortillas was in Xochimilco, a system of canals in Mexico City that was founded by the Xochimilcas in the tenth century. It is a popular tourist destination where you can travel the canals in colorful gondolas called trajineras. My parents took me there when I was about nine years old and they tell me I refused to eat the blue corn tortillas because they were too weird. I feel deeply sorry for nine-year-old me, because I missed out on tortillas made from freshly ground blue corn cooked on a comal right in front of you on a floating trajinera. Fresh blue corn masa is very hard to find outside of Mexico, so for this recipe we will be using blue corn masa harina. You can use these tortillas to make Huitlacoche and Zucchini Blossom Quesadillas (page 126), Bean and Nopal Tostadas (page 117), or any recipe in this book that calls for tortillas.

MAKES: 4 servings (12 tortillas)

TOTAL TIME: 20 minutes

2 cups (285 g) blue corn masa harina

¼ teaspoon salt

1. Place the masa harina and salt in a large bowl and gradually pour in 1¾ cups (414 mL) warm water while mixing with your hand. Knead for 5 minutes, or until there are no dry spots in the masa and it is soft like Play-Doh, pliable but not sticky. To test if the masa is too dry, roll a small piece into a ball and lightly press it; if the edges crack, the dough is too dry. Add an additional ¼ cup (59 mL) warm water and knead again.

2. Preheat a comal or heavy-bottomed skillet over medium heat.

3. Divide the masa into twelve balls about the size of a golf ball (1.7 ounces/50 g). Lay a plastic liner (I like to cut squares out of grocery bags) on the bottom of a tortilla press. Place a ball of masa in the center of the liner and lay a second liner on top of the ball. Use your fingers to lightly press down on the masa ball and close the press, pushing down the lever to apply pressure. The tortilla should be about ¹⁄₁₆ inch (1.5 mm) thick.

4. Open the tortilla press and peel off the top liner. Flip the exposed corn tortilla onto your fingers and with your opposing hand, peel off the remaining plastic liner.

5. Lay the tortilla directly on the hot comal. If the tortilla bubbles, it means the skillet is too hot; if this happens, reduce the heat to medium-low. Let it cook for 30 seconds, or until the edges change color and there is some light spotting, then flip. The tortilla should easily flip. If your tortilla is stuck, it means the heat is too low and the tortilla is not cooked yet, or your pan is not properly seasoned. Cook for 20 to 30 seconds, until you see some light spotting on this side. Flip one more time, and here is when you should start seeing the tortilla puff up. Let cook for another 20 seconds, then transfer to a tortilla warmer. Don't worry if your tortilla doesn't puff

(CONTINUED)

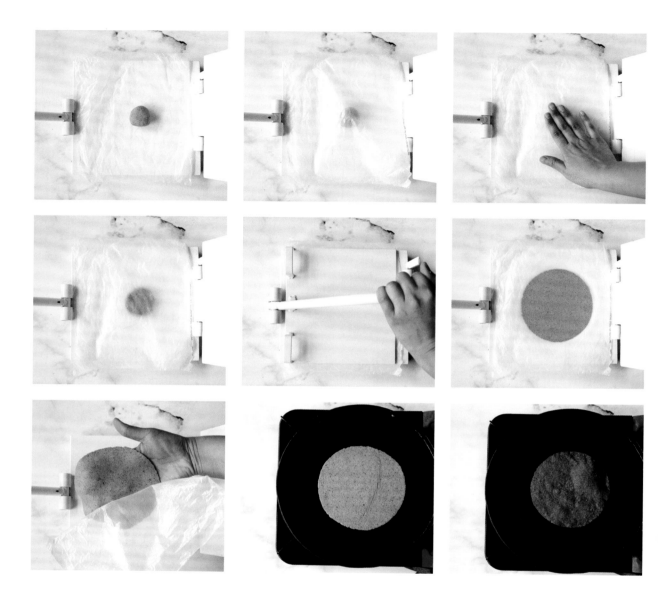

up. It will take some time to figure out the right heat on your stove and skillet to perfect your tortilla-making. Repeat this process with the rest of the masa. Serve warm.

6. Once cool, store in an airtight container in the fridge for up to 3 days or in the freezer for up to 3 months.

NOTE

If you don't have a tortilla press, you can use two heavy, flat-bottomed objects (books will work). To reheat the tortillas, spray with some water and reheat for 30 seconds on each side on a comal or skillet over medium-high heat.

YUCATÁN WHITE SPICE PASTE

Recado Blanco

Recado blanco is a spice paste used as a flavor base for Yucatecan dishes, like Pumpkin Seed Meatballs in Chaya Broth (page 71). There are three kinds: negro, rojo, and blanco. The red one is also known as achiote paste and is the one most commonly found. Every family has their own recipe, so there are many variations; this is Bruno Cocom's family recipe. Don Bruno is a Mayan priest and cocinero tradicional who promotes Yucatecan cuisine throughout Mexico.

MAKES: ¾ cup (60 g)

TOTAL TIME: 20 minutes

1 tablespoon dried oregano
1 teaspoon black peppercorns
3 whole cloves

1 large red onion (232 g), cut in half
3 garlic cloves (9 g), unpeeled
1 teaspoon salt

1. Heat a comal or medium skillet over medium-low heat. Put in the oregano, peppercorns, and cloves and toast for 20 to 30 seconds, shaking the pan occasionally, until you begin to smell the aroma of the spices. Transfer them to a molcajete or spice grinder and process into a fine powder.

2. Increase the heat to medium-high and place the onion halves and garlic on the comal. Once the onion and garlic are charred and blackened, about 1 minute for the garlic and 4 minutes for the onion, flip them over and cook until they are soft and have black spots all over.

3. Peel the garlic and transfer it to the molcajete with the spices, add the onion and salt, and grind in a circular motion until a thick paste forms. Alternatively, you can use a food processor and pulse for about 1 minute to turn it into a paste. Store in an airtight container in the fridge for up to 5 days or in the freezer for up to 3 months.

3

THE INDIGENOUS KITCHEN

I can't talk about Mexican cuisine without acknowledging the Indigenous cultural heritage that is its basis. To this day, the Indigenous communities hold the knowledge of the ritual practices, traditions, and culinary techniques that existed since before the Spanish conquest. To properly honor the Indigenous community in Mexico, I collaborated with six cocineras tradicionales and one cocinero tradicional: Liliana Palma Santos (Zapotec), Florinda Vásquez Palma (Zapotec), Evangelina Aquino Luis (Zapotec), Francisca Maurilio Godinez (Mixe), Isabel Lazo Chavez (Zapotec), Ariadna Pinacho Cruz (Zapotec), and Bruno Cocom (Maya). Our goal was to record for posterity the naturally plant-based traditional foods that have been passed down in their families and communities for generations.

One of their main concerns is that the knowledge of these recipes is at risk of being lost, since the newer generations don't want to learn them and they are being prepared less and less. Another concern is the cultural extractivism that is happening in the community by foreigners, chefs, and foodies who travel to Mexico in search of recipes and experiences, and contribute nothing to the community, often not even paying the cocineras for their time. That's why I contacted Liliana (Lily) Palma Santos (@zapotectravelbylily), and she coordinated a meeting with the cocineras in Oaxaca, acting as an intermediary and advocate for the community. We reached an agreement that includes compensation and recognition of cocineras as the authors of the recipes, and agreed that every time I mention, publish, or distribute these recipes, they will be attached to the name and Indigenous community where they originated. And so my family and I traveled to Tlacolula de Matamoros, Teotitlán del Valle, and San José del Pacifico in Oaxaca and later to Chetumal and Bacalar in Quintana Roo.

At first I think we were all a little nervous, as most of the cooking we did was in the cocineras' homes, but as we began cooking, we found that we had a common language: food. I brought a scale, timer, and camera, and together we weighed every ingredient, timed every step, and took videos. The challenge for me was keeping my kids occupied, but the cocineras included them in the preparations. My oldest is fascinated by fire and was constantly asking about the fogón (wood-fired stove) and eventually was given the task of adding wood to the fire; my daughter made her first nixtamal tortilla; and my little one help spread beans on masa to make a tamal. The best part was sitting down together once the cooking was done and sharing a meal.

It is important to say that Indigenous communities in Mexico continue to be marginalized and discriminated against, and are still fighting for their sovereignty. We can support them by educating ourselves about Indigenous culture, shopping directly from Indigenous artisans and paying them fairly, and supporting the fight for Indigenous rights. The recipes that follow are the original recipes as they were recorded, but I do include in the notes tips on how you can re-create them at home with the ingredients and tools available in the US.

RAINBOW TORTILLAS

Tortillas de Arcoíris

Forty-five minutes from Oaxaca City is Tlacolula de Matamoros, a small town known for its colorful market. Here Liliana (Lily) Palma Santos runs a farm-to-table restaurant called Criollito. Criollito is famous for its rainbow tortillas, which are made with native dried corn that has been cooked and ground into masa with three different colors. The colors are ground into the masa on a metate, a large volcanic rock grinding stone, by using spinach, beets, and guajillo chiles. She cooks the tortillas on a clay comal over an open fire, preserving the cooking tradition practiced by her mother and grandmother before her. The rainbow part is a reflection of the creativity of Lily and Florinda Vásquez Palma (Criollito's cocinera). Lily takes immense pride in her culture and Zapotec heritage and wants to bring Oaxaca to the world one rainbow tortilla at a time. She also runs a tour company that offers responsible tourist experiences in the Zapotec community. You can find her at @zapotectravelbylily.

MAKES: **24 tortillas**

TOTAL TIME: **1 hour**

GREEN MASA
4 large spinach leaves
9 ounces (250 g) fresh
   white corn masa
   (about 1 cup)

RED MASA
3 dried guajillo chiles
   (25 g), seeds and
   stems removed
1 pound (450 g) fresh
   white corn masa
   (about 1¾ cups)

PINK MASA
1 small beet (47 g),
   peeled, roughly
   chopped
14 ounces (400 g) fresh
   white corn masa
   (about 1⅔ cups)

1. To make the green masa, using a metlapil (an elongated stone), grind down the spinach leaves on the metate, grinding back and forth until a green puree forms, in about 2 minutes. Start adding the masa in batches and continue to grind back and forth with the metlapil, incorporating the green puree into the masa. As you grind, the masa will spread out on the metate; gather it with your hands, form it back into a ball, and keep grinding. Continue this process until you have run out of masa and the masa on the metate is completely green. If there are large pieces of spinach left in the masa, pick them out. Transfer the masa to a bowl and cover with a damp towel. Clean the metate with water to remove all traces of green.

2. To make the red masa, place the guajillo chiles in a bowl and pour boiling water over them. Let them soak for 15 minutes. Drain the chiles and transfer them to the metate. Start grinding back and forth on the metate until a thick puree forms, in 5 to 6 minutes. Add the masa in batches and continue to grind back and forth with the metlapil, incorporating the red puree into the masa. As you grind, the masa will spread out on the metate; gather it with your hands, form it back into a ball, and keep grinding. Continue this process until you have run out of masa and the masa on the metate is completely red. If there are large pieces of chile left in the masa, pick them out. Transfer the masa to a bowl and cover with a damp towel. Clean the metate with water to remove all traces of red.

(CONTINUED)

3. To make the pink masa, grind down the beet on the metate, grinding back and forth until a pink puree forms, in 3 to 5 minutes. Start adding the masa in batches and continue to grind back and forth with the metlapil, incorporating the pink puree into the masa. As you grind, the masa will spread out on the metate; gather it with your hands, form it back into a ball, and keep grinding. Continue this process until you have run out of masa and the masa on the metate is completely pink. If there are large pieces of beet left in the masa, pick them out. Transfer the masa to a bowl and cover with a damp towel. Clean the metate with water to remove all traces of pink.

4. To make the tortillas, preheat a clay comal or skillet over medium heat. Take a 1-ounce (28 g) piece of each masa and roll them into one ball. Lay a plastic liner (I like to cut squares out of grocery bags) on the bottom of a tortilla press. Place a ball of masa in the center of the liner and lay a second liner on top of the ball. Use your fingers to lightly press down on the masa ball and close the press, pushing down the lever to apply pressure. The tortilla should be about 1/16 inch (1.5 mm) thick.

5. Open the tortilla press and peel off the top liner. Flip the exposed corn tortilla onto your fingers and with your opposing hand, peel off the remaining plastic liner.

6. Lay the tortilla directly on the hot skillet. If the tortilla bubbles, it means the skillet is too hot; if this happens, reduce the heat to medium-low. Let it cook for 30 seconds, or until the edges change color and there is some light spotting, then flip. The tortilla should easily flip. If your tortilla is stuck, it means the heat is too low and the tortilla is not cooked yet, or your pan is not properly seasoned. Cook for 20 to 30 seconds, until you see some light spotting on this side. Flip one more time, and here is when you should start seeing the tortilla puff up. Let cook for another 20 seconds, then transfer to a tortilla warmer. Don't worry if your tortilla doesn't puff up. It will take some time to figure out the right

heat on your stove and skillet to perfect your tortilla-making. Repeat this process with the rest of the masa. Serve warm.

7. Once cool, store in an airtight container in the fridge for up to 3 days or in the freezer for up to 3 months.

VARIATIONS

Food processor instructions: When making this with a food processor, puree the vegetables first, pulsing until a coarse puree forms, then add the masa and process for about a minute. The masa will turn the color of the vegetable, but there will still be some small vegetable pieces. If the masa is too dry, you can add 1 tablespoon water.

Masa harina instructions: Place 4⅓ cups (1 pound/453 g) masa harina in a large bowl and gradually pour in 3 cups (710 mL) warm water while mixing with your hand. Knead for 5 minutes, or until there are no dry spots in the masa and it is soft like Play-Doh, pliable but not sticky. To test if the masa is too dry, roll a small piece into a ball and lightly press it; if the edges crack, the dough is too dry. Add an additional ¼ cup (59 mL) water and knead again. Use this to replace the amount of fresh masa in the recipe.

Florinda Vásquez Palma and Liliana Palma Santos

Isabel Lazo Chavez

THICKENED SQUASH VINE SOUP

Espesado de Guías

Isabel Lazo Chavez is a Zapotec cocinera tradicional from Teotitlán del Valle, a small town located in the Valles Centrales region, about 12 miles east of Oaxaca City. In a town known for its handwoven textiles, Doña Isabel and her family are expert weavers, as well as excellent cooks. She has a small restaurant called Comedor Jaguar; her specialty is this farmer's soup, made with fruits of the milpa: squash, young squash vines, zucchini blossoms, and wild greens (quelites), simmered in a corn-thickened broth. Doña Isabel grinds the corn in her metate just the way her mom showed her when she was nine years old. She likes to serve this soup with warm corn tortillas.

MAKES: 6 servings

TOTAL TIME: 1 hour

---

2 cups (192 g) young squash vines
10 small young native yellow ears of corn (1.2 kg), shucked, divided
6 small round zucchini (497 g), stems removed, cut into large cubes
1½ cups (50 g) chepil or watercress, picked off the stem

17 zucchini blossoms (76 g), pistils removed
1 fresh or dried pipicha sprig *or* 1 cilantro sprig + 1 mint sprig
1 teaspoon salt
Warm corn tortillas, for serving

NOTE

I had to make some modifications to re-create this at home since American corn is less starchy and sweeter than native Mexican corn, and doesn't have the same thickening properties. Use six medium yellow ears of corn, cut two of them into thirds, and simmer them in the water (step 2). Cut off the kernels of the other four ears and pulse them in a food processor until a thick paste forms. Add 3 tablespoons masa harina and pulse again to incorporate, then continue to step 3.

1. To prep the squash vines, select only the stems closest to the flowers, remove the leaves and reserve them, and cut the stems into 2-inch (5 cm) pieces. Rinse and transfer them to separate bowls.

2. Bring 8 cups (1.9 L) water to a simmer in a large pot over medium heat. Add five ears of corn, cover the pot, and simmer for 6 to 7 minutes, until the corn changes to a deep yellow color. Add the zucchini and squash vine stems, cover, and simmer for 12 to 15 minutes, until the vines are tender.

3. While the vines and zucchini are simmering, cut the kernels off the five remaining corn cobs and grind them to a fine paste on a metate, grinding back and forth with a metlapil for 8 to 10 minutes. Alternatively, you can use a food processor for 2 to 3 minutes, until a fine paste forms. Transfer the paste to a bowl and add 3 cups (700 mL) water to dilute it.

4. With a slotted spoon remove the zucchini and vine stems from the pot, but leave the corn. Add the chepil, squash vine leaves, and zucchini blossoms and simmer for 15 minutes, or until the squash leaves are very tender and fall apart when touched with your fingers.

5. Pour the diluted corn paste, pipicha sprig, and salt into the pot and bring to a simmer for 15 minutes, or until the soup thickens enough to coat the back of the spoon.

6. To serve, ladle about 1 cup (60 g) of the zucchini and vine stems in each bowl and pour the thickened corn soup over it. Serve with warm corn tortillas. Store in an airtight container in the fridge for up to 5 days or in the freezer for up to 3 months.

WILD GREENS SOUP

Guisado de Quelites

Quelites in Mexico is a blanket term for any edible wild green; there are over 350 different edible species that are eaten throughout the country. Quintoniles (amaranth greens) are only one of them. They are mostly consumed in central Mexico; in the northern states, where meat is king, we think of them as weeds. Doña Isabel Lazo Chavez, a Zapotec cocinera tradicional, makes this beautiful soup of purslane and amaranth greens in her restaurant, Comedor Jaguar. She serves it with a wedge of lime, homemade corn tortillas, and a fiery chile de árbol salsa.

MAKES: 6 servings

TOTAL TIME: 40 minutes

4 cups (415 g) quintoniles (amaranth greens)
2½ cups (291 g) verdolaga (purslane), tough stems removed, rinsed
2 teaspoons salt

CHILE DE ÁRBOL SALSA
10 dried árbol chiles (7 g), stems removed
2 garlic cloves (6 g), peeled
½ teaspoon salt

TO SERVE
2 limes, cut into quarters

Isabel Lazo Chavez

1. To prepare the quintoniles, gently tear off the leaves from the stems and rinse them really well, then transfer them to a large bowl.

2. Bring 10 cups (2.3 L) water to a simmer in a large pot over medium heat. Drop in the purslane, cover, and simmer for 6 to 7 minutes, until it wilts. Add the quintoniles and salt, cover, and continue to simmer for 12 to 13 minutes, until all the greens are falling-apart tender.

3. To make the salsa, heat a comal or heavy-bottomed skillet over medium-high heat. Put in the chiles and toast for 30 to 40 seconds on each side, until they brown in spots and become fragrant. Transfer the chiles to a heatproof bowl. Pour 1 cup (236 mL) hot water over them and let them soak for 10 minutes. Drain the chiles, but reserve the soaking liquid. Transfer the chiles and the garlic to a molcajete and grind down in a circular motion until a thick paste forms, in 3 to 4 minutes. Add about ½ cup (118 mL) reserved soaking liquid and the salt to the molcajete to get the paste to a salsa consistency. If you don't have a molcajete, you can use a blender or food processor.

4. With a ladle, spoon a generous portion of the soup into each bowl and serve with a wedge of lime and the chile de árbol salsa. Store in an airtight container in the fridge for up to 5 days or in the freezer for up to 3 months.

NOTE

If you can't find amaranth greens or purslane, use 2 pounds (900 g) spinach, Swiss chard, or mustard greens instead.

Ariadna Pinacho Cruz

FOREST MUSHROOM SOUP

Sopa del Bosque

Three hours south of Oaxaca City, nestled in the Sierra Sur, is San José del Pacífico, a small mountain town. It is truly a magical place with twisting trails in thick pine forests, and in the fall months it becomes a mushroom foraging paradise. There Zapotec chef Ariadna Penacho Cruz creates culinary magic at Huitzil, a small restaurant on the mountaintop focused on mushroom cuisine. I visited Chef Ariadna when it wasn't mushroom season, so everything we prepared was made with dried mushrooms. We made a hearty yellowfoot mushroom soup simmered with native potatoes and chile tuxta, onion, garlic, and oregano. It is a very special soup because it was made with all local ingredients, but you can re-create it at home with minimal substitutions.

MAKES: **6 servings**

TOTAL TIME: **45 minutes**

1 tablespoon vegetable oil

2 garlic cloves (6 g), finely chopped

½ medium red onion (70 g), finely chopped

2 large Roma tomatoes (220 g), cut into small cubes

13 small papas criolla or baby Yukon Gold potatoes (360 g), cut into small cubes

1 teaspoon ground tuxta chile or ground chipotle powder

2 teaspoons chopped fresh oregano

2 cups (60 g) dried yellowfoot mushrooms (*Craterellus tubaeformis*) or dried chanterelle mushrooms

2 teaspoons salt

⅛ teaspoon freshly ground black pepper

FRIED TORTILLA STRIPS

½ cup (118 mL) vegetable oil

5 corn tortillas, cut into thin strips

TO SERVE

1 cup (33 g) alfalfa sprouts

1. Heat the oil in a large pot over medium-low heat. Add the garlic and cook for 30 seconds, or until it begins to brown, then add the onion and cook until it begins to soften and brown around the edges, in 2 to 3 minutes. Add the tomatoes, stir, and cook for 4 to 5 minutes, until they begin to break down and release their juices. Add the potatoes and cook for 2 to 3 minutes, then pour in 2 quarts (2 L) water and add the tuxta chile. Increase the heat to medium-high and bring to a simmer. As soon as it simmers, add the oregano, mushrooms, salt, and pepper and stir. Reduce the heat to low and let it simmer for about 30 minutes, or until the mushrooms and potatoes are tender.

2. Meanwhile, to make the tortilla strips, heat the oil in a small skillet over medium heat to 350°F (175°C). Add a handful of the tortilla strips to the hot oil and cook until golden brown, stirring occasionally, for about 1 minute. Use a slotted spoon to transfer to a plate lined with paper towels. Repeat with the rest of the tortilla strips.

3. Serve the soup in bowls topped with the fried tortilla strips and the sprouts. Store the soup in an airtight container in the fridge for up to 5 days or in the freezer for up to 3 months. The fried tortilla strips can be stored in an airtight container at room temperature for up to 2 days.

VARIATIONS

Oil-free: Omit the oil when cooking the garlic and onion and start with ¼ cup (59 mL) vegetable broth. Use toasted tortilla strips.

Fresh mushrooms: To make this with fresh mushrooms, substitute 10 ounces (283 g) fresh chanterelle or cremini mushrooms for the dried mushrooms.

LOBSTER MUSHROOM MOLOTES

Molotes de Hongos Langosta

Zapotec chef Ariadna Penacho Cruz and her family are exceptionally well versed in all things mushrooms. They do guided foraging tours and offer temazcal ritual experiences. They forage mushrooms during the rainy season, then dehydrate them and eat them all year long. They also have a deep knowledge of medicinal herbs and their uses. These molotes (a filled savory corn-based pastry) are made with blue corn masa, but they are very similar in technique to the Plantain Molotes in Black Mole (page 138). They are filled with an amanita basii mushroom filling. Amanita basii is a mushroom endemic to the mountains of Oaxaca. I had never tried them before and was blown away by their meatiness. As a substitute you can use dried lobster mushrooms or 1½ pounds (680 g) fresh mushrooms (see note). Chef Ariadna tops her molotes with radishes, pickled onions, and pasta de frijol.

MAKES: **6 servings**

TOTAL TIME: **30 minutes + soaking time**

FILLING

5 cups (10 ounces/300 g) dried bas' Caesar (amanita basii) mushrooms or dried lobster mushrooms
2 tablespoons vegetable oil
1 medium red onion (170 g), finely chopped
2 garlic cloves (6 g), peeled
4 large Roma tomatoes (375 g), diced
1 teaspoon salt
⅛ teaspoon freshly ground pepper
2 dried bay leaves
8 fresh epazote leaves
1¼ cups (40 g) watercress, fibrous stems removed

MOLOTES

1⅓ pounds (600 g) fresh blue corn masa
Vegetable oil, for frying

TO SERVE

1 cup (247 g) Oaxacan Refried Black Beans (page 20)
½ cup (118 mL) vegetable broth
1 head (360 g) green leaf lettuce
1 recipe Pickled Onions (page 111)
3 red radishes (12 g), thinly sliced

1. Place the mushrooms in a small bowl and pour enough water to cover them by 2 inches (5 cm). Let them soak for 1 hour.

2. Heat the oil in a large skillet over medium-high heat. Add the onion and garlic and cook until they begin to brown, in 2 to 3 minutes. Add the tomatoes and cook for 3 to 4 minutes, until they begin to soften and release their juices. Add the salt and pepper and stir.

3. Drain the mushrooms and add them to the skillet with the bay leaves and epazote. Continue to cook for 4 to 5 minutes, until the mushrooms are tender. Stir in the watercress and cook for 3 to 4 minutes, until it is completely wilted. Remove the pan from the heat.

4. Form the masa into twelve equal balls. Take one ball between your palms and flatten it to a ¾-inch-thick (2 cm) disk. Place about 1 tablespoon of the mushroom filling in the center of the disk. Close it so the ends touch, almost like you're making an empanada. Cup both hands together, with the masa ball in the center, to give it a football shape, then seal the edges. Repeat this process with the rest of the balls and arrange them on a rimmed baking sheet.

5. Pour 3 inches (7.5 cm) of oil into a large, deep pot and heat over medium heat to 350°F (175°C). Drop two or three molotes in the oil and fry them for 1 to 2 minutes on each side, until they are golden brown all over. Transfer them to a plate lined with paper towels and let them cool for 5 minutes. Repeat with the rest of the molotes.

6. To assemble, heat the refried beans in a medium skillet over low heat and add the vegetable broth to thin them out to the consistency of a cream

Ariadna Pinacho Cruz

sauce. In Oaxaca they call this pasta de frijol. Place a lettuce leaf on each plate, top with two or three molotes, drizzle some of the pasta de frijol on top, and add the pickled onions and sliced radishes.

7. Molotes do not store well, so it is best to eat them the day you fry them.

NOTES

You can substitute 1½ pounds (680 g) fresh cremini or button mushrooms for the dried mushrooms.

To make the molotes with masa harina, combine 2¼ cups (259 g) blue corn masa harina with 2 cups (473 mL) warm water and ½ teaspoon salt and mix, just like we did for the Blue Corn Tortillas (page 48). This makes about twelve small molotes.

TIME-SAVING TIPS

Use 1 (15-ounce/425 g) can black beans, drained, to make the pasta de frijol. Simply puree the beans in a blender, then heat in a small skillet over low heat.

The molotes can be shaped and stored in the fridge overnight, then fried the next day.

VARIATION

Oil-free: Instead of making the molote shape, flatten the masa disk to ½ inch (2.5 cm) thick, add the filling in the center, and fold so the ends meet together, then seal with a fork like an empanada. Air-fry at 400°F (205°C) for 20 minutes, flipping halfway through. To make the filling, replace the oil with ¼ cup of water or vegetable broth.

THICK CACTUS

Nopal Grueso

In Oaxaca a variety of cactus known as nopal de castilla (*Opuntia ficus-indica*) grows to monstrous proportions, with the cactus pads reaching 12 inches (30 cm) long and 2 inches (5 cm) thick. To cook this gentle giant, first the thorns must be cut off as well as the outer skin, revealing the heart of the cactus (corazón de nopal). This is then cooked in a simple broth and served as a soup with a spicy chile pasilla salsa and thinly sliced onions. Among the Zapotec this dish is sometimes lovingly referred to as "carnita," or little meat, because it is so substantial and filling. Cocinera tradicional Evangelina Aquino Luis shares with us this traditional Zapotec recipe from Tlacolula de Matamoros. Since the cactus is hard to find outside of Oaxaca, I have included a way to adapt it at home with small cactus paddles (see note). Just a warning, because I know it's not everyone's cup of tea: the broth is meant to be a little bit slimy.

MAKES: 6 servings

TOTAL TIME: 45 minutes

1 small head garlic (16 g), top cut off
1 large white onion (232 g), cut in half, divided
5 small avocado leaves
2½ pounds (1.1 kg) nopal de castilla, thorns removed, skin cut off, cut into 2-inch (5 cm) cubes
2 teaspoons salt

SALSA

9 dried pasilla chiles (35 g), stems removed
10 small avocado leaves
1 teaspoon salt

1. Heat 3 quarts or 12 cups (3 L) water in a large pot over medium heat. Add the garlic, half the onion, and the avocado leaves. Before the water comes to a boil, add the nopal and cook, not quite simmering, for 30 to 35 minutes, until tender.

2. Meanwhile, to make the salsa, heat a large clay comal or heavy-bottomed skillet over medium-low heat. Place the chiles on the center of the comal and the avocado leaves on the edge. Toast for 3 to 4 minutes on each side, until the chiles have turned a bright red-brick color and are lightly toasted. The avocado leaves should be lightly toasted as well.

3. Transfer the toasted chiles to a heatproof bowl and pour boiling water over them. Let them soak for 15 minutes. Drain the chiles and transfer them to a blender with the avocado leaves. Add 1 cup water and the salt and puree until smooth.

4. To serve, thinly slice the remaining half onion. Scoop the nopal from the pot with some of the broth into each bowl. Add a sprinkling of the sliced onion and serve with the salsa on the side. The outer layer of the nopal is tough and fibrous, so you can smash the nopal cubes to get to the tender part, or if you get a bit of fibrous skin, you can suck on it and then discard it.

NOTE

The thick cactus is difficult to find outside of Oaxaca. Instead, you can use four thin nopal paddles (about 2½ pounds/1.1 kg), which you can find at your local Mexican grocery store. Remove the spines (see page 17) and cut them into 1-inch (5 cm) squares. Decrease the cooking time in step 1 to 20 to 25 minutes.

Evangelina Aquino Luis

CHICHILO MOLE
FROM TLACOLULA DE MATAMOROS
Chichilo Tradicional de Tlacolula de Matamoros

This is sometimes known as a sad mole, a ceremonial mole prepared for funerals in the Zapotec tradition. Others call it a mystic mole, because it is believed that the taste of it changes according to your mood. For those who have lost a loved one, it always has a tinge of bitterness. This recipe is from Evangelina Aquino Luis, a Zapotec cocinera tradicional from Tlacolula de Matamoros, Oaxaca; it has been passed down by the women in her family for generations. It is also what she calls a "receta de rescate," a recipe on the verge of extinction that needs to be rescued since it is prepared less and less within the community. She dedicates her time to teaching this recipe every opportunity that she has, serving it in her restaurant La Cocina de Nana Vira, and participating in national competitions. In 2022 she won the cooking competition at the Fourth Encounter of Oaxacan Cocineras Tradicionales with this recipe. Evangelina serves it with white rice and cooked quelites formed into patties.

MAKES: 6 to 8 servings

TOTAL TIME: 2 hours

9 to 10 ancho negro chiles (250 g), stems and seeds removed
1 medium white onion (167 g), cut in half
1 small head garlic (19 g), left whole
⅛ cup (20 g) raw almonds
2 teaspoons cumin seeds
2½ teaspoons dried thyme
2 teaspoons dried Mexican oregano
1⅓ cups (200 g) raw sesame seeds
¼ cup (59 mL) vegetable oil
14 ounces (400 g) fresh white corn masa
1 tablespoon salt
2 pounds (907 g) quintoniles (amaranth greens) or any other greens, such as Swiss chard or spinach
Freshly cooked rice, for serving

1. Heat a large clay comal or heavy-bottomed skillet over medium heat. Slice open the chiles so you can lay them completely flat. Working in batches, toast the chiles until they are deeply toasted, in 5 to 6 minutes. At first, the inside of the chiles will turn a brick-red color, then as you continue toasting, it will become a dark brown color. The outside of the chiles will crisp up. You want the chiles to be very toasted but not burned. Transfer to a large heatproof bowl, pour boiling water over them, and let them soak while you toast the rest of the ingredients.

2. Place the onion, cut side down, and garlic on the edge of the comal, where the heat is not as intense. Reduce the heat to medium-low and toast the almonds in the center of the comal until they are brown in spots and begin to crack, in about 3 minutes. Transfer them to a small bowl. On the edge of the comal, toast the cumin seeds, thyme, and Mexican oregano until lightly toasted and aromatic, while stirring, for 1 to 2 minutes. Transfer to the bowl with the almonds.

3. Reduce the heat to low. Place the sesame seeds in a small bowl and pour in ½ cup (118 mL) water, then transfer the moist sesame seeds to the comal and stir, letting the water evaporate, for about 3 minutes. Once the water evaporates, the seeds will begin to toast; continue to stir for 4 more minutes. The sesame seeds shouldn't pop; if they do, your heat is too high, so reduce the heat and continue to toast. Transfer to the bowl with the chiles. Remove the onion and garlic, peel the garlic, and transfer both to the bowl with the almonds.

(CONTINUED)

4. Drain the chiles and sesame seeds, transfer them to a blender, and add the rest of the toasted ingredients, plus enough water to get the blender going. Blend until smooth.

5. Heat the oil in a large pot over medium-low heat. Reduce the heat to low and pour in the puree while stirring; be careful as it might splash. Continuing to stir constantly, simmer the chile puree for 45 minutes, or until it thickens, becomes shiny, and pulls away from the sides of the pot. The puree will splatter as it cooks, so if you have a splatter screen, place it so it covers most of the pot. **This step is very important, so please do not skip it! It is during this process that the mole flavors deepen.** Remove the pot from the heat and scrape the mole paste off the sides of the pot, making a ball of paste in the center of the pot. You can let it cool and store it in an airtight container in the fridge for up to 3 months or in the freezer for up to 1 year. If you are using it now, keep it in the pot.

6. In a large bowl, dissolve the masa in 4¼ cups (1 L) water, then strain through a fine-mesh sieve. Place the pot with the mole paste back on the stove over low heat and add 8½ cups (2 L) water and the salt. Slowly stir to dissolve the paste, increase the heat to medium-low, and bring to a simmer for 10 minutes. Pour in the dissolved masa and simmer for 20 more minutes; if it begins to splash, lower the heat and partially cover the pot with a lid.

7. To cook the quintoniles, bring a pot of water to a boil and drop in the greens. Simmer for 1 minute, then drain.

8. To serve, with your hands form the greens into patties the size of your palm, squeezing out any excess liquid. Place on a plate and bathe it with mole. Serve with rice. Store the prepared mole in an airtight container in the fridge for up to 5 days or in the freezer for up to 6 months.

NOTE

If you don't have a large comal, toast each of the elements individually in a large skillet over medium-high heat.

TIME-SAVING TIP

Make the chichilo mole paste the day before and continue with step 6 the next day.

VARIATIONS

Oil-free: Omit the oil when simmering the chile puree.

Masa harina instruction: Instead of fresh masa, you can use ½ cup (59 g) masa harina dissolved in 1½ cups (354 mL) water.

Evangelina Aquino Luis

PUMPKIN SEED MEATBALLS
IN CHAYA BROTH
Chee Sikil

Bacalar is the home of the Lagoon of the Seven Colors, a crystal-clear, bright blue and turquoise lagoon in the far south of the Yucatán peninsula. This beautiful city is where I met Bruno Cocom and his family. Don Bruno is a Mayan priest, the last of his line, who dedicates his life to the preservation of Mayan culture, traditions, and cuisine. He is also a preservationist of the Melipona bee and its honey. Don Bruno learned to make chee sikil from his grandfather, also a Mayan priest; the best I can describe it is as a pumpkin seed patty simmered in a broth with chaya leaves. This dish is unique because the pumpkin seed patty is so meaty and packed with umami that it's almost like a meatball. The pumpkin seeds are toasted and ground, then kneaded until they release their oil, which is key to flavoring the broth. Just a little bit of a warning: Mayan tradition says that while making this dish, if a visitor stops by and interrupts you, your patties will fall apart in the broth and all your work will be for nothing. So no visitors allowed! Don Bruno uses a pepita that is very hard to find in the US, but you can substitute hulled pumpkin seeds (see notes).

MAKES: **8 to 10 servings**

TOTAL TIME: **1 hour 10 minutes**

5¼ cups (500 g) pepita menuda (raw whole small squash seeds)

3 teaspoons salt, divided

10 large chaya leaves (50 g), stems removed

1 tablespoon achiote paste

2 tablespoons Yucatán White Spice Paste (page 51)

Warm corn tortillas, for serving

Lime wedges, for serving

1. Heat a large skillet or comal over medium heat. Put in the pumpkin seeds and lightly toast them while stirring often for 5 to 6 minutes. The seeds will be slightly browned but will not pop. Remove from the heat and transfer them to a rimmed baking sheet to cool for 6 to 7 minutes, until they are cool enough to handle. Pass the seeds in between your fingers to cool them down quicker. Transfer the seeds to a grain mill or metate and grind them until a fine powder forms. (Alternatively, you can do this in a food processor.) Transfer them to a large bowl.

2. Fill a pot with 10 cups (2.4 L) water and bring to a boil over high heat. Reduce the heat to low and add 1 teaspoon of the salt and the chaya. Let it simmer for 18 to 20 minutes while you prepare the meatballs.

3. Place the achiote paste, spice paste, and remaining 2 teaspoons salt in a small bowl and pour in 1¾ cups (415 mL) water. Use your hands to dissolve the paste. Transfer the ground seeds to a large baking pan and slowly pour the dissolved spices on top. Using your hands, knead together until a rough dough forms, in 3 to 4 minutes. The dough will be crumbly and hard. Keep kneading for 4 to 5 more minutes, until the dough starts leaking oil. The dough will get even harder to knead, but keep kneading for 2 to 3 more minutes. If you don't knead long enough to remove the oil, the dough will be soft and fall apart in the broth.

(CONTINUED)

4. Divide the dough into eight equal portions and, using your hands, squeeze each portion as hard as you can to get every last bit of oil out of the dough. Do this over a small bowl to reserve the oil. Form the dough into oblong patties about 2 inches (5 cm) long; you should have about twenty-eight patties.

5. Drop the patties into the simmering broth with the chaya. Pour in the pumpkin seed oil and bring to a simmer. Do not stir until it comes to a simmer to prevent the patties from falling apart. Cover and simmer for 35 minutes, or until the meatballs are the same color all the way through and the center is not oily.

6. Serve with warm corn tortillas and lime wedges. Store the soup in an airtight container in the fridge for up to 5 days. This does not freeze well.

NOTES

If you can't find chaya leaves, use 3½ cups (4 ounces/131 g) chopped Swiss chard.

Instead of the small raw pumpkin seeds with their shell that Don Bruno used in Bacalar, you can use the hulled pumpkin seeds (pepitas) that are often found in grocery stores. Use 3½ cups (250 g) hulled pumpkin seeds. When you get to step 3, use only 1½ teaspoons achiote paste, 1 tablespoon white spice paste, 1 teaspoon salt, and ½ cup (118 mL) water. Pour the water with the dissolved spices in slowly, mixing with your hand. The dough that forms isn't as crumbly as the one made with the pepita menuda; it starts off with the texture of a thick paste, and as you start kneading. it will firm up. Only knead until you see the first bit of oil, in about 5 minutes. You won't be able to reserve much oil. Divide the dough into ten balls about the size of a golf ball and form into oblong patties. Continue with step 5.

Bruno Cocom

CHARRED WHITE BEAN AND PUMPKIN SEED MASH

Tok Sel

Bruno Cocom stirs vigorously while his wife holds the pot. Plumes of smoke and steam waft out and the aroma of garlic, toasted pumpkin seed, and charred beans permeates the air. Don Bruno, a Mayan cocinero tradicional, is making tok sel, a sort of bean mash made with ibes (a small white bean), cebollín (chives), garlic, ground pumpkin seeds, and rocks. Yes, rocks! The rocks are heated in a fire until they are red-hot and added to the pot with the beans, then you stir very quicky so your beans don't burn. The result is a flavor combination unlike any other: the rocks char some of the beans and add a smokiness to the whole dish, which is very hard to replicate. Don Bruno learned how to make this from his grandparents; he serves this on warm corn tortillas, with limes and habanero chiles. I have documented the recipe as it was prepared that day with Don Bruno, but I have included a way to make it at home in the notes.

MAKES: **4 to 6 servings**

TOTAL TIME: **2 hours**

2¼ cups (500 g) ibes or any small dried white beans, such as navy or alubia blanca, rinsed

5¼ cups (500 g) pepita menuda (raw whole small squash seeds)

¼ cup (20 g) fresh chives, cut into ¼-inch (6 mm) pieces

2 garlic cloves (6 g), minced

1½ teaspoons salt

TO SERVE

12 corn tortillas

4 limes, cut into quarters

1 habanero chile, sliced

1. Place the ibes in a large pot and pour in enough water to cover them by 3 inches (7.5 cm). Bring to a simmer over high heat, reduce the heat to medium-low, and simmer for 1½ hours, until the beans are tender but still firm.

2. An hour into the beans' cooking time, place seven medium rocks right on an open fire.

3. Heat a large skillet or comal over low heat. Put in the squash seeds and toast them, stirring often, until they are golden brown and begin to pop, in about 20 minutes. Remove from the heat and transfer to a rimmed baking sheet to cool for 6 to 7 minutes. Pass the seeds in between your fingers to cool them down quicker. Transfer the seeds to a grain mill, metate, or food processor and grind them until a fine powder forms. Transfer them to a large bowl.

4. When the beans are done, remove them from the heat and drain some of the liquid, leaving about 1 inch (5 cm) of broth in the pot. Add the chives, garlic, ground seeds, and salt and mix vigorously with a wooden spoon (Don Bruno did this with a large stick). Add the hot rocks and stir as fast as you can for 5 to 6 minutes. Place a clean kitchen towel over the pot and cover with a lid. Let it sit for 2 minutes. Carefully take out the rocks and cover the pot again for 5 minutes.

5. Serve with warm corn tortillas, lime wedges, and slices of habanero.

NOTES

The pepita menuda can be replaced with 3½ cups (250 g) hulled pumpkin seeds (pepitas).

If you have a grill, you can place the rocks directly on the grill to get them hot, and follow the recipe as is. If this isn't a possibility for you, then preheat the oven broiler to high. After you mix the cooked beans, chives, garlic, ground seeds, and salt, spread the mixture on a rimmed baking sheet and broil for 1 to 2 minutes, until it begins to char in spots.

4

A FONDA BREAKFAST

Fondas are small family-run restaurants that feed whole neighborhoods for a decent price. The food is simple, unpretentious—and delightful. During colonial times small inns, called mesones, appeared. Each mesón had a small kitchen, not quite a restaurant, that would feed the travelers. These restaurants were called fondas. During the Porfiriato period (1876–1911) fondas were not necessarily attached to a hotel or mesón; they flourished and became the go-to place for people of low income to find a delicious home-cooked meal.

Today, fondas are well-known for their quick and filling breakfasts and their three-course lunches. In this chapter, I use simple substitutions to re-create traditional fonda breakfasts as vegan. I show how tofu can replace scrambled eggs, delve into the heartiness of chilaquiles, and prove that mushroom-tofu chorizo can fool even the most die-hard meat eater. I also include regional dishes like papadzules from Yucatán and chilorio burritos from Sinaloa. This shows beautifully that vegan breakfast goes way beyond overnight oats, especially if it's prepared in a fonda.

MEXICAN-STYLE TOFU SCRAMBLE

Tofu Huevo a la Mexicana

After becoming vegan I quickly realized that I did not enjoy tofu scrambles. I would keep trying them at restaurants but would be disappointed every time—until I decided to make it myself. I know it can seem daunting to eat just scrambled tofu, but I promise you will be changed after having this tofu scrambled Mexican-style. I recommend you eat it in tacos with Molcajete Salsa (page 36), avocado slices, and Oaxacan Refried Black Beans (page 20). If you happen to have any leftovers, you can use them to fill Pumpkin Seed Enchiladas (page 90).

MAKES: **4 servings**

TOTAL TIME: **30 minutes**

1 (14- to 16-ounce/ 397 g) block firm tofu, drained

SEASONING SAUCE
1 teaspoon salt
1 teaspoon garlic powder
½ teaspoon yellow mustard
⅛ teaspoon ground turmeric
⅛ teaspoon freshly ground black pepper

SCRAMBLE
1 tablespoon avocado oil
⅓ large white onion (91 g), chopped (about ½ cup)
1 serrano chile (23 g), finely chopped
2 medium Roma tomatoes (148 g), chopped (about 1 cup)

1. To press the tofu, place it between two large plates, then place a heavy object on top. Let sit for 15 minutes. Discard the liquid that came out of the tofu. Crumble the tofu with your hands over a bowl.

2. To make the seasoning sauce, whisk together 2 tablespoons water, the salt, garlic powder, mustard, turmeric, and pepper in a small bowl.

3. Heat the oil in a large skillet over medium-low heat. Add the onion and serrano chile and cook until the onion is tender and translucent, for 4 to 5 minutes. Add the tomatoes and continue to cook until they break down and release some of their juices, in 3 to 4 minutes.

4. Stir in the tofu, increase the heat to medium, and let cook until the tofu begins to brown, in 4 to 5 minutes. Reduce the heat to low, pour the seasoning sauce over the tofu, and stir to completely coat the tofu in the sauce. Let cook for 1 minute. Serve hot or store in an airtight container in the fridge for up to 3 days or in the freezer for up to 3 months.

VARIATIONS

Oil-free: Replace the oil with ¼ cup (59 mL) water or broth to cook the onion and chile.

Eggy taste: Decrease the salt in the seasoning sauce to ¾ teaspoon and add ⅛ teaspoon kala namak.

SOY CURL MACHACA
Machaca de Soya

Machaca is a salted dried beef that is commonly enjoyed in northern Mexico. It has been around since the eighteenth century, when salting and drying were used as a method of preservation. I'm from the state of Coahuila, where without fail you can find machaca on the breakfast table. This vegan version is made with soy curls, a meat substitute made with dehydrated soybeans. I added no-beef bouillon to give it a beefy flavor, but that is completely optional. I typically like to eat this in a Spicy Machaca Tofu Scramble (page 82), but you can also cook it with onion, garlic, and jalapeños and eat it in tacos or burritos. I like to make this in big batches so I can freeze it and use it to make a quick breakfast.

MAKES: **6 to 8 servings**

TOTAL TIME: **1 hour 40 minutes**

½ cup (118 mL) soy sauce

3 garlic cloves (9 g), peeled

3 tablespoons avocado oil

½ teaspoon smoked paprika

1½ tablespoons no-beef bouillon

8 ounces (227 g) soy curls

1. Preheat the oven to 250°F (120°C). Line a rimmed baking sheet with a silicone mat or parchment paper.

2. To make the marinade, place the soy sauce, garlic, oil, smoked paprika, bouillon, and 2 cups (473 mL) hot water in a blender and puree until smooth. Pour the mixture into a large bowl and add the soy curls. With a wooden spoon, press down on the soy curls so they are submerged in the marinade. Let them soak for 10 minutes, stirring halfway through.

3. Drain and discard the marinade, using your hands to squeeze out any excess liquid left in the soy curls. Spread the soy curls on the prepared baking sheet and bake for 1½ hours, turning every half hour. Remove from the oven and let cool on the baking sheet. As they cool they will become crisp on the edges and chewy.

4. Once completely cool, place one-third of the soy curls in the blender and pulse to shred into small pieces. Be careful not to blend too much or you will end up with a very meaty powder. Repeat with the rest of the soy curls. **Do not do this in the food processor or it will turn the soy curls into powder!** Store in an airtight container in the refrigerator for up 2 weeks or in the freezer for up to 6 months.

VARIATION

Oil-free: Replace the oil with vegetable broth or water.

SPICY MACHACA TOFU SCRAMBLE
Machacado Ranchero

This is my mother's favorite breakfast. It's a saucy, savory, and protein-filled dish that takes you straight to northern Mexico. Machaca is a salted dried beef, but I use a soy version. The machaca is cooked until crisp and then incorporated into a tofu scramble, which is simmered in a spicy roasted tomato salsa ranchera. This is perhaps the best way to enjoy machaca, at least in our house. Try this with tortillas and refried beans or make burritos with it.

MAKES: **4 servings**

TOTAL TIME: **30 minutes**

1 (14- to 16-ounce/ 397 g) block firm tofu, drained

SALSA RANCHERA
4 medium Roma tomatoes (309 g), cored
1 or 2 jalapeño chiles (72 g), stems removed
¼ large white onion (65 g)
2 garlic cloves (6 g), unpeeled
½ teaspoon salt

SEASONING SAUCE
1 teaspoon salt
1 teaspoon garlic powder

½ teaspoon yellow mustard
⅛ teaspoon ground turmeric
⅛ teaspoon freshly ground black pepper

TOFU SCRAMBLE
1 tablespoon avocado oil
½ cup (50 g) Soy Curl Machaca (page 81)
⅓ large white onion (91 g), chopped (about ½ cup)

TO SERVE
Warm tortillas
Refried Pinto Beans (page 20)

VARIATIONS

Oil-free: Omit the oil and start by dry-toasting the machaca in a skillet over medium heat for 1 to 2 minutes, until it begins to crisp around the edges. Reduce the heat to low and add the onion and ¼ cup (59 mL) broth or water.

Eggy taste: Reduce the salt in the seasoning sauce to ¾ teaspoon and add ⅛ teaspoon kala namak.

1. To press the tofu, place it between two large plates and place a heavy object on top. Let sit for 15 minutes. Discard the liquid that came out of the tofu. Crumble the tofu with your hands over a bowl.

2. To make the salsa ranchera, preheat the broiler to high. Line a rimmed baking sheet with aluminum foil.

3. Place the tomatoes, jalapeños, onion, and garlic on the prepared baking sheet and place on the rack closest to the broiler. Broil for 3 to 4 minutes on each side, until the vegetables have softened and have black spots all over. Remove the garlic 2 minutes in and peel it. Transfer the vegetables to a blender, add the salt, and puree until completely smooth.

4. To make the seasoning sauce, whisk together 2 tablespoons water, the salt, garlic powder, mustard, turmeric, and pepper in a small bowl.

5. Heat the oil in a large skillet over medium heat. Add the machaca and cook until it begins to crisp on the edges, in about 2 minutes. Reduce the heat to low, add the onion, and let cook until the onion is tender and translucent, for 3 to 4 minutes. Stir in the tofu and the seasoning sauce and stir to completely coat the tofu in the sauce. Pour in the salsa ranchera, stir, and let simmer slowly until the salsa slightly thickens, in 5 to 6 minutes.

6. Serve hot with tortillas and refried beans. Store the tofu scramble in an airtight container in the fridge for up to 3 days or in the freezer for up to 3 months.

TIME-SAVING TIP

Use leftover soy curl machaca for a quick breakfast or make the soy curl machaca the day before.

RED CHILAQUILES

Chilaquiles Rojos

I swear to you this might be the most crowd-pleasing and filling Mexican breakfast out there. Crispy tortillas are tossed in a spicy tomato sauce and topped with seasonal vegetables, almond crema, and ripe avocado slices. The beauty of it all is that you can change the toppings to your preference, or you could even add Mexican-Style Tofu Scramble (page 78), Mushroom Chorizo (page 93), or Almond Queso Fresco (page 31) for a heartier meal. You can make ahead by prepping the sauce, the tortillas, and almond crema the day before.

MAKES: 4 to 6 servings

TOTAL TIME: 50 minutes

FRIED TORTILLAS
- 1 cup (236 mL) vegetable oil
- 18 corn tortillas, each cut into 8 triangles

SAUCE
- 4 dried guajillo chiles (35 g), stems and seeds removed
- 1 or 2 dried árbol chiles, stems and seeds removed
- 2 (14.5-ounce/411 g) cans diced roasted tomatoes
- ⅓ large white onion (91 g), roughly chopped (about 1 cup)
- 3 garlic cloves (9 g), peeled
- ½ teaspoon salt
- ⅛ teaspoon freshly ground black pepper

VEGETABLE SAUTÉ
- 1 teaspoon avocado oil
- 1 small zucchini (124 g), diced (about 1¼ cups)
- 2 medium Roma tomatoes (154 g), chopped
- 2 garlic cloves (6 g), minced
- ½ head broccoli (182 g), cut into florets (about 2 cups)
- ¼ cup (59 mL) vegetable broth or water
- ½ cup (90 g) cooked or canned black beans, drained
- 1 cup (30 g) chopped spinach
- ½ teaspoon salt
- ⅛ teaspoon freshly ground black pepper

CHILAQUILES
- 1 teaspoon avocado oil
- ¼ cup (12 g) chopped fresh cilantro
- 1 avocado (215 g), pitted, peeled, and sliced
- ½ cup (118 mL) Almond Crema (page 28) or vegan sour cream

1. To make the fried tortillas, heat the oil in a large, heavy-bottomed skillet over medium-high heat until the oil reaches 350°F (175°C) or a tortilla sizzles when it touches the oil. Fry the tortilla triangles in batches until golden brown, for about 1 minute on each side. Remove them from the skillet, place them on a paper towel–lined plate, and let them cool.

2. To make the sauce, place the guajillo and árbol chiles in a small pot and add enough water to cover them by 2 inches (5 cm). Bring the water to a boil over high heat, turn the heat off, and let them sit for 15 minutes. Drain the chiles and transfer them to a blender. Add the tomatoes with their juices, onion, garlic, salt, and pepper and puree until completely smooth. Pass the sauce through a fine-mesh sieve. Reserve until you are ready to assemble the chilaquiles.

3. To make the vegetable sauté, heat the oil in a large skillet over medium heat. Add the zucchini and cook for 2 to 3 minutes, until the zucchini begins to soften. Add the tomatoes and garlic and cook for 2 to 3 minutes, until the tomatoes begin to release their juices. Reduce the heat to medium-low, add the broccoli and broth, and cover. Let the broccoli steam for 5 to 6 minutes, until it starts to get tender. Add the black beans, spinach, salt, and pepper and stir. Cook for 1 minute to wilt the spinach.

4. To assemble the chilaquiles, heat the oil in a large pot over low heat. Pour in the sauce while stirring constantly—be careful because it could splash. Let it simmer for 5 minutes, or until it thickens slightly and becomes a deep red color.

5. Add the fried tortillas to the pot and stir to completely coat them. The tortillas will begin to soften, but we don't want them to be completely soft, so you have to work fast! Transfer the

coated tortillas to serving plates and top with the vegetable sauté, chopped cilantro, avocado slices, and a drizzle of Almond Crema. Serve immediately. I do not recommend you store the chilaquiles, but you can store the sauce and vegetable sauté in separate airtight containers in the fridge for up to 3 days. The fried tortillas will stay crisp in an airtight container at room temperature for up to 2 days.

NOTE

You can use any leftover sauce to make enchiladas.

TIME-SAVING TIPS

You can use store-bought vegan sour cream instead of the Almond Crema; just add a little bit of water to thin it out to the consistency of a thick heavy cream. Use frozen broccoli and spinach to cut down on prep time.

VARIATION

Oil-free: Bake the tortilla triangles on a rimmed baking sheet at 425°F (220°C) for 8 to 10 minutes, flipping halfway through. Replace the oil in the vegetable sauté with ¼ cup (59 mL) vegetable broth, and omit the oil when simmering the sauce.

GREEN CHILAQUILES
Chilaquiles Verdes

Remember the Roasted Tomatillo Salsa (page 39) from the family restaurant? This is where it really shines. Crisp tortillas are tossed in the salsa, then topped with Almond Crema (page 28) and Almond Queso Fresco (page 31). This is the simple version, but you can customize it to your liking by adding a vegetable sauté, avocado slices, Mexican-Style Tofu Scramble (page 78), or your favorite chicken substitute. If you plan to make this for a crowd, you can work ahead by making the sauce, frying or baking the tortillas, and making the Almond Crema and queso fresco the day before.

MAKES: **4 to 6 servings**

TOTAL TIME: **40 minutes**

1 cup (236 mL) vegetable oil
18 corn tortillas, each cut into 8 triangles
1 tablespoon avocado oil
Double recipe Roasted Tomatillo Salsa (page 39; about 4 cups/946 mL)
½ cup (118 mL) Almond Crema (page 28) or vegan sour cream

¾ cup (88 g) Almond Queso Fresco (page 31) or vegan feta cheese
¼ cup (12 g) chopped fresh cilantro
½ large white onion (116 g), thinly sliced (about 1¼ cups)

1. Heat the vegetable oil in a large, heavy-bottomed skillet over medium-high heat until the oil reaches 350°F (175°C) or a tortilla sizzles when it touches the oil. Fry the tortilla triangles in batches until golden brown, for about 1 minute on each side. Remove them from the skillet, place them on a paper towel–lined plate, and let them cool.

2. Heat the avocado oil in a large pot over medium-low heat and pour the sauce in, stirring constantly. Be careful as it might splash. Let it simmer for 5 minutes, or until it slightly thickens.

3. Add the fried tortillas to the pot with the sauce and stir to coat. The tortillas will begin to soften, but we don't want them to be completely soft, so you have to work fast! Transfer the coated tortillas to serving plates and top with the Almond Crema, queso fresco, cilantro, and onion.

4. Serve immediately. I do not recommend you store the chilaquiles, but you can store the sauce in an airtight container in the fridge for up to 3 days. The fried tortillas will stay crisp in an airtight container at room temperature for up to 2 days.

TIME-SAVING TIP

You can use store-bought vegan feta cheese to replace the Almond Queso Fresco, and vegan sour cream instead of the Almond Crema; just add a little bit of water to thin out the sour cream to the consistency of a thick heavy cream.

VARIATION

Oil-free: Bake the tortilla strips on a rimmed baking sheet at 425°F (220°C) for 8 to 10 minutes, flipping halfway through. Omit the oil when simmering the sauce.

CHILORIO BURRITOS

Burritas de Chilorio

Burritos in Mexico are quite different from what you might imagine: They are made with a medium-size flour tortilla and simply rolled, leaving the edges open. Chilorio, a shredded meat stew, is a very typical dish in the state of Sinaloa, the land of wheat and flour tortillas. In this meat-free version, shredded oyster mushrooms and tofu are stewed in an adobo sauce made with chile guajillo and chile pasilla. I tested this recipe many times with many different meat substitutes and tofu was the clear winner, but if you like, you can substitute TVP or shredded jackfruit.

MAKES: **4 servings**

TOTAL TIME: **40 minutes**

ADOBO SAUCE
- **5 dried guajillo chiles (46 to 54 g), stems and seeds removed**
- **2 dried pasilla chiles (11 g), stems and seeds removed**
- **¼ large white onion (65 g), roughly chopped**
- **5 garlic cloves (17 g), roughly chopped**
- **1 small dried bay leaf**
- **1 teaspoon salt**
- **½ teaspoon dried Mexican oregano**
- **½ teaspoon coriander seeds**
- **¼ teaspoon cumin seeds**
- **⅛ teaspoon freshly ground black pepper**
- **2 tablespoons (29 mL) white vinegar**

CHILORIO
- **1 (14- to 16-ounce/ 397 g) block extra-firm tofu, drained**
- **2 tablespoons avocado oil, divided**
- **1 pound (453 g) oyster mushrooms, shredded, or your favorite mushrooms, sliced**
- **¾ teaspoon salt**
- **½ large white onion (136 g), chopped (about 1¼ cups)**
- **1 large Anaheim chile (120 g), stems and seeds removed, diced (about 1 cup)**
- **3 medium Roma tomatoes (332 g), diced (about 2 cups)**

TO SERVE
- **8 medium flour tortillas**
- **1½ cups (370 g) Refried Pinto Beans (page 20)**
- **1 recipe Molcajete Salsa (page 36)**

1. To make the adobo sauce, place the guajillo and pasilla chiles in a small pot and pour in enough water to cover them by 2 inches (5 cm). Bring to a boil over medium-high heat. Turn the heat off and let them soak for 15 minutes. Drain, reserving 1½ cups (354 mL) of the soaking liquid. Transfer the chiles and reserved soaking liquid to a blender and add the onion, garlic, bay leaf, salt, oregano, coriander seeds, cumin seeds, pepper, and vinegar. Puree until smooth, then pass through a fine-mesh sieve.

2. To make the chilorio, first place the tofu between two large plates, then place a heavy object on top. Let sit for 15 minutes. Discard the liquid that came out of the tofu. Use the large holes of a box grater to shred the tofu. Place the tofu on a clean kitchen towel to absorb any excess liquid for 5 minutes.

3. Heat 1 tablespoon of the oil in a large skillet over medium-high heat. Add the mushrooms and cook, stirring occasionally, until golden brown, for 7 to 8 minutes. Reduce the heat to medium-low, add the tofu, stir to combine, and let cook for 3 to 4 minutes, until the tofu begins to brown. Reduce the heat to low and pour in the adobo sauce. Simmer until it slightly thickens and deepens in color, in 12 to 15 minutes.

4. Heat the remaining 1 tablespoon oil in another large skillet over medium heat. Add the onion and Anaheim chile and cook until the onion is tender and translucent, in 4 to 5 minutes. Add the tomatoes and cook until they begin to soften, in about 3 minutes. Add the tofu mixture and cook until heated through, for 5 to 6 minutes.

5. To assemble, one by one heat the tortillas in a skillet or comal over medium-low heat for 1 minute on each side. Spread 2 tablespoons refried beans on each tortilla and spoon some chilorio in the center. Roll the tortilla around the filling. The ends of the burrito should be open. Serve hot with the salsa.

6. You can freeze the assembled burritos in an airtight container for up to 3 months or store the chilorio in the fridge for up to 4 days.

TIME-SAVING TIP

Make the adobo sauce the day before and store in an airtight container in the fridge. Use 1 (16-ounce/453 g) can refried beans.

VARIATION

Oil-free: To make this without oil, cook the mushrooms and tofu in a nonstick pan until golden brown. If they begin to stick, add a little bit of water or vegetable broth. Cook the onion and Anaheim chile in ¼ cup vegetable broth.

PUMPKIN SEED ENCHILADAS
Papadzules

The first time I tried to make this dish I was a newlywed. I had found a first-edition copy of Diana Kennedy's *The Cuisines of Mexico* in a used bookstore and was cooking my way through it. I don't remember specifically where I went wrong when making her recipe, but something was definitely not right! I am happy to say that I have learned a thing or two since then, and I hope you will try this Mayan dish, which is prepared throughout the state of Yucatán. Corn tortillas are filled with a tofu scramble (this is traditionally filled with hard-boiled eggs) and bathed in an earthy pumpkin seed sauce that is topped with a bright and spicy habanero tomato sauce.

MAKES: **4 servings**

TOTAL TIME: **50 minutes**

HABANERO TOMATO SAUCE
- **5 medium Roma tomatoes (485 g), cored and roughly chopped (about 3 cups)**
- **¼ large white onion (65 g), roughly chopped (about ⅓ cup)**
- **1 garlic clove (3 g), peeled**
- **1 teaspoon salt**
- **1 teaspoon avocado oil**
- **1 habanero chile (8 g), stem removed**

PUMPKIN SEED SAUCE
- **1 bunch (85 g) epazote (about 3 cups) *or* ½ cup (6 g) dried epazote**
- **¼ large white onion (65 g)**
- **1 habanero chile (8 g), halved and seeds removed**
- **2 cups (258 g) hulled pumpkin seeds (pepitas)**
- **1 teaspoon salt**

TO SERVE
- **12 corn tortillas**
- **1 recipe Mexican-Style Tofu Scramble (page 78)**

1. To make the habanero tomato sauce, place the tomatoes, onion, garlic, and salt in a blender and puree until smooth. Heat the oil in a medium saucepot over medium-low heat and pour in the sauce while stirring constantly; be careful as it might splash. With a sharp knife, score an X on the tip of the habanero, then add it whole to the sauce. Reduce the heat to low and simmer for 12 to 15 minutes, until the sauce thickens and turns a deep red color.

2. To make the pumpkin seed sauce, you will first have to make an epazote-habanero broth. In a small pot, bring 3½ cups (830 mL) water to a boil, then add the epazote, onion, and habanero. Reduce the heat to low and simmer for 6 to 7 minutes. Remove the pan from the heat and let it steep for 15 minutes. Pass through a fine-mesh sieve and reserve the broth; you should have about 3 cups (710 mL).

3. In a medium skillet, toast the pepitas over medium-low heat, constantly stirring, until they become golden brown and begin to pop, in 3 to 4 minutes. Be careful not to overtoast them or the sauce will be bitter. Transfer them to a plate and let them cool for 5 minutes. Place the pepitas and salt in a blender with 2½ cups (590 mL) of the epazote-habanero broth and puree until the sauce has the consistency of a crepe batter. If it is too thick, add the remaining ½ cup (118 mL) broth. Transfer the sauce to a large skillet and heat over low heat.

4. To assemble, one by one warm the corn tortillas in a skillet or comal over medium heat for 1 minute on each side. Place 2 tablespoons of the tofu scramble on the center of each tortilla. Roll up the tortilla, like you're making enchiladas, and transfer it to a serving plate.

5. Pour the pumpkin seed sauce on top of the enchiladas, and spoon the habanero tomato sauce on top. Serve immediately.

6. The dish as a whole does not store well, but the different components do. Store the pumpkin seed sauce, habanero tomato sauce, and tofu scramble in separate airtight containers in the fridge for up to 3 days. To reheat the pepita sauce, you will need to add a little water or vegetable broth to thin it out to the consistency it had before.

TIME-SAVING TIP

Make the habanero tomato sauce and the epazote broth the day before and store in separate airtight containers in the fridge. Use leftover Mexican-Style Tofu Scramble (page 78) to fill the enchiladas.

NOTE

Epazote is key to flavoring the pumpkin seed sauce, but if you can't find it, you can use ½ bunch cilantro (39 g) and 2 oregano sprigs.

VARIATION

Oil-free: Omit the oil when simmering the habanero tomato sauce.

MUSHROOM CHORIZO
Chorizo de Champiñones

Inevitably, there comes a time when new friends or acquaintances find out I'm vegan and they ask me to prepare something for them. When this happens I usually make this mushroom chorizo. It is liked by meat eaters and vegans alike because it is prepared in the same manner as traditional chorizo, which means it is packed with the spices and flavor we know and love. Mexican breakfast without chorizo is most certainly not breakfast, so now you don't have to miss out and you can enjoy a morning feast of Poisoned Tacos (page 98), potato and chorizo tacos, or even Mexican Bean and Cheese Toast (page 94). Freezing the tofu is optional, but it does result in a firmer, chewier texture.

MAKES: 4 servings (1¼ pounds/534 g)

TOTAL TIME: 1 hour

---

1 (14- to 16-ounce/ 397 g) block extra-firm tofu, frozen overnight and thawed

ADOBO SAUCE
6 dried guajillo chiles (44 g), stems and seeds removed
2 dried ancho chiles (20 g), stems and seeds removed
2 to 4 dried árbol chiles, stems and seeds removed
4 garlic cloves (12 g), peeled
2 whole cloves
1 tablespoon dried Mexican oregano

1 tablespoon paprika
1½ teaspoons salt
½ teaspoon ground cumin
½ teaspoon ground coriander
⅛ teaspoon freshly ground black pepper
¼ cup apple cider vinegar

CHORIZO
2 tablespoons vegetable oil
8 ounces (226 g) cremini mushrooms, finely chopped (about 2 cups)
⅓ cup (38 g) walnuts, finely chopped

TIME-SAVING TIP

Make the adobo sauce the day before and store in an airtight container in the fridge.

1. To press the tofu, drain the tofu and place it between two large plates, then place a heavy object on top. Let it sit for 30 minutes. Discard the liquid that came out of the tofu, then crumble the tofu with your hands into a bowl.

2. To make the adobo sauce, place all the chiles in a small pot and pour in enough water to cover them by 2 inches (5 cm). Bring to a boil over medium-high heat. Turn the heat off and let them soak for 15 minutes. Drain, but reserve ¾ cup (180 mL) of the soaking liquid. Transfer the chiles and reserved soaking liquid to a blender and add the garlic, cloves, oregano, paprika, salt, cumin, coriander, pepper, and vinegar. Puree until completely smooth. Pass through a fine-mesh sieve.

3. Heat the oil in a large skillet over medium heat. Add the mushrooms and cook until they begin to brown and crisp up, in 6 to 7 minutes. Add the tofu and cook until the tofu begins to brown, for 3 to 4 minutes. If it starts to stick to the pan, add a little bit of water and, with a wooden spoon, scrape the bottom of the pan to loosen the crisp pieces. Reduce the heat to low and add the walnuts and adobo sauce, stirring constantly; be careful as it might splash. Simmer for 6 to 7 minutes, until the sauce has thickened and been absorbed by the tofu.

4. Serve hot or store in an airtight container in the fridge for up to 4 days or in the freezer for up to 3 months.

VARIATIONS

Oil-free: Omit the oil and use a nonstick pan. Add a little vegetable broth or water if the mushrooms stick to the pan.

Mild: Omit the árbol chiles.

MEXICAN BEAN AND CHEESE TOAST

Molletes

In northern Mexico, we love our flour tortillas and our bolillo rolls! This is evident in this quick breakfast, where Refried Pinto Beans (page 20) are spread on a crusty bolillo, topped with Cashew Queso Asadero (page 32), then baked until the cheese is melted and the bread is a golden-brown color. I like to top molletes with pico de gallo, but they are also excellent with Molcajete Salsa (page 36). This can be a very easy breakfast to make, and if you're looking for an even quicker version, you could use canned refried beans and your favorite vegan cheese and have this on the table in less than 10 minutes.

MAKES: **4 servings**

TOTAL TIME: **20 minutes**

PICO DE GALLO

- 4 Roma tomatoes (338 g), chopped (about 2 cups)
- ½ large white onion (116 g), finely chopped (about 1 cup)
- 1 jalapeño chile (39 g), finely chopped (about 3 tablespoons)
- ¼ cup (12 g) chopped fresh cilantro
- 2 tablespoons fresh lime juice
- 1 teaspoon salt

MOLLETES

- 4 large bolillo or ciabatta rolls, cut in half
- 1½ cups (370 g) Refried Pinto Beans (page 20), warmed
- 8 ounces (225 g) Cashew Queso Asadero (page 32) or vegan cheese, thinly sliced

1. Preheat the oven to 400°F (205°C). Line a rimmed baking sheet with aluminum foil.

2. To make the pico de gallo, in a large bowl, combine the tomatoes, onion, jalapeño, cilantro, lime juice, and salt. Mix well and let sit in the fridge while you prepare the molletes.

3. Place the bolillo halves cut side up on the prepared baking sheet and bake for 2 minutes, or until they are lightly toasted. Remove from the oven.

4. Spread about 3 tablespoons refried beans on each bolillo half, top with about three slices of cheese, enough to cover the surface of the bolillo, and bake for 10 minutes, or until the edges of the bolillo are golden brown and the cheese has melted. Transfer the bolillos to a plate and let them cool for 5 minutes.

5. Top with pico de gallo and serve immediately.

TIME-SAVING TIPS

Use 1 (16-ounce/453 g) can refried beans and store-bought vegan mozzarella cheese. Instead of making pico de gallo, top with your favorite store-bought salsa.

VARIATIONS

Chorizo molletes: After spreading the beans, add ⅓ cup (56 g) Mushroom Chorizo (page 93) to each bolillo half, then add the cheese.

Avocado molletes: Add two avocado slices on top of the cheese once it comes out of the oven and top with the pico de gallo or Molcajete Salsa (page 36).

CREAMY POBLANO AND CORN TACOS

Tacos de Rajas con Crema

These are one of my favorite breakfast tacos: Poblano chiles are sautéed with onion, garlic, and corn and tossed in a silky vegan crema. The poblanos bring a smokiness and heat to the dish that is subdued by the creaminess of the sauce. Every time I make this dish I think back to when I worked in the family restaurant as a teenager. I had to roast and peel sacks of poblano chiles. I ended up in tears because my hands burned so badly from handling them without gloves, and the cooks made fun of me. I will forever appreciate gloves in the kitchen.

MAKES: **4 servings**

TOTAL TIME: **30 minutes**

1 tablespoon avocado oil
1 large white onion (296 g), thinly sliced (about 2 cups)
2 garlic cloves (6 g), minced
2¼ cups (304 g) fresh or frozen corn kernels (about 3 ears corn)
½ cup (118 mL) vegetable broth
5 poblano chiles (617 g), roasted (see page 14), peeled, seeded, and cut into strips
1 cup (236 mL) Almond Crema (page 28)
1 teaspoon salt
¼ teaspoon freshly ground black pepper
12 corn tortillas

1. Heat the oil in a large skillet over low heat. Add the onion and cook for 5 to 6 minutes, stirring often, until it is tender and translucent. Add the garlic, corn, and vegetable broth, increase the heat to medium, cover, and let steam until the corn is tender, for 3 to 4 minutes.

2. Stir in the poblano chiles and cook for 1 minute, or until they are heated through. Reduce the heat to low and pour in the crema. Add the salt and pepper and stir.

3. To assemble, one by one heat the tortillas on a skillet or comal over medium heat for 1 minute on each side. Fill each tortilla with 2 tablespoons of the filling and serve immediately.

4. I do not recommend you store the assembled tacos, but you can store the rajas con crema in an airtight container in the fridge for up to 3 days or in the freezer for up to 3 months.

TIME-SAVING TIP

Roast the poblanos and make the crema the day before and store in separate airtight containers in the fridge.

VARIATION

Oil-free: Substitute ¼ cup (59 mL) water or broth for the oil.

POISONED TACOS

Tacos Envenenados

Legend says that in the 1940s a man named Don Lauro would sell these crisp tacos near the local railroad station in the city of Zacatecas. He had a particular sense of humor, which showed in the sign he placed outside his establishment that said, "If you want to poison yourself, eat tacos." Thus the name "poisoned tacos." While there is nothing poisonous about this recipe, you will find a satisfyingly filling breakfast taco you can make with mashed potatoes, refried beans, mushroom chorizo, and a slice of Cashew Queso Asadero (page 32). If you happen to have leftover mashed potatoes, you can make this recipe in less than 30 minutes. Serve with Blistered Serranos (page 44) and a squeeze of lime juice.

MAKES: 4 servings

TOTAL TIME: 40 minutes

FILLING
- 1 pound (453 g) russet potatoes, peeled and cut into 1-inch (5 cm) chunks (about 3 cups)
- 3 dried guajillo chiles (22 g), stems and seeds removed
- 1½ teaspoons salt, divided
- 2 cups (337 g) cooked or canned pinto beans, drained
- ⅔ cup (160 mL) bean broth or vegetable broth
- 1 tablespoon avocado oil
- 1 cup (170 g) Mushroom Chorizo (page 93)

TO SERVE
- 12 corn tortillas
- 4 ounces (115 g) Cashew Asadero Cheese (page 32) or vegan mozzarella cheese, thinly sliced
- ¼ cup (59 mL) vegetable oil
- 2 limes, cut in half
- 1 recipe Blistered Serranos (page 44) or Roasted Tomatillo Salsa (page 39)

1. To make the filling, place the potatoes, chiles, and 1 teaspoon of the salt in a medium pot and add enough cold water to cover the potatoes by 2 inches (5 cm). Bring to a boil over high heat, reduce the heat to low, and simmer for 15 to 18 minutes, until the potatoes are tender. Drain and transfer the chiles to a blender and the potatoes to a bowl. Mash the potatoes with a potato masher or a fork.

2. Add the beans, broth, and remaining ½ teaspoon salt to the blender with the chiles and puree until smooth.

3. Heat the avocado oil in a large skillet over medium-low heat. Add the chorizo and cook until it begins to brown, in 2 to 3 minutes. Add the mashed potatoes and bean puree and stir to incorporate everything together. Cook for another 2 to 3 minutes, until the mixture thickens to the consistency of refried beans.

4. To assemble, one by one heat the tortillas on a comal or skillet over medium-high heat for 30 to 40 seconds on each side, or wrap the tortillas in a moistened paper towel and cook them for 1 minute in the microwave, until they are soft and pliable. Fill each tortilla with 2 tablespoons of the filling and a small slice of the asadero cheese and fold in half to make a taco.

5. Heat the vegetable oil in another large skillet over medium-high heat. To test if the oil is hot enough, drop a piece of tortilla in the oil; if it sizzles, the oil is ready. Working in batches, add the tacos and pan-fry until golden brown, about 1 minute on each side. Transfer to a plate lined with paper towels.

6. Serve immediately with a side of limes and Blistered Serranos. I don't recommend you store the assembled tacos, but you can store the filling in an airtight container in the fridge for up to 4 days.

TIME-SAVING TIP

To make these tacos in less than 20 minutes, use 2 cups (420 g) leftover mashed potatoes, replace the guajillos with 1 teaspoon ancho chile powder, and use 1 cup (170 g) store-bought vegan chorizo.

VARIATION

Oil-free: Omit the oil and cook the chorizo in a nonstick pan. Instead of pan-frying the tacos, air-fry them at 400°F (205°C) for 12 to 15 minutes, until crispy, flipping them halfway through.

A FONDA BREAKFAST

5

STREET FOOD

Undoubtedly, some of Mexico's best food is eaten hunched over a plate of tacos on the closest street corner. There's something about street tacos that just hits the spot every time. I don't know if it's the shiny tortilla that has been dipped in grease, the crunchiness of the onion, the aroma of the cilantro, or the creaminess of the avocado salsa that makes them so irresistible. I also love that street food is for everyone, from the business guy in an expensive suit to the starving student. But street food goes way beyond tacos; in many ways it is a celebration of the legacy of corn in Mexico. You can find gorditas filled with stewed nopales and potatoes, mushroom tlacoyos topped with a fiery salsa, potato flautas, and itacates filled with papas con rajas. All of these are corn-based antojitos (hand-held snacks), and as I found out when I visited Doña Silvia, a food vendor outside the San Juan Market in Mexico City, these seemingly simple antojitos are made with fresh nixtamalized corn masa, local mushrooms and vegetables, and homemade salsa. I've had food on the streets of Mexico City that is better than any fine-dining Mexican restaurant in the US.

In this chapter, I explore the magic and versatility of plant proteins. Hibiscus becomes barbacoa, oyster mushrooms become carnitas, and TVP (textured vegetable protein) becomes a meaty filling for an empanada from Hidalgo. There's even a recipe for chicharron made with rice! There's also plenty of vegetables, but there's something to be said about using meat substitutes. I didn't stop eating meat because I didn't like the flavor of it, and the truth is sometimes I miss it, and I especially did in the beginning. So I am in favor of using meat substitutes like TVP, soy curls, and tofu. I think anything that will make your transition to veganism easier is valid—plus who doesn't enjoy a good taco?

PORCINI MUSHROOM CHICHARRONES

Chicharrones de Hongo Porcini

My great-grandfather was a pig butcher. I don't remember ever meeting him, but I do remember my grandmother's deep love for crispy, crackling chicharrones. She would eat them while they were still warm, on a soft corn tortilla with a slice of avocado and topped with a fiery salsa. In an attempt to re-create chicharrones without the pork, I am relying on a technique I first saw while I was spending a week staging as a young cook in the kitchen at José Andrés's Minibar in Washington, DC. A puree of overcooked rice and spices is dehydrated and then fried to make the most amazing chicharron, which I think even my grandmother would have loved. The porcini mushroom powder gives it a slightly porky flavor, but any mushroom powder will work as well. You can eat them as a snack with lime and hot sauce, or you can use them as a topping for Bean and Nopal Tostadas (page 117) or Fava Bean and Mushroom Stuffed Blue Corn Cakes (page 123).

MAKES: **4 servings**

TOTAL TIME: **2 hours 20 minutes**

½ cup (92.5 g) long-grain rice
1½ teaspoons porcini mushroom powder
⅛ teaspoon smoked paprika
⅛ teaspoon garlic powder

¼ teaspoon salt
½ to 1 chipotle chile in adobo
2 cups (473 mL) canola oil

1. Preheat the oven to 200°F (95°C). Line two rimmed baking sheets with silicone mats or parchment paper.

2. In a medium saucepot, combine the rice and 2½ cups (591 mL) water. Bring to a boil over high heat, reduce the heat to low, and simmer for 15 to 20 minutes, stirring occasionally, until almost all the water has evaporated and the rice is completely overcooked.

3. Remove from the heat and transfer to a blender. Add the porcini mushroom powder, smoked paprika, garlic powder, salt, and chipotle. Blend until completely smooth; it should have the consistency of a thin pancake batter. If the mixture is too thick, add ¼ cup (59 mL) water to get it going. You should have about 2 cups (473 mL) of puree.

4. Divide the puree equally between the prepared baking sheets, using a spatula to spread it to ¼ inch (6 mm) thick. It's OK if it is a little uneven. Bake for 2 hours, rotating the pan halfway through. The puree will become the texture of fruit leather in some places and hard in others. If you find that the puree hasn't dried out completely on the side that is touching the tray, peel it off the tray, flip it, and put it back in the oven for 15 minutes. Remove from the oven and let cool. It will continue to harden and dry out as it cools.

(CONTINUED)

5. Heat the oil in a medium saucepot to 375°F (190°C). Break the dehydrated puree into 3- to 4-inch (7.5 to 10 cm) pieces and drop them into the hot oil. The pieces will immediately puff up as they hit the oil. If they don't, it means your oil is not hot enough. Flip them and let them fry on the other side until golden and crispy; this will all take 15 to 20 seconds.

6. Remove from the oil and place on a wire cooling rack. Store in an airtight container at room temperature for up to 2 days.

TIME-SAVING TIP

Dehydrate the puree the day before, break it into pieces, and store in an airtight container at room temperature. Fry the chicharrones the next day.

VARIATION

Oil-free: Place four or five (3-inch/7.5 cm) pieces of the dehydrated puree on a plate and microwave for 30 to 40 seconds, until they puff up and are hard to the touch.

AL PASTOR TACOS

Tacos al Pastor

Al pastor tacos are the quintessential street food, sold on vendor carts or shops on the street where you can see the meat roasting on a spit. While this vegan version may not be roasted on a spit, it is so packed with flavor that you won't miss a thing. Sometimes I struggle to find a balance between looking for realistic meat substitutes or forgoing them altogether and just using vegetables. Here I have decided to do a little bit of both by using a combination of textured vegetable protein and cauliflower marinated in an adobo of dried chiles, pineapple, spices, and herbs. Mushrooms would also work very well with this recipe, as would grilling the cauliflower after it has been marinated. Serve with Roasted Tomatillo Salsa (page 39) or Chile de Árbol Salsa (page 43).

MAKES: **4 to 6 servings**

TOTAL TIME: **40 minutes**

TVP

- 1½ cups (113 g) textured vegetable protein
- 1 large white onion (232 g), cut in half, divided
- 1 dried bay leaf

ADOBO SAUCE

- 4 dried guajillo chiles (38 g), stems and seeds removed
- 1 dried ancho chile (15 g), stem and seeds removed
- 1 dried morita chile (3 g), stem and seeds removed, *or* 1 small chipotle chile in adobo
- 1 tablespoon achiote paste
- 3 garlic cloves (12 g), peeled
- ½ teaspoon ground cumin
- ½ teaspoon dried Mexican oregano
- ⅛ teaspoon black peppercorns
- 2 whole cloves
- ¾ cup (123 g) diced (½-inch/1.25 cm pieces) fresh pineapple, divided
- 1 tablespoon apple cider vinegar
- 1½ teaspoons salt
- ½ head (350 g) medium cauliflower, cut into small florets (about 3 cups)
- 1 tablespoon avocado oil

TO SERVE

- 12 corn tortillas
- ½ large white onion (152 g), sliced (about 1 cup)
- ½ cup (25 g) packed fresh cilantro, roughly chopped
- 1 recipe Roasted Tomatillo Salsa (page 39) or your favorite salsa

(CONTINUED)

1. Preheat the oven to 450°F (230°C). Line a rimmed baking sheet with a silicone mat or parchment paper.

2. To prepare the TVP, place the TVP, half the onion, and the bay leaf in a medium saucepot with enough water to cover the TVP by 3 inches (7.5 cm). Bring to a boil over high heat, reduce the heat to low, and simmer for 10 minutes. Drain and discard the onion and bay leaf. When the TVP is cool enough to handle, use your hands to squeeze out any excess liquid, then transfer it to a bowl.

3. To make the adobo sauce, heat a cast-iron pan or comal over medium-high heat. Toast the chiles for 30 seconds on each side, or until they are slightly darker in color and become fragrant. Place them in a pot and add enough water to cover them by 2 inches (5 cm). Bring the water to a boil, then turn off the heat and let them soak for 15 minutes. Once the chiles are soft and pliable, drain them but reserve 1 cup (236 mL) of the soaking liquid. Transfer the chiles to a blender and add the reserved chile soaking liquid, achiote paste, remaining half onion, garlic, cumin, oregano, peppercorns, cloves, ¼ cup (41 g) of the pineapple, the vinegar, and salt. Puree until smooth. Pass the sauce through a fine-mesh sieve. You should have about 2½ cups (591 mL).

4. In a medium bowl, combine the cauliflower florets and 1 cup (236 mL) of the adobo sauce and stir to completely coat the cauliflower. Transfer to the prepared baking sheet and bake for 20 to 25 minutes, until the cauliflower is tender but not mushy.

5. While the cauliflower is baking, heat the oil in a large skillet over medium heat. Add the TVP and cook until the TVP begins to brown, in 5 to 6 minutes. Reduce the heat to low, pour in the adobo sauce, and simmer until the sauce has almost completely evaporated, for about 15 minutes. Remove the cauliflower from the oven and add it to the skillet with the TVP. Stir to evenly distribute the cauliflower.

6. To serve, one by one heat the tortillas on a comal or heavy-bottomed skillet over medium heat for 30 to 40 seconds on each side. Place 1½ to 2 tablespoons of the al pastor filling on each tortilla and sprinkle some of the chopped onion and cilantro on top. Add a couple of pieces of the remaining fresh pineapple and serve with the salsa.

7. Store the al pastor filling in an airtight container in the fridge for up to 5 days or in the freezer for up to 6 months.

TIME-SAVING TIP

Make the adobo sauce the day before and store in an airtight container in the fridge.

VARIATIONS

Oil-free: Omit the oil and use a nonstick skillet to cook the TVP.

Mild: Omit the chile morita.

HIBISCUS FLOWER BARBACOA
Barbacoa de Jamaica

There is only one place where I have had a hibiscus flower taco that I have truly enjoyed, and it was at Nuno's Tacos in Dallas. Nuno himself graciously gave me some tips on cooking the hibiscus without revealing his secret recipe. Traditional barbacoa is very fatty, so to mimic the fat I use mashed grilled eggplant, which adds a smoky flavor and a creamy texture. Adding baking soda to the second water bath the hibiscus is cooked in mellows the acidity. The quality of the hibiscus flower does matter for this recipe, as some brands of hibiscus have a lot of debris; you can find my recommendations in the Resources (page 309). Last, in the variations I include instructions to make a refreshing drink called agua de jamaica with the leftover cooking liquid.

MAKES: **4 servings**

TOTAL TIME: **1 hour 10 minutes + marinating time**

HIBISCUS
3 cups (70 g) dried hibiscus flowers
¼ teaspoon baking soda
½ cup (118 mL) vegetable broth or water
1 tablespoon soy sauce
½ teaspoon dried thyme
½ teaspoon garlic powder
¼ teaspoon smoked paprika
½ teaspoon dried Mexican oregano
¼ teaspoon ancho chile powder
¼ teaspoon salt
¼ teaspoon freshly ground black pepper

BARBACOA
1 large eggplant (424 g)
2 tablespoons avocado oil
1 large white onion, finely chopped, divided (232 g)
3 garlic cloves (9 g), finely chopped
¼ teaspoon salt
⅛ teaspoon freshly ground black pepper
½ cup (118 mL) vegetable broth (optional)

TO SERVE
12 corn tortillas
½ cup fresh (25 g) cilantro, finely chopped
1 recipe Chile de Árbol Salsa (page 43) or your favorite salsa

1. Pick over the flowers and remove any stems or twigs. Place in a colander and rinse really well. Depending on the quality of your flowers, you might need to do this several times.

2. Transfer the hibiscus flowers to a large pot and add enough water to cover them by 4 inches (10 cm), about 2 quarts (1.8 L). Bring to a boil over high heat, reduce the heat to low, and simmer for 45 minutes. Drain the hibiscus flowers, but save the liquid to make agua de jamaica (see variations).

3. Return the flowers to the pot and fill it with enough fresh water to cover them by 4 inches (10 cm). Add the baking soda and simmer over low heat for 10 to 15 minutes, until the hibiscus flowers are al dente. You should be able to easily bite through them, but they shouldn't be completely mushy. Drain and rinse them. Discard the water and transfer the flowers to a medium bowl.

4. To make the marinade, in a small bowl, whisk together the broth, soy sauce, thyme, garlic powder, smoked paprika, oregano, ancho chile powder, salt, and pepper. Pour the marinade over the flowers, stir to coat, and transfer to a reusable food bag or zip-top bag and let rest overnight in the refrigerator.

5. Preheat a grill to 450°F (230°C).

6. Using a fork, poke holes in the eggplant. Place the eggplant on the grill, close the lid, and let it cook for 15 to 20 minutes, until the skin is charred and it looks deflated and soft. Flip it and cook for 5 more minutes, or until it is completely soft to the touch.

(CONTINUED)

7. Remove the eggplant from the grill and let cool for 5 to 6 minutes. Remove the skin with your hands and cut the eggplant in half, then use a spoon to remove half of the seeds. Chop the flesh of the eggplant until it resembles a coarse puree.

8. Heat the oil in a large skillet over medium-low heat. Add half the chopped onion and cook for 4 to 5 minutes, stirring often, until it begins to brown. Add the garlic and cook for 1 minute, stirring occasionally.

9. Add the eggplant and cook until it is soft and a grayish color, for about 3 minutes. Add the hibiscus with the marinade and the salt and pepper, and stir to evenly combine. Increase the heat to medium and cook, stirring occasionally, for 3 to 4 minutes, until the hibiscus starts to brown. Be careful not to burn or overcook it, because it can become tough again. If there are browned bits stuck to the bottom of the skillet, add the broth and scrape them off with a wooden spoon, then stir them into the mixture. These browned bits have a lot of flavor, so we don't want to leave them in the pan.

10. To serve, one by one heat the tortillas on a comal or heavy-bottomed skillet over medium heat for 30 to 40 seconds on each side. Fill each tortilla with 1½ to 2 tablespoons of the barbacoa and sprinkle some of the remaining chopped onion and cilantro on each taco, then top with salsa.

11. Store the barbacoa in an airtight container in the fridge for up to 5 days or in the freezer for up to 6 months.

NOTE

If you don't have a grill, preheat the broiler to high. Cut off the stem of the eggplant and cut it into quarters lengthwise, then cook the eggplant in a steamer over medium-high heat for 8 to 10 minutes, until completely soft. Remove from the steamer and transfer it to a rimmed baking sheet, skin side down. Brush the cut side with 1 tablespoon avocado oil and broil for 1 to 2 minutes, until browned. Remove it from the oven, let cool for 5 minutes, and scoop out the flesh with a spoon.

VARIATIONS

Oil-free: Omit the oil and use a nonstick skillet to cook your barbacoa.

Agua de jamaica: Add 1 quart (1 L) water and ½ cup (100 g) sugar to the reserved hibiscus cooking water and stir. Let cool completely in the fridge. Serve over ice.

REQUESÓN AND CARROT CRISPY TACOS

Tacos Dorados de Requesón con Zanahoria

These crispy tacos filled with cashew requesón and carrot are inspired by the tacos dorados sold on the streets of Nayarit. They are usually filled with shrimp, but it is not uncommon to see them filled with requesón as well. They are always accompanied by a consomé, which is a tomato broth that can be used as a salsa or as a dipping sauce. You could say these are the original hard shell tacos, but so much better! The best part is that you can fill them with almost anything—leftover mashed potatoes, beans, or veggies. I like to serve them with Chile Morita Salsa (page 40) for an extra spice kick.

MAKES: **4 servings**

TOTAL TIME: **45 minutes**

PICKLED ONIONS
- 1 large red onion (356 g), divided
- ¼ cup (59 mL) fresh lime juice
- ½ teaspoon salt

CONSOMÉ
- 2 Roma tomatoes (203 g), cored and cut into quarters
- 1 dried guajillo chile, stem and seeds removed
- 1 garlic clove, peeled
- 1 dried bay leaf
- 1 teaspoon dried Mexican oregano
- ½ teaspoon salt

CARROT FILLING
- 4 medium carrots (273 g), grated (about 2 cups), divided
- ½ teaspoon garlic powder
- ½ teaspoon onion powder
- ½ teaspoon ancho chile powder
- ¼ teaspoon salt
- ⅛ teaspoon freshly ground black pepper

TACOS
- 12 corn tortillas
- 1 recipe Cashew Requesón (page 35) or ¾ cup (184 g) vegan ricotta cheese
- ½ cup (118 mL) vegetable oil
- 1 head romaine lettuce (226 g), thinly sliced

1. To make the pickled onions, cut the onion into quarters. Reserve one-quarter for the consomé and thinly slice the remaining onion. Transfer the sliced onion to a small bowl and combine with the lime juice and salt. Let marinate in the fridge, stirring occasionally, until the tacos are ready.

2. To make the consomé, in a small pot, combine the reserved quarter onion, tomatoes, guajillo, garlic, bay leaf, oregano, salt, and 2¼ cups (532 mL) water. Bring to a boil over high heat, reduce the heat to low, and simmer for 15 minutes. Discard the bay leaf. Transfer everything to the blender, including the water, and puree until smooth.

3. To make the carrot filling, reserve ⅓ cup (46 g) of the grated carrots to use as a garnish. In a large bowl, combine the remaining grated carrots, garlic powder, onion powder, ancho chile powder, salt, and pepper.

4. To assemble, one by one heat the tortillas on a comal or heavy-bottomed skillet over medium-high heat for 30 to 40 seconds on each side, or wrap the tortillas in a moistened paper towel and cook them for 1 minute in the microwave, until they are soft and pliable. Fill each tortilla with 1 tablespoon of the requesón and 1 tablespoon of the carrot filling and fold in half.

5. Heat the oil in a large skillet over medium-high heat. Fry the tacos until golden brown, about 1 minute on each side. Transfer to a paper towel–lined plate. Arrange the tacos on plates and top with romaine lettuce, reserved grated carrot, and pickled onions. You can pour some of the consomé on top of the tacos or serve it on the side as a dipping sauce.

(CONTINUED)

6. These tacos do not store well after they are cooked.

TIME-SAVING TIP

You can make the consomé and pickled onions the day before.

VARIATIONS

Oil-free: Air-fry the tacos at 400°F (205°C) for 15 to 20 minutes, flipping them halfway through, until golden brown and crispy.

Potato tacos dorados: Instead of requesón and carrots, use 1½ cups (315 g) leftover mashed potatoes to fill your tacos, and follow the rest of the recipe as is.

MUSHROOM CARNITAS
Carnitas de Setas

This recipe is inspired by the famous pork carnitas of the state of Michoacán. If you hadn't noticed already, I have a deep love for mushrooms, and there is no better recipe than this one to showcase them. The meaty texture and umami flavor in the mushrooms combined with the crisp yuba make this taco simply irresistible. There are two ingredients you might not recognize: yuba, which is tofu skin, and porcini mushroom powder. The mushroom powder gives the mushrooms a pungent pork-like flavor, and the yuba adds a crunch to the taco. If you can't find yuba, you can omit it and increase the oyster mushrooms to 2 pounds (900 g) instead. This recipe uses more oil than I usually use to mimic the fat in the carnitas. Serve on warm corn tortillas topped with onion, chopped cilantro, and Chile de Árbol Salsa (page 43).

MAKES: 4 servings

TOTAL TIME: 40 minutes

YUBA
5 ounces (140 g) fresh or frozen yuba sheets, torn into 1 × 2-inch (2.5 × 5 cm) strips
1 tablespoon soy sauce
1 tablespoon orange juice
1 garlic clove (3 g), minced

MUSHROOMS
½ cup (118 mL) fresh orange juice
1 teaspoon onion powder
1 teaspoon garlic powder
1 teaspoon porcini mushroom powder
½ teaspoon smoked paprika

½ teaspoon + ⅛ teaspoon salt
4 tablespoons avocado oil, divided
1½ pounds (680 g) oyster mushrooms, stems trimmed, torn into large pieces

TO SERVE
12 corn tortillas
½ large white onion (152 g), minced (about 1 cup)
½ cup (25 g) packed fresh cilantro, roughly chopped
1 recipe Chile de Árbol Salsa (page 43)

1. Place the yuba in a medium bowl and add the soy sauce, orange juice, 2 tablespoons water, and the garlic. Toss the yuba with your hands to make sure it is coated with the marinade. Let it marinate for 15 minutes.

2. For the mushrooms, in a small bowl, whisk together the orange juice, onion powder, garlic powder, porcini mushroom powder, smoked paprika, and salt; set aside.

3. Heat 3 tablespoons of the oil in a large skillet over medium-high heat. Add half the mushrooms and cook for 4 to 5 minutes, stirring occasionally, until golden brown. Transfer them to a small plate. Add the rest of the mushrooms to the pan and cook until golden brown. Return the first batch of mushrooms to the pan and pour in the orange juice mixture. Simmer for 3 to 4 minutes, until most of the liquid evaporates.

4. Heat the remaining 1 tablespoon oil in another large skillet over medium-high heat. Add the yuba and cook for 4 minutes, stirring occasionally, until it becomes golden brown and crispy in some spots. Transfer it to the pan with the mushrooms and stir.

5. To serve, one by one heat the tortillas on a comal or heavy-bottomed skillet over medium heat for 30 to 40 seconds on each side. Fill each tortilla with 1½ to 2 tablespoons of the carnitas, sprinkle some chopped onion and cilantro on each taco, and top with salsa.

6. Store the filling in an airtight container in the fridge for up to 5 days or in the freezer for up to 6 months.

VARIATION

Oil-free: In a large bowl, toss the mushrooms with the orange juice mixture, then place on a rimmed baking sheet lined with a silicone mat or parchment paper. Bake at 400°F (205°C) for 15 minutes, stirring halfway through. Place the marinated yuba on another rimmed baking sheet lined with a silicone mat or parchment paper. Reduce the oven temperature to 375°F (190°C) and add the yuba to the oven. Bake for 15 minutes, or until golden brown and crispy, then remove the yuba and mushrooms from the oven and combine them on one of the baking sheets.

BEAN AND NOPAL TOSTADAS
Tostadas de Arriero

In the town of Amealco, Querétaro, you can find a very special tostada made from thickly ground nixtamalized blue corn and topped with beans and nopal salad, and sometimes queso fresco. The tostadas were often cooked directly on the embers of wood-burning stoves. Tradition says that arrieros—people who would move goods across the countryside on pack animals—would eat these tostadas on their way through Amealco because they were easy to make and carry with the ingredients on hand. The best way to make these at home is by toasting homemade Blue Corn Tortillas (page 48). You can also make these with store-bought tostadas or by toasting store-bought blue corn tortillas.

MAKES: **4 servings**

TOTAL TIME: **30 minutes**

1 recipe Blue Corn
   Tortillas (page 48)
½ recipe Refried Pinto
   Beans (page 20) *or* 1
   (16-ounce/453 g) can
   refried beans
1 recipe Cactus Salad
   (page 47)

1 recipe Almond Queso
   Fresco (page 31) or
   vegan feta cheese
½ cup (100 g) canned
   pickled jalapeños and
   carrots

1. Preheat the oven to 400°F (205°C). Line two rimmed baking sheets with silicone mats or parchment paper.

2. Divide the tortillas equally between the prepared baking sheets and bake for 15 to 20 minutes, flipping them halfway through, until hard to the touch and crunchy.

3. Spread 2 to 3 tablespoons beans on each tostada, top with ⅓ cup (53 g) nopales salad, 1 tablespoon crumbled queso fresco, and as many pickled jalapeños and carrots as you like.

TIME-SAVING TIP

Use store-bought blue corn tortillas, canned refried beans, and vegan feta cheese instead of the Almond Queso Fresco.

117

POTATO AND POBLANO STUFFED CORN CAKES

Itacates de Rajas con Papas

Tepoztlán, Morelos, is famous for its itacates. *Itacates* comes from the Nahuatl word *ihtacatl*, which roughly translates to "food for the journey." They are similar to gorditas but have a characteristic triangle shape. The masa differs from that of a gordita, due to the addition of cheese and lard; in our case we are adding avocado oil, which results in a soft, flavorful masa. The filling is poblano chiles and potatoes simmered in a garlicky tomato sauce. You can also fill them with papas con chorizo, mushrooms in mole, or practically anything you would fill a taco with.

MAKES: 4 servings

TOTAL TIME: 35 minutes

RAJAS CON PAPAS

1 large russet potato (423 g), cut into small dice (about 2 cups)
2 teaspoons salt, divided
4 medium Roma tomatoes (453 g), cored
3 garlic cloves (9 g), peeled
2 teaspoons avocado oil
1 large white onion (232 g), chopped (about 1½ cups)
4 poblano chiles (477 g), roasted (see page 14), peeled, and cut into thin strips
½ teaspoon chopped fresh thyme
½ teaspoon dried marjoram
⅛ teaspoon freshly ground black pepper

ITACATES

2 cups (242 g) masa harina
⅛ teaspoon baking powder
½ teaspoon salt
¼ cup (59 mL) avocado oil

TO SERVE

½ cup (118 mL) Almond Crema (page 28) or vegan sour cream
¾ cup (88 g) Almond Queso Fresco (page 31) or vegan feta cheese
1 recipe Chile de Árbol Salsa (page 43) or your favorite salsa

1. To make the filling, put the potato in a medium saucepot and add enough water to cover by 3 inches (7.5 cm). Add ½ teaspoon of the salt and bring to a boil over high heat. Reduce the heat to low and simmer for 10 minutes, or until the potato begins to soften. Drain.

2. Put the tomatoes in another saucepot and add enough water to cover them by 2 inches (5 cm). Bring to a boil over high heat, reduce the heat to low, and simmer for 5 to 6 minutes, until the tomato skins burst and the tomatoes begin to soften. Drain the tomatoes and transfer them to a blender. Add the garlic and puree until completely smooth. You should have about 2½ cups (591 mL) of puree.

3. Heat the oil in a large skillet over medium-low heat. Add the onion and cook until tender and translucent, for about 7 minutes. Add the potato and stir to combine. Add the tomato puree, poblanos, thyme, marjoram, remaining 1½ teaspoons salt, and pepper and simmer for 8 to 10 minutes, until the puree thickens and becomes a deep red color and the potato is cooked through. Remove from heat.

4. Preheat the oven to 350°F (175°C). Line a rimmed baking sheet with a silicone mat or parchment paper.

5. To make the itacates, in a large bowl, combine the masa harina, baking powder, and salt. Add the avocado oil and slowly pour in 1⅔ cups (394 mL) warm water while mixing with your hands. Knead for 5 minutes, until the masa is soft like Play-Doh, pliable but not sticky. Roll a small piece of masa into a ball and lightly press it; if the edges crack, the dough is too dry. Add an additional ¼ cup (59 mL) water and knead again.

(CONTINUED)

6. Divide the dough into six equal balls. Pat each ball to flatten it while rotating it between your hands until it is ⅓ inch (8.5 mm) thick. Use your hands to shape the ball into a flat triangle about ½ inch (1.25 cm) thick.

7. Heat a comal or heavy-bottomed skillet over medium heat. Reduce the heat to medium-low, add the itacates to the pan, and let them cook for 2 to 3 minutes on each side, until they are browned in spots. Transfer them to the prepared baking sheet and bake for 5 to 6 minutes, until the center is cooked. Remove from the oven and let sit for 5 minutes. Cut the itacates in half and top one side with the potato mixture. Add 1 tablespoon Almond Crema, 1 tablespoon queso fresco, and salsa on top of the filling, then top with the other half of the itacate. Serve hot.

8. You can store the filling in an airtight container in the fridge for up to 4 days or in the freezer for up to 3 months. The itacates can be stored, after they are cooked and before cutting them, in an airtight container in the fridge for up to 2 days. To reheat them, spray them with water to moisten the surface and bake at 350°F (175°C) for 6 to 8 minutes.

TIME-SAVING TIPS

Make the rajas con papas the day before and store in an airtight container in the fridge. Use store-bought vegan feta cheese to replace the Almond Queso Fresco and vegan sour cream instead of the Almond Crema; just add a little bit of water to thin out the sour cream to the consistency of a thick heavy cream.

VARIATION

Oil-free: Omit the oil and use ¼ cup (59 mL) broth to cook the onion. Omit the oil in the masa and add additional water as needed to reach the Play-Doh consistency.

FAVA BEAN AND MUSHROOM STUFFED BLUE CORN CAKES

Tlacoyos de Habas y Setas

Tlacoyos are football-shaped masa pockets that are stuffed with seasonal vegetables and cooked on a comal right on the streets of Mexico City. They are topped with nopales and queso fresco and are meant to be eaten with your hands. I thought I knew how to make tlacoyos—until I met Doña Silvia Díaz. Doña Silvia is from Xalatlaco, a small town 36 miles away from Mexico City. Her family has been making tlacoyos, quesadillas, and gorditas on the streets of Mexico City for years. Her tlacoyos are made with a beautiful indigo-colored masa that they make fresh every day, and are filled with your choice of fresh fava beans, mushrooms stewed in epazote, huitlacoche, or wilted zucchini blossoms. Doña Silvia and her family got a kick out of watching me try to shape tlacoyos, but I promise with a little practice you can shape them too. To make these at home, we are using a blue corn masa harina. I have given you two choices of fillings. Choose one filling to make 4 servings of tlacoyos or make both fillings and double the masa for 8 servings. If you are lucky enough to find fresh fava beans, see the notes for instructions. You can find Doña Silvia's recipe for Huitlacoche and Zucchini Blossom Quesadillas on page 126.

MAKES: 4 servings (6 large tlacoyos)

TOTAL TIME: 45 minutes + soaking time

FAVA BEAN FILLING

- ¾ cup (113 g) dried shelled fava beans, soaked in water overnight and drained
- ¼ large white onion (65 g), roughly chopped (about ⅓ cup)
- 1 garlic clove (3 g), roughly chopped
- ½ teaspoon salt

MUSHROOM FILLING

- 2 teaspoons avocado oil
- ½ large white onion (152 g), finely chopped (about 1 cup)
- 2 garlic cloves (6 g), minced
- 1 pound (453 g) oyster mushrooms, trimmed and shredded
- 1 epazote sprig, chopped (about 2 tablespoons) *or* 2 teaspoons dried epazote
- ½ cup (118 mL) vegetable broth
- ¾ teaspoon salt

MASA

- 2 cups (284 g) blue corn masa harina

TO SERVE

- ½ recipe Cactus Salad (page 47)
- ½ cup (58 g) Almond Queso Fresco (page 31) or vegan feta cheese
- 1 recipe Chile de Árbol Salsa (page 43) or your favorite salsa

Silvia Diaz

(CONTINUED)

1. To make the fava bean filling, place the beans in a medium saucepot and fill with enough water to cover them by 2 inches (5 cm). Bring to a boil over high heat, reduce the heat to low, and simmer for 20 minutes. The fava beans should be cooked but still have some bite to them. Drain and transfer them to a food processor. Add the onion, garlic, and salt and process for 1 to 2 minutes, until the fava beans turn into a chunky paste. Transfer to a bowl and let cool.

2. To make the mushroom filling, heat the oil in a large skillet over medium-low heat. Add the onion and cook, stirring occasionally, for 4 to 5 minutes, until the onion is tender and translucent. Add the garlic and cook for 1 minute. Add the mushrooms and epazote and cook for 2 to 3 minutes, until the mushrooms begin to soften. Reduce the heat to low, add the vegetable broth and salt, cover, and continue to cook for 8 to 10 minutes, until the mushrooms are tender and almost all the liquid is gone. Transfer to a bowl and let cool.

3. To make the masa, place the masa harina in a large bowl and gradually pour in 1½ cups (354 mL) warm water while mixing with your hand. Knead for 5 minutes, or until there are no dry spots in the masa and it is soft like Play-Doh, pliable but not sticky. Roll a small piece of masa into a ball and lightly press it; if the edges crack, the dough is too dry. Add an additional ¼ cup (59 mL) water and knead again.

4. Preheat a comal or heavy-bottomed skillet over medium heat.

5. Divide the dough into six equal balls. Rub your hands with a little bit of oil and flatten one ball into a circle about ½ inch (1.25 cm) thick. Place 1 tablespoon of either filling in the center and fold it in half so the edges of the masa touch, like you are making an empanada. Pinch the edges closed. Place the ball of filled masa in your hands and cup both hands together, with the masa in the center, to give the ball a football shape. Carefully flatten the tlacoyo by patting it between your hands until it is ¼ inch (6 mm) thick. It is OK if some of the filling escapes or shows through the masa. Repeat with the rest of the masa and filling.

6. Reduce the heat under the comal to medium-low and cook the tlacoyos, one at a time, for 4 to 5 minutes on each side, until firm to the touch.

7. Serve the warm tlacoyos topped with 2 to 3 tablespoons of the nopales salad, queso fresco, and salsa.

8. You can store the fillings in separate airtight containers in the fridge for up to 4 days or in the freezer for up to 3 months. The cooked tlacoyos can be stored in an airtight container in the fridge for up to 2 days or in the freezer for up to 6 months. To reheat them, spray them with water to moisten the surface and bake them at 350°F (175°C) for 6 to 8 minutes.

TIME-SAVING TIP

Make the fillings the day before and store in the fridge.

VARIATIONS

Oil-free: Omit the oil when making the fillings and rub your hands with a little bit of water instead of oil when shaping the tlacoyos. To make the filling, replace the oil with ¼ cup of water or vegetable broth.

Fresh fava beans: Use 2½ pounds (1.13 kg) fresh fava beans in their pods. You should end up with 2 cups (256 g) shucked fava beans. Add them to a food processor with the onion, garlic, and salt and pulse for 30 to 60 seconds to form a paste, similar to making falafel. This is your filling.

HUITLACOCHE AND ZUCCHINI BLOSSOM QUESADILLAS

Quesadillas de Huitlacoche y Flor de Calabaza

Doña Silvia, the tlacoyo expert, also makes quesadillas. She uses the same masa to make blue tortillas and makes them right there on the spot, then fills them with cheese and a filling of huitlacoche (corn fungus) or zucchini blossoms stewed in onion, garlic, chile, and epazote. Her tortillas have a characteristic elongated oval shape, making every bite the perfect ratio of tortilla to filling. I have given you two choices of fillings. Choose one filling to make 4 servings of quesadillas or make both fillings and masa for 8 servings. Look for huitlacoche at your local Mexican market and zucchini blossoms at farmers' markets in the early summertime. Serve these with Chile de Árbol Salsa (page 43) or Molcajete Salsa (page 36).

MAKES: **4 servings**

TOTAL TIME: **1 hour**

HUITLACOCHE FILLING
- 2 teaspoons avocado oil
- ¼ large white onion (65 g), finely chopped (about ⅓ cup)
- 2 garlic cloves (6 g), minced
- 1 red jalapeño chile, finely chopped
- 8 ounces (226 g) fresh huitlacoche, rinsed and cut into ½-inch (1.25 mm) pieces
- 1 epazote sprig, chopped (about 2 tablespoons), *or* 2 teaspoons dried epazote
- ½ teaspoon salt
- ⅛ teaspoon freshly ground black pepper

ZUCCHINI BLOSSOM FILLING
- 2 teaspoons avocado oil
- ⅓ large white onion (91 g), finely chopped (about ½ cup)
- 2 garlic cloves (6 g), minced
- 1 or 2 serrano chiles (43 g), finely chopped
- 10 zucchini blossoms (45 g), pistils removed, rinsed, and cut into strips
- 1 epazote sprig, chopped (about 2 tablespoons), *or* 2 teaspoons dried epazote
- ½ teaspoon salt
- ⅛ teaspoon freshly ground black pepper

QUESADILLAS
- 1 recipe Blue Corn Tortillas (page 48)
- 1 recipe Cashew Requesón (page 35) or vegan ricotta cheese
- 1 recipe Chile de Árbol Salsa (page 43) or your favorite salsa

1. To make the huitlacoche filling, heat the oil in a large skillet over medium-low heat. Add the onion and cook, stirring often, until tender and translucent, for 4 to 5 minutes. Add the garlic and jalapeño and cook for 3 to 4 minutes, until the jalapeño softens. Add the huitlacoche, epazote, salt, and pepper and cook for 8 to 10 minutes, stirring occasionally. As it cooks the huitlacoche will release some liquid, but by the time you are done cooking, most of the liquid will be gone.

2. To make the zucchini blossom filling, heat the oil in another large skillet over medium-low heat. Add the onion and cook, stirring often, until tender and translucent, for 4 to 5 minutes. Add the garlic and serranos and cook for 3 to 4 minutes, until the serranos soften. Add the zucchini blossoms, epazote, salt, and pepper and cook for 3 to 4 minutes, stirring occasionally, until the blossoms wilt.

3. To assemble, one by one heat the tortillas on a comal or heavy-bottomed skillet over medium heat for 30 to 40 seconds on each side. Place 1 tablespoon of either filling and 1 tablespoon Cashew Requesón on each tortilla. Fold in half and cook for 1 to 2 minutes on each side, until the requesón is warm. Serve with the salsa.

TIME-SAVING TIP

Make the fillings and cheese the day before and use store-bought blue corn tortillas.

VARIATIONS

Oil-free: Omit the oil when cooking the filling and replace it with ¼ cup (59 mL) vegetable broth.

Canned huitlacoche: If you can't find fresh huitlacoche, use 1 (7.5-ounce/212 g) can huitlacoche, drained.

MEXICAN CORNISH PASTIES

Pastes Hidalguenses de Carne de Soya con Papas

I find the history of food so fascinating, and the story behind these pastes (pasties) is one of my favorite culinary crossovers. In 1824 a group of English miners arrived in the state of Hidalgo to work the silver mines of Real del Monte. With them came a wave of Cornish immigrants who formed tight-knit communities and brought the food of the miners, the pasty. The community thrived until the company's financial failure and dissolution in 1849, when most of the immigrants returned to England. The legacy of the pasty remains to this day in Hidalgo, where you can find pasties filled with classic meat and potatoes with a spicy twist, and various sweet and savory fillings. One of my favorite versions is filled with arroz con leche. In this vegan version I use TVP to replace the beef, but you can fill this with practically anything. Serve with Roasted Tomatillo Salsa (page 39) or your favorite salsa.

MAKES: 13 medium pasties

TOTAL TIME: 1 hour + resting time

DOUGH
- 4 cups (500 g) bread flour
- 1 teaspoon salt
- 1 cup (226 g) unsalted vegan butter, cold

TVP
- 1 cup (62 g) textured vegetable protein
- ½ large white onion (152 g)
- 1 dried bay leaf

FILLING
- 1 tablespoon avocado oil
- 2 cups (210 g) button mushrooms, finely chopped
- ½ large white onion (152 g), chopped (about 1 cup)
- 1 large leek (300 g), dark green top cut off, thinly sliced
- 1 or 2 serrano chiles (8 g), finely chopped
- 1 medium russet potato (242 g), peeled and cut into small cubes
- ½ large carrot (100 g), cut into small cubes (about ⅔ cup)
- ¾ cup (177 mL) vegetable broth
- ¼ teaspoon salt
- ⅛ teaspoon freshly ground black pepper
- 1 tablespoon chopped fresh parsley

SEASONING SAUCE
- 2 tablespoons soy sauce
- 2 teaspoons vegan Worcestershire
- 1 teaspoon nutritional yeast
- ¼ teaspoon smoked paprika
- 1 teaspoon garlic powder
- ⅛ teaspoon ground coriander

TO GLAZE
- ½ cup (118 mL) unsweetened almond milk

(CONTINUED)

1. To make the dough, in a large bowl, mix the flour and salt. Using your hands, rub the vegan butter into the flour until it resembles breadcrumbs. Add ¾ cup (177 mL) cold water and mix with your hands, forming the dough into a ball. If the dough is too dry, add an additional ¼ cup (59 mL) cold water. Transfer the dough to a floured surface and knead for 5 to 6 minutes, until the dough becomes smooth and slightly elastic. Place in an airtight container and let it rest in the fridge for at least 3 hours, or up to overnight. The resting time is very important; otherwise the dough will be very difficult to roll out.

2. To prepare the TVP, place the TVP, 3 cups (709 mL) water, the onion, and bay leaf in a medium saucepot. Bring to a boil over high heat, reduce the heat to low, and simmer for 10 minutes. Drain and discard the onion and bay leaf. When the TVP is cool enough to handle, use your hands to squeeze out any excess liquid, then transfer it to a bowl.

3. To make the filling, heat the oil in a large skillet over medium-high heat. Add the mushrooms and cook for 3 to 4 minutes, until they begin to brown. Reduce the heat to low and add the onion, leek, and serranos and cook until they soften, stirring occasionally, for 4 to 5 minutes. Add the potato, carrot, and vegetable broth, cover, and cook, stirring occasionally, for 5 to 6 minutes, until the potato begins to soften and the liquid completely evaporates.

4. While the potato is cooking, make the seasoning sauce. In a small bowl, whisk together the soy sauce, vegan Worcestershire, nutritional yeast, smoked paprika, garlic powder, coriander, and ½ cup (118 mL) water.

5. Increase the heat under the potato mixture to medium and add the TVP and seasoning sauce. Stir to coat the TVP with the sauce, add the salt and pepper, cover, and let simmer for 12 to 14 minutes, until the potato is almost cooked through. Remove from the heat, stir in the parsley, transfer to a bowl, and let cool in the fridge while you roll out the dough.

6. Preheat the oven to 350°F (175°C). Line a rimmed baking sheet with a silicone mat or parchment paper.

7. On a floured surface, divide the dough into thirteen equal pieces, each about the size of a golf ball. Using a rolling pin, roll out each piece of dough to make a 6-inch (15 cm) circle about ⅛ inch (3 mm) thick. Place 1 heaping tablespoon of the filling on one-half of the circle, moisten the edges with water, and fold over the dough, forming a half-moon. Seal the edges with your fingers, then crimp with a fork. Alternatively, you can make a decorative seal: Start at one end, pinch and slightly twist the dough diagonally across the seam between your thumb and index finger, and continue pinching and twisting until you have sealed all of the dough.

8. Place the pasties on the prepared baking sheet 2 inches (5 cm) apart and brush with almond milk. Bake for 40 to 50 minutes, until the bottoms of the pasties are golden brown. Remove from the oven and let cool for 5 to 6 minutes before serving. Store leftovers in an airtight container in the fridge for up to 2 days. Reheat in a 350°F (175°C) oven for 15 minutes.

TIME-SAVING TIPS

Use the food processor to chop the mushrooms. Make the dough and filling the night before. The pasties can also be filled, shaped, and frozen, then taken out at a later date and baked from frozen at 350°F (175°C) for 40 to 45 minutes. You can also use store-bought puff pastry to make these; bake at 400°F (205°C) for 20 to 25 minutes, until golden brown on the bottom.

6

MOLE FROM THE MARKET

Every time I travel to a new city in Mexico, the first thing I do is visit the market. I could spend a whole day there, enthralled by its colorful vendors who offer everything from fruits and vegetables to prepared meals, as well as artesanías (handicrafts) and souvenirs. The markets' origins can be traced back to precolonial Mexico. When Hernán Cortés arrived in Tlatelolco, a neighboring city to Tenochtitlan, he was blown away by the sheer size of the market. In his letters to King Carlos V of Spain, he describes it as twice as big as the city of Salamanca, where more than 60,000 souls assembled daily and were engaged in buying and selling. The markets were a center of trade, social life, and economy in Mesoamerica. Even after the Spanish conquest, markets continued to thrive and were later enriched with imports brought by the Manila galleons starting in 1565. Markets in Mexico are relevant to this day; Mexico City alone has over 300 different markets! So if you happen to find yourself in Mexico and want to try authentic local cuisine, visit the market first.

I often get asked what my favorite Mexican dish is, and I always respond mole! Mole is one of the shining stars of the market. Vendors sell different-colored mole pastes by the kilo there, as well as the many dried chiles and spices needed to make this complex sauce. Mole, like the market, has pre-Hispanic origins, but the first moles, or mullis as they were known, were less complicated: thick sauces made with a diverse variety of chiles, tomatoes, and seeds. This changed in the colonial period with the arrival of products like cinnamon, cloves, anise, nuts, and bread. These ingredients transformed mole into the sauce we know today, but regionally there are still many moles that are closer to their pre-Hispanic counterparts.

The *Larousse Diccionario Enciclopédico de la Gastronomía Mexicana* by Ricardo Muñoz Zurita names seventy-one different types of regional moles! In this chapter I explore seven types of mole, how to make them, and what to serve them with. You can replicate the flavors of the mole from the market at home; all you need is a little time and patience.

Perhaps no one has expressed the beauty of Mexican markets as well as the famous Chilean poet Pablo Neruda in his book *Memoirs*: "Mexico with its prickly pear and its serpent; Mexico blossoming and thorny, dry and lashed by hurricane winds, violent in outline and color, violent in eruption and creation, surrounded me with its magic and its extraordinary light. I traveled through it for years, from market to market. Because Mexico is to be found in its markets. Not in the guttural songs of the movies or in the false image of the Mexican in sombrero, with moustache and pistol. Mexico is a land of crimson and phosphorescent turquoise shawls. Mexico is a land of earthen bowls and pitchers, and fruit lying open to a swarm of insects. Mexico is an infinite countryside of steel-blue century plants with yellow thorns. The most beautiful markets in the world have all this to offer. Fruit and wool, clay and weaving looms, give evidence of the incredible skill of the fertile and timeless fingers of the Mexicans."

BLACK MOLE

Mole Negro

Mole negro is the most complex of all the moles. It takes time and practice to learn how much toasting the chiles and nuts need, and to achieve the right balance between sweet and bitter. This sauce has a sweet aromatic quality and a richness, along with a hint of bitterness, which makes it one of the best. To experience mole negro in the most authentic way, I encourage you to visit Oaxaca, where it is traditionally made on a wood-burning stove (cocina de humo), which adds a hint of smokiness to the mole that is hard to replicate. That being said, I think it is still worth your time to make it at home; the process is not difficult, but it is time-consuming. I have included notes on how you can work ahead to make this more manageable. As far as the ingredients go, the chile chilhuacle is hard to find outside of Oaxaca (see Resources, page 309), but chile ancho can be used as a substitute. Serve it over hearty vegetables, use it to make mole enchiladas, or make the Plantain Molotes in Black Mole (page 138). This recipe makes a large quantity because I believe all your time and effort deserve abundant results.

MAKES: **10 to 12 servings**

TOTAL TIME: **5 hours**

8 dried chilhuacle negro chiles (56 g) *or* 4 dried ancho chiles
6 to 8 dried pasilla chiles (85 g)
7 dried mulato chiles (200 g)
3 dried avocado leaves
1 dried bay leaf
1 (3-inch/7.5 cm) Ceylon cinnamon stick, broken into pieces, *or* ½ teaspoon ground cinnamon
½ teaspoon dried Mexican oregano
½ teaspoon anise seeds
¼ teaspoon dried thyme
¼ teaspoon dried marjoram
¼ teaspoon cumin seeds
2 whole cloves
2 whole allspice berries
¼ teaspoon black peppercorns
¼ cup (41 g) raw almonds
¼ cup (44 g) raw peanuts
¼ cup (28 g) pecans

¼ cup (40 g) sesame seeds
3 tablespoons (34 g) hulled pumpkin seeds (pepitas)
⅓ cup (57 g) raisins
2 medium Roma tomatoes (247 g)
4 medium tomatillos (254 g), husks removed, rinsed
1 large white onion (232 g), cut in half, divided
6 garlic cloves (18 g)
5 tablespoons (78 mL) avocado oil, divided
1 ripe plantain (198 g), peeled and cut into quarters
½ bolillo *or* 4-inch (10 cm) piece of baguette (52 g)
1 corn tortilla, cut into quarters
5 cups (1.2 L) vegetable broth
1 (3-ounce/85 g) tablet Mexican chocolate
¼ cup (50 g) sugar
1 tablespoon salt

(CONTINUED)

135

MOLE FROM THE MARKET

1. Remove the stems and seeds from the chiles, but reserve ¼ cup (24 g) of the seeds. Open the chiles so you can lay them completely flat.

2. Heat a large comal or heavy-bottomed skillet over medium-low heat. Working in batches, toast the chilhuacle and pasilla chiles until they are deeply toasted, for 10 to 12 minutes. At first, the inside of the chile will turn a brick red color, then as you continue toasting, it will become a dark brown color. The outside of the chile will crisp up. You want the chiles to be very toasted but not burned. Transfer the chiles to a large bowl of hot water.

3. In the same comal, toast the mulato chiles until they are deeply toasted, for 15 to 16 minutes. Similar to the previous chiles, the inside will first turn brick red, then dark brown. The outside of the chile should be crisp to the touch but not burned. Transfer them to the bowl with the other chiles, place a heatproof plate on top of the chiles to submerge them in the water, and let them soak for 45 minutes.

4. In a small skillet, toast the reserved chile seeds over medium heat until they are black, stirring often, for 4 to 5 minutes. Be sure to open a window because the spicy fumes of the chile seeds toasting will make you cough. Transfer the seeds to a small bowl of water and let them sit for 5 minutes. Drain and transfer to a large bowl and pour 2 cups (473 ml) of hot water over them.

5. In the same skillet, toast the avocado leaves and bay leaf over medium heat for about 1 minute, or until fragrant, then reserve for later use.

6. In the same skillet, toast the cinnamon, oregano, anise, thyme, marjoram, cumin, cloves, allspice, and peppercorns over medium heat for 1 minute, or until fragrant. Transfer the spices to the bowl with burnt seeds.

7. In the same skillet, toast the almonds over medium heat until they are brown in spots and begin to crack, in about 3 minutes; transfer to the large bowl with the toasted spices. Toast the peanuts until deep golden brown, in about 2 minutes; transfer to the bowl. Toast the pecans until they are golden brown, in about 2 minutes; transfer to the bowl. Toast the sesame seeds until they begin to pop and are golden brown, in 3 to 4 minutes; transfer to the bowl. Toast the pumpkin seeds until they are brown in spots and begin to pop, in about 2 minutes; transfer to the bowl. Finally, toast the raisins for 1 minute, or until they plump up and become a reddish color; transfer to the bowl.

8. Preheat the broiler to high.

9. Place the tomatoes, tomatillos, onion, and garlic on a rimmed baking sheet and broil for 3 to 4 minutes, flipping them halfway through, until they soften and are covered with black spots. Remove the garlic 2 minutes in, and peel it. Transfer everything to the large bowl with the spices and nuts.

10. Heat 2 tablespoons of the oil in a large skillet over medium heat and fry the plantain and bread until golden brown, for about 2 minutes on each side. Transfer to the same large bowl. In the same skillet, toast the tortilla until it has black spots all over and is crispy, for about 3 minutes on each side. Transfer to the same bowl.

11. Drain the chiles and transfer them to a blender. Add 3 cups (720 mL) hot water and puree until smooth. Pass through a fine-mesh sieve into a medium bowl.

12. Transfer the contents of the large bowl to the blender and puree until smooth, then pass through a fine-mesh sieve into another medium bowl.

13. Heat the remaining 3 tablespoons oil in a large pot over low heat. Pour in the chile puree while stirring, taking care as it might splash. Simmer the chile puree for 20 minutes, while constantly stirring, or until it thickens and pulls away from the sides of the pot. The puree will continue to splatter as it cooks, so I recommend you use a splatter screen if you have one.

14. Pour in the second puree and simmer for 20 minutes while constantly stirring, until it thickens and darkens to a dark brown, almost black color. Be careful with the splattering. Pour in the vegetable broth, chocolate, toasted avocado leaves and bay leaf, sugar, and salt and bring to a simmer. Simmer for 30 minutes, or until the sauce thickens enough to coat the back of a spoon. Let cool, then transfer to an airtight container and let it mellow in the fridge overnight before using. Store in the fridge for up to 5 days or in the freezer for up to 6 months.

TIME-SAVING TIPS

Day 1: Do steps 1 through 4, leaving the chiles and seeds out at room temperature.

Day 2: Do steps 5 through 12 and store the purees in separate airtight containers in the fridge.

Day 3: Do steps 13 and 14.

Day 4: Enjoy your mole.

VARIATION

Oil-free: Dry-toast the bolillo and tortilla. Bake the plantain in the oven at 425°F (220°C) for 10 minutes. Omit the oil when cooking the chile puree.

MOLE FROM THE MARKET

PLANTAIN MOLOTES IN BLACK MOLE

Molotes de Plátano Macho en Mole Negro

Molotes are golden-brown, fried snacks made with mashed plantain, filled with Oaxacan Refried Black Beans (page 20) and Cashew Queso Asadero (page 32), and topped with Almond Crema (page 28) and Almond Queso Fresco (page 31). You can find them in the southern states of Veracruz and Oaxaca. In the central states of Puebla, Hidalgo, and Tlaxcala, they are made with corn masa, like the Lobster Mushroom Molotes (page 64). I have a deep love for the sweetness that ripe plantains bring to every dish, which is why I like to serve them with mole negro; it is a symphony of sweet, spicy, and savory. The plantains for this recipe need to be very ripe, with their skins more black than yellow, and soft to the touch. Serve the molotes as appetizers or for brunch.

MAKES: **4 servings**

TOTAL TIME: **1 hour + resting time**

---

4 ripe plantains (797 g), cut into thirds, peel on
Avocado oil, for frying
1 cup (247 g) Oaxacan Refried Black Beans (page 20)
½ recipe Cashew Queso Asadero (page 32), cut into 1-inch (2.5 cm) pieces, *or* 5 ounces (141 g) vegan mozzarella

2 cups (473 mL) Black Mole (page 135)
½ cup (118 mL) Almond Crema (page 28)
½ cup (58 g) Almond Queso Fresco (page 31) or vegan feta cheese

1. Place the plantain pieces in a medium pot and fill with enough water to cover them by 3 inches (7.5 cm). Bring to a boil over high heat, reduce the heat to low, and simmer for about 15 minutes, or until the plantain pieces swell and begin to burst out of their skins. Drain. To peel them, squeeze the skins and the plantain should pop right out. Transfer them to a medium bowl and mash into a puree with a fork. Let cool in the fridge for 30 to 60 minutes.

2. Heat about 3 inches (7.5 cm) of oil in a large, heavy-bottomed skillet over medium heat to about 350°F (175°C). If you don't have a thermometer, you can test the oil by dropping in a small piece of plantain puree. If it sizzles, then the oil is ready.

3. To form the molotes, divide the plantain mash into ten equal balls. Flatten a ball in your hand to a ½-inch (1.25 mm) thick round. Place 1 tablespoon beans in the center and a piece of cheese. Close it so the ends touch, almost like you're making an empanada. Cup both hands together, with the plantain ball in the center, to give it a football shape. Repeat this process with the rest of the plantain mash.

4. Fry the molotes for 1 to 2 minutes on each side, until they are golden brown all over. Transfer them to a plate and let cool for 5 minutes.

5. To assemble, in a medium saucepot, bring the mole to a simmer over medium-low heat.

6. Pour ¼ cup (59 mL) mole on each plate, place two molotes on top, drizzle Almond Crema over them, and sprinkle with queso fresco.

VARIATION

Oil-free: Air-fry the molotes at 400°F (205°C) until they are golden brown, for 15 to 20 minutes, flipping them halfway through.

TIME-SAVING TIPS

Use store-bought vegan feta cheese, vegan mozzarella, and 1 (16-ounce/453 g) can refried beans. Make the molotes and store them in the fridge, then fry them the next day.

MOLE POBLANO

Mole poblano is the most well-known and celebrated of the moles. It is a rich and complex sauce that is both savory and sweet, fragrant and spicy. Unlike mole negro, mole poblano has no bitter undertones, making it a favorite among people all over the world. While mole dates back to pre-Hispanic times, mole poblano as we know it today was invented in the seventeenth century after the Spanish arrived and brought with them bread and spices. Whenever I am asked what my favorite food is, I always answer mole poblano, and after making this recipe you will see that even though it is a labor of love, it is well worth every minute spent making it. This recipe makes a large amount, but I urge you not to decrease the quantities, as you can freeze the mole for up to 6 months. Serve it over hearty vegetables or make Mole Poblano Enchiladas (page 147).

MAKES: **8 to 10 servings**

TOTAL TIME: **2 hours**

½ cup (118 mL) avocado oil, divided
5 dried ancho chiles (73 g), stems and seeds removed
6 dried mulato chiles (77 g), stems and seeds removed
6 dried pasilla chiles (41 g), stems and seeds removed
4 dried chipotle meco chiles (28 g), stems and seeds removed
½ bolillo *or* 4-inch (10 cm) piece of baguette (61 g)
1 corn tortilla (26 g), cut into quarters
¼ cup (44 g) raw peanuts
¼ cup (44 g) raisins
1 ripe plantain (190 g), peeled and sliced
7 cups (1.65 L) vegetable broth, warm, divided
3 tablespoons (30 g) raw almonds
3 tablespoons (30 g) hulled pumpkin seeds (pepitas)

¼ cup (40 g) sesame seeds
1 (3-inch/7.5 cm) Ceylon cinnamon stick, broken into pieces, *or* ½ teaspoon ground cinnamon
¼ teaspoon anise seeds
¼ teaspoon coriander seeds
3 whole allspice berries
3 whole cloves
⅛ teaspoon black peppercorns
⅛ teaspoon dried thyme
2 medium Roma tomatoes (125 g)
1 small white onion (193 g), cut into quarters
3 garlic cloves (9 g), peeled
1½ (3-ounce/85 g) tablets Mexican chocolate
1 teaspoon no-chicken bouillon
2 teaspoons salt

(CONTINUED)

1. Heat ¼ cup (59 mL) of the oil in a large skillet over medium-low heat. Working in batches, fry the chiles for 1 minute on each side, or until they become a deep red color and are lightly toasted. Transfer to a medium bowl filled with hot water and let them soak while you toast the rest of the ingredients.

2. In the same skillet, toast the bread and tortilla until golden brown, for about 2 minutes on each side; transfer to a large bowl. Toast the peanuts for 2 to 3 minutes, until golden brown; transfer to the same bowl. Toast the raisins for 1 minute, stirring constantly, until they plump up and become a reddish color; transfer to the bowl. Toast the plantain slices for 2 minutes on each side, until golden brown; transfer to the bowl. Add 2 cups (473 mL) of the warm vegetable broth to the bowl and let everything soak.

3. In a small skillet, toast the almonds over medium heat for 2 to 3 minutes, stirring constantly, until they are deeply toasted and begin to crack; transfer to the bowl with the bread and plaintains. Toast the pumpkin seeds for 1 to 2 minutes, until they begin to pop and become golden brown; transfer to the same bowl. Toast the sesame seeds for 2 to 3 minutes, until they begin to pop and become golden brown; transfer to the same bowl. Toast the cinnamon, anise, coriander, allspice, cloves, peppercorns, and thyme for about 1 minute, or until they are fragrant; transfer to the bowl.

4. Preheat the broiler to high.

5. Place the tomatoes, onion, and garlic on a rimmed baking sheet and broil for 3 minutes, flipping them halfway through, or until they soften and are covered with black spots. Transfer them to the bowl with the nuts and spices.

6. Drain the chiles, but reserve 1 cup (236 mL) of the soaking liquid. Transfer the chiles and reserved soaking liquid to a blender and puree until smooth. Pass through a fine-mesh sieve into a medium bowl.

7. Transfer the contents of the large bowl to the blender and puree until smooth, then pass through a fine-mesh sieve into another medium bowl.

8. Heat the remaining ¼ cup (59 mL) oil in a large pot over medium-low heat. Reduce the heat to low and pour in the chile puree while stirring, taking care as it might splash. Simmer the chile puree for 10 minutes, while constantly stirring, or until it thickens and pulls away from the sides of the pot. The puree will continue to splatter as it cooks, so I recommend you use a splatter screen if you have one.

9. Pour in the second puree and simmer for 15 minutes while constantly stirring, until it thickens and darkens to a dark brown color. Be careful with the splattering. Pour in the remaining 5 cups (1.2 L) vegetable broth, chocolate, bouillon, and salt and bring to a simmer. Simmer for 15 to 20 minutes, until the sauce thickens enough to coat the back of a spoon.

TIME-SAVING TIP

Day 1: Do steps 1 through 7 and store the purees in separate airtight containers in the fridge.

Day 2: Do steps 8 and 9.

VARIATION

Oil-free: Dry-toast the chiles, tortilla, bolillo, peanuts, and raisins instead of frying them. Bake the plantain at 425°F (220°C) for 10 minutes. Omit the oil when cooking the chile puree.

PUMPKIN SEED GREEN MOLE

Pipián Verde

Pipián is a pumpkin seed–based sauce with pre-Hispanic origins that has earthy, herbal, and spicy notes. The Mexicas would prepare pumpkin seed–based sauces to serve over fish, wild game, and vegetables. In the colonial cuisine of the seventeenth century, aromatic herbs and spices were added to it. There are many regional variations, but this version is inspired by the state of Puebla, where they make it with hoja santa and epazote. If you have trouble finding hoja santa, you can use the dried version, or a combination of basil and fennel leaves. Pipián is also sold at the markets in paste form just like mole negro and mole poblano. Mexican green onions are a variety of green onion with a larger white bulb. If you can't find them, they can be replaced with regular green onions. You can serve it with hearty vegetables like the Red Almond Mole (page 148) and rice, but I like to serve it as a dipping sauce for a large platter of grilled vegetables.

MAKES: 4 servings

TOTAL TIME: 40 minutes

PIPIÁN VERDE

- 1½ cups (195 g) hulled pumpkin seeds (pepitas)
- ½ cup (55 g) sesame seeds
- 4 teaspoons avocado oil, divided
- ½ large white onion (152 g), sliced (about 1 cup)
- 2 to 3 serrano chiles (37 g), stems removed, chopped
- 2 garlic cloves (3 g), chopped
- 8 medium tomatillos (453 g), husks removed, cut into quarters
- 1 large fresh or dried hoja santa leaf *or* 1 teaspoon chopped fresh basil and fennel leaves
- 1 cup (30 g) packed spinach
- ½ cup (17 g) packed fresh cilantro
- 2 epazote sprigs (16 g) *or* 1 tablespoon dried epazote
- 1½ teaspoons salt
- ⅛ teaspoon freshly ground black pepper
- 2 cups (473 mL) vegetable broth

GRILLED VEGETABLES

- 1 cup cremini mushrooms (110 g)
- 1 yellow squash (196 g), cut into ½-inch (1.25 cm) slices
- 1 large zucchini (144 g), cut into ½-inch (1.25 cm) slices
- 7 baby bell peppers (187 g)
- 1 bunch asparagus (340 g), trimmed
- 2 Mexican green onions (210 g)
- ¼ cup (59 mL) olive oil
- 1 teaspoon salt
- ¼ teaspoon freshly ground black pepper

(CONTINUED)

1. To make the sauce, heat a medium skillet over medium heat. Put in the pumpkin seeds and toast, stirring often, for 1 to 2 minutes, until the seeds begin to pop and become brown in spots. Remove from the heat, reserve 1 tablespoon, and transfer the rest to a blender.

2. In the same skillet, toast the sesame seeds over medium heat, stirring often, for 2 to 3 minutes, until they begin to pop and are golden brown. If your sesame seeds are bouncing out of your skillet before they are ready, sprinkle some water on them and continue toasting. Transfer to the blender.

3. Heat 2 teaspoons of the avocado oil in a large skillet over medium heat. Add the onion and serranos and cook until they begin to brown, for 4 to 5 minutes. Add the garlic and cook for 1 minute. Add the tomatillos and cook until they soften and begin to brown, in 6 to 7 minutes. Transfer to the blender.

4. Add the hoja santa, spinach, cilantro, epazote, salt, pepper, and vegetable broth to the blender and puree until smooth.

5. Heat the remaining 2 teaspoons oil in the same large skillet over medium heat. Reduce the heat to low and pour in the sauce, while stirring, taking care as it may splash, and simmer for 5 to 6 minutes, until the sauce thickens slightly.

6. Preheat a grill to medium-high heat.

7. Brush the vegetables with the olive oil and sprinkle with the salt and pepper. Working in batches, grill the vegetables until tender and charred in spots, for 7 to 8 minutes for the mushrooms, 5 to 6 minutes for the yellow squash, zucchini, and bell peppers, and 3 to 4 minutes for the asparagus and green onions. Transfer all the grilled vegetables to a platter and serve with the green pipián on the side, topped with the reserved pumpkin seeds.

8. Store the sauce in an airtight container in the fridge for up to 5 days or in the freezer for up to 6 months. The grilled vegetables can be stored in an airtight container in the fridge for up to 3 days.

VARIATION

Oil-free: Use ¼ cup (59 mL) vegetable broth instead of the oil when cooking the onion, and omit the oil when simmering the sauce. If your grill is well seasoned, there is no need to add oil to the vegetables before grilling.

MOLE POBLANO ENCHILADAS
Enmoladas de Mole Poblano

Enmoladas, also known as mole enchiladas, can be filled with any vegetable combination imaginable, but I like mine filled with braised greens (quelites) and potatoes, and topped with avocado slices, Almond Queso Fresco (page 31), and toasted sesame seeds. They are my favorite way of eating mole; they are hearty and savory, with a touch of sweetness, and provide an ideal balance between vegetables, mole, and corn tortillas. They are often served for breakfast or brunch, but they make an excellent lunch or dinner served with Mexican Red Rice (page 24). Any of the moles in this chapter can be used to make enmoladas, so feel free to play around with the fillings and the moles to make your favorite combination.

MAKES: 4 servings

TOTAL TIME: 30 minutes

FILLING
1 large russet potato (450 g), peeled and cut into dice (about 2½ cups)
2½ teaspoons salt, divided
2 teaspoons avocado oil
½ large white onion (152 g), finely chopped (about 1 cup)
2 garlic cloves, minced (6 g)
4 cups (238 g) quelites or Swiss chard, purslane, beet greens, or radish greens
¼ cup (59 mL) vegetable broth
⅛ teaspoon freshly ground black pepper

TO ASSEMBLE
3 cups (720 mL) Mole Poblano (page 141)
12 corn tortillas
1 avocado (215 g), pitted, peeled, and sliced
1 recipe Almond Crema (page 28)
2 tablespoons toasted sesame seeds
½ cup (58 g) Almond Queso Fresco (page 31) or vegan feta cheese

1. To make the filling, place the potato and 2 teaspoons of the salt in a medium pot and fill with enough water to cover them by 3 inches (7.5 cm). Bring to a boil over high heat, reduce the heat to low, and simmer for about 6 minutes, or until the potato is tender but not mushy. Drain the potato and transfer to a medium bowl.

2. Heat the oil in a large skillet over medium-low heat. Add the onion and cook for 4 to 5 minutes, or until it is tender and translucent. Add the garlic and cook for 1 minute. Add the greens and vegetable broth, cover, and cook until the greens have wilted and are tender, stirring occasionally, for about 3 minutes. Add the potato, remaining ½ teaspoon salt, and pepper and stir.

3. To assemble, in a medium saucepot bring the mole to a simmer over medium-low heat. One by one heat the tortillas on a comal over medium-high heat for 30 to 40 seconds on each side, or wrap the tortillas in a moistened paper towel and cook them for 1 minute in the microwave, until they are soft and pliable. Fill each tortilla with 1½ tablespoons of the filling and fold in half.

4. Pour ⅓ cup (78 mL) mole on each plate and spread it to cover the width of the plate. Place 3 filled tortillas on top of the mole, then cover with more mole. Top with avocado slices, Almond Crema, toasted sesame seeds, and Almond Queso Fresco. Serve immediately.

5. You can store the filling in an airtight container in the fridge for up to 4 days or in the freezer for up to 3 months. I don't recommend you store the enmoladas after they have been assembled.

VARIATION
Oil-free: Omit the oil when cooking the onion and use ¼ cup (59 mL) vegetable broth instead.

RED ALMOND MOLE

Pipián Rojo de Almendra

Like the Pumpkin Seed Green Mole (page 143), this is a thick, earthy sauce, a distant cousin of mole, but in this case, I am making it in the style of San Luis Potosí, with toasted almonds instead of pumpkin seeds. Toasted guajillo chiles, árbol chiles, cloves, and bay leaf make this a spicy, aromatic sauce that complements the hearty potatoes and carrots and the starchy and creamy ayocote morado bean. Serve with rice and warm corn tortillas. This would also make an excellent tamal filling, or you can use the sauce to make the Nixtamalized Butternut Squash in Almond Pipián (page 248).

MAKES: 4 servings

TOTAL TIME: 35 minutes

PIPIÁN
15 dried guajillo chiles (116 g), stems and seeds removed
5 dried árbol chiles (5 g), stems and seeds removed
¾ cup raw almonds (114 g)
2 whole cloves
¼ large white onion (65 g), roughly chopped (about ⅓ cup)
2 garlic cloves (6 g), peeled
1 teaspoon salt
⅛ teaspoon freshly ground black pepper
2 teaspoons avocado oil
1 cup (236 mL) vegetable broth
1 dried bay leaf

VEGETABLES
2 cups red-skin potatoes (296 g), cut into quarters
1 large chayote (316 g), peeled and diced (about ¾ cup)
½ teaspoon salt
2 medium carrots (169 g), cut into half-moons (about 1½ cups)
1½ cups (266 g) cooked ayocote morado beans

TO SERVE
Freshly cooked white rice or Mexican Red Rice (page 24)
Corn tortillas, warm

1. Heat a large, heavy-bottomed skillet over medium heat. Put in the chiles and toast for 30 seconds on each side. Transfer to a medium pot and fill with enough water to cover them by 2 inches (5 cm). Bring to a boil over high heat, turn the heat off, and let them soak for 15 minutes. Drain, but reserve 2½ cups (590 mL) of the soaking liquid. Transfer the chiles and reserved soaking liquid to a blender.

2. Heat a small skillet over medium-low heat. Put in the almonds and toast for 2 to 3 minutes, stirring occasionally, until brown spots appear and the almonds begin to crack. Transfer to the blender.

3. In the same small skillet, toast the cloves over medium-low heat for 1 minute, or until they become fragrant; transfer to the blender. Add the onion, garlic, salt, and pepper to the blender and puree until smooth.

4. Heat the oil in a large pot over medium-low heat. Reduce the heat to low and pour in the puree while stirring, taking care as it may splash. Simmer for 5 minutes, or until the puree thickens and darkens in color. Add the vegetable broth and bay leaf and simmer for 10 to 12 minutes, stirring occasionally, until the sauce is thick enough to coat the back of a spoon.

5. While the pipián is simmering, place the potatoes and chayote in a medium pot and pour in enough water to cover the vegetables by 2 inches (5 cm). Add the salt and bring to a boil over high heat, then reduce the heat to medium-low and simmer for 9 minutes. Add the carrots and simmer for 6 minutes, or until the vegetables are tender. Drain and transfer to the pot with the pipián. Add the ayocotes and stir.

6. Serve immediately with rice and warm corn tortillas.

7. Store in an airtight container in the fridge for up to 4 days or in the freezer for up to 3 months.

VARIATIONS

Oil-free: Omit the oil when cooking the chile puree.

Roasted veggies: Roast 1 acorn squash, sliced; ½ head cauliflower, cut into florets; and 1 large sweet potato, peeled and cut into cubes, on a rimmed baking sheet lined with a silicone mat or parchment paper at 400°F (205°C) for 30 minutes, or until the vegetables are tender. Add this to the pot with the pipián.

PINK MOLE

Mole Rosa

This rose-colored mole from the state of Guerrero was invented in the 1980s by Chef Alicia Gironella De'Angeli for a local cooking competition. The recipe takes the traditional cooking techniques from mole but uses ingredients local to Guerrero like mezcal and sesame seeds. The color comes from a flavorful stock made from beets, which makes this a unique sauce that is spicy, sweet, aromatic, creamy, and deeply savory. I have adapted this recipe from De'Angeli's book *El Gran Larousse de la Cocina Mexicana, Volume 3*.

You can use it as you would any mole sauce: Serve it over hearty vegetables, make enmoladas (mole enchiladas), or make the Onion Tarte Tatin in Pink Mole (page 246). If you can't find pink pine nuts, you can substitute regular pine nuts.

MAKES: 4 servings

TOTAL TIME: 1½ hours

BEET BROTH

- ½ large white onion (136 g)
- 1 head garlic (30 g), unpeeled, with the top cut off
- 2 large beets (464 g), peeled and cut into quarters
- 2 fresh or dried hoja santa leaves *or* 2 teaspoons chopped fresh basil and fennel leaves
- 1 (3-inch/7.5 cm) Ceylon cinnamon stick *or* ½ teaspoon ground cinnamon
- 1 tablespoon anise seeds

MOLE

- ½ cup (118 mL) mezcal
- ¼ large white onion (65 g), finely chopped (about ⅓ cup)
- 2 garlic cloves (6 g), minced
- 1 tablespoon vegan butter
- ⅔ cup (100 g) raw almonds
- ⅔ cup (100 g) pink pine nuts
- ¾ cup (100 g) sesame seeds
- 1 fresh or dried bay leaf
- 1 thyme sprig *or* ½ teaspoon dried thyme
- 1 marjoram sprig *or* ½ teaspoon dried marjoram
- ⅛ teaspoon cumin seeds
- 2 whole cloves
- 2 chipotle chiles in adobo
- ¼ cup (51 g) dairy-free white chocolate
- 2 teaspoons avocado oil
- 1 teaspoon salt

TO SERVE

- Cooked hearty vegetables, such as potatoes, cauliflower, mushrooms, or squash
- 3 tablespoons pomegranate seeds
- 2 tablespoons pink pine nuts

(CONTINUED)

1. To make the beet broth, preheat the broiler to high.

2. Place the onion and garlic on a rimmed baking sheet and broil for 2 to 3 minutes, until charred, flipping the onion halfway through. Transfer them to a medium saucepot; there is no need to peel the garlic. Add the beets, hoja santa, cinnamon, and anise, then pour in 6 cups (1.4 L) water. Bring to a boil over high heat, reduce the heat to low, and simmer for 1 hour. Strain and reserve all of the broth. (We won't be using the beets in the mole, but they would be great in a salad.)

3. To make the mole, place the mezcal, onion, and garlic in a small skillet and bring to a boil over high heat, then reduce the heat to low and simmer for 8 minutes, or until the onion is tender and translucent and the mezcal almost evaporates. Transfer to a small bowl.

4. Melt the butter in a large skillet over medium heat. Add the almonds, pine nuts, and sesame seeds and toast until the sesame seeds start to pop and brown, in about 4 minutes. Reduce the heat to low and add 1½ cups (354 mL) of the beet broth, the bay leaf, thyme, marjoram, cumin, and cloves. Add the onion and garlic and simmer for about 8 minutes, or until the sesame seeds begin to soften. Remove and discard the bay leaf. Remove the thyme and marjoram sprigs, pull off the leaves, and return them to the skillet; discard the stems. Transfer the contents of the skillet to a blender, add another 2 cups (473 mL) of the beet broth, the chipotles, and white chocolate and blend until smooth. Pass through a fine-mesh sieve.

5. Heat the oil in a large pot over medium-low heat. Reduce the heat to low and pour in the mole while stirring, being careful as it may splash. Add the remaining ½ cup (118 mL) beet broth and the salt and simmer for 8 to 10 minutes, until the sauce thickens slightly.

6. Serve over the cooked vegetables, topped with the pomegranate seeds and pine nuts. Store in an airtight container in the fridge for up to 5 days or in the freezer for up to 6 months.

TIME-SAVING TIP

Make the beet broth the day before. Pass through a fine-mesh sieve and store in an airtight container in the refrigerator.

VARIATION

Oil-free: Omit the oil when simmering the sauce.

Francisca Maurilio Godinez

YELLOW MOLE

Mole Amarillo

Mole amarillo is perhaps the most overlooked of the moles in Oaxaca. Its name is deceiving; it's more of a bright orange sauce. This is a very special recipe, because it was shared with me by Indigenous cocinera tradicional Francisca Maurilio Godinez. She is from the Mixe region of Oaxaca, also known as the Sierra Mixe, where the Mixe people still practice the culinary traditions and rituals of their ancestors. She thickens her mole amarillo with maíz criollo, a native variety of heirloom corn grown in Oaxaca. You can instead use dried white Olotillo corn (see Resources, page 309). This recipe has been documented and shared with her specifications; in the notes I include my observations from when I re-created the recipe at home, and have included a version made with masa harina. You can use this mole to make Yellow Mole Empanadas (page 156).

MAKES: 4 servings

TOTAL TIME: 30 minutes + soaking time

¾ cup (173 g) dried maíz criollo (white heirloom corn)

3 dried guajillo chiles (24 g), seeds and stems removed

5 to 10 dried árbol chiles (4 to 8 g)

2 large Roma tomatoes (248 g), cored

6 garlic cloves (18 g), peeled

2 mint sprigs, leaves only

2 teaspoons salt

1. Soak the corn in a bowl of room-temperature water overnight. Drain and transfer to a small bowl.

2. Place the chiles and tomatoes in a small pot and add enough water to cover them by 2 inches (5 cm). Bring the water to a boil over high heat, reduce the heat to low, and let them simmer for 7 minutes, or until the chiles are soft and pliable. Drain the chiles and tomatoes, but reserve 1½ cups (354 mL) of the soaking liquid. Transfer the chiles, tomatoes, and reserved soaking liquid to a blender, add the garlic and mint, and puree until completely smooth. You should have about 3½ cups (828 mL) of puree. Transfer the chile puree to a large pot and heat over medium-low heat.

3. Place the corn and 2 cups (473 mL) water in the blender and puree until smooth. Pass through a fine-mesh sieve right into the pot of chile puree. Transfer the leftover corn solids in the sieve back into the blender, add 1 cup (236 mL) water, and puree until smooth. Pass through the sieve again right into the pot.

4. Add the salt and bring to a simmer over low heat. Cook for 8 to 10 minutes, stirring often, until it thickens to the consistency of a thick cream soup. It should be a shiny bright orange color.

5. Store in an airtight container in the fridge for up to 3 days or in the freezer for up to 3 months.

VARIATION

Masa harina: To make this with masa harina, in a small bowl, whisk together ¼ cup (30 g) masa harina and 1 cup (236 mL) water until the masa harina completely dissolves. If there are still lumps, you can pass it through a fine-mesh sieve. Heat the chile puree in a medium saucepot over medium heat. Slowly pour in the masa mixture while whisking. Bring to a simmer and cook for 8 to 10 minutes, until the sauce is a deep orange color and has thickened enough to coat the back of a spoon. Use only 1 teaspoon salt for this version.

YELLOW MOLE EMPANADAS

Empanadas de Mole Amarillo

In Mexico empanadas don't necessarily need to be made with wheat flour, like these empanadas de mole amarillo from Oaxaca, which are made with corn masa and filled with stewed beans and mustard greens. Making these will take some practice because they are made with handmade tortillas and are filled while they are still cooking on the comal, but don't worry, it isn't impossible. In Oaxaca they seal the edges with their fingers, but I recommend you use a spoon to avoid burning yourself. What I love the most about these empanadas are the crisp and toasted edges that add a smokiness and firmness to the masa. You can eat these for breakfast or as a midafternoon snack.

MAKES: **4 servings**

TOTAL TIME: **30 minutes**

2 teaspoons avocado oil
½ large white onion (152 g), finely chopped (about 1 cup)
2 garlic cloves (6 g), finely chopped
1 bunch mustard greens or Swiss chard (286 g), tough stems removed, roughly chopped
⅓ cup (78 mL) vegetable broth
1 (15-ounce/425 g) can cannellini or navy beans, drained and rinsed (about 1½ cups)
½ teaspoon salt
⅛ teaspoon freshly ground black pepper
1½ cups (175 g) masa harina
½ recipe Yellow Mole (page 155)

1. Heat the oil in a large skillet over medium-low heat. Add the onion and cook until tender and translucent, for 4 to 5 minutes. Add the garlic and cook for 1 more minute, or until it is fragrant.

2. Add the mustard greens and vegetable broth, cover, and cook for 2 to 3 minutes, stirring occasionally, until the greens have wilted. Add the beans, salt, and pepper and cook, uncovered, for 5 minutes, or until almost all the broth has evaporated.

3. Preheat a comal or heavy-bottomed skillet over medium heat.

4. To make the empanadas, place the masa harina in a large bowl and gradually pour in 1¼ cups (295 mL) water while mixing with your hand. Knead for 5 minutes, or until there are no dry spots in the masa and it is soft like Play-Doh, pliable but not sticky. To test the masa, roll it into a small ball and lightly press it; if the edges crack, the dough is too dry. Add an additional ¼ cup (59 mL) water and knead again. If the dough sticks to your fingers, it is too wet; add 1 tablespoon masa harina and knead again.

5. Divide the masa into eight equal balls. Lay a plastic liner (I like to cut squares out of grocery bags) on the bottom of a tortilla press. Place a ball of masa in the center of the liner and lay a second liner on top of the ball. If you don't have a tortilla press, you can also use two heavy flat-bottomed objects (books will work). Use your fingers to lightly press down on the masa ball and close the press, pushing down the lever to apply pressure. The tortilla should be about ¹⁄₁₆ inch (1.5 mm) thick.

6. Open the tortilla press and peel off the top liner. Flip the exposed corn tortilla onto your fingers and with your opposing hand, peel off the remaining plastic liner.

7. Lay the tortilla directly on the hot comal. If the tortilla bubbles, it means your comal is too hot; if this happens, reduce the heat to medium-low. Let it cook for 30 seconds, or until the edges change color and there is some light spotting, then flip. The tortilla should easily flip. If your tortilla is stuck, it means the heat is too low and the tortilla is not cooked yet, or your pan is not properly seasoned. Cook for 20 to 30 seconds.

8. While your tortilla is cooking, place 1½ tablespoons of the filling and 1 tablespoon of the mole amarillo on one-half of the tortilla. With a spatula, lift the other side and close it over the filling. Use a spoon to seal the edges, flip the empanada, and cook for 2 minutes, or until the edges crisp and change color and there is some dark spotting. Remove from the comal and repeat this process with the rest of the masa and filling.

9. Let the empanadas cool for a minute or two before biting into them. The filling will be hot.

10. You can store the filling in an airtight container in the fridge for up to 4 days or in the freezer for up to 3 months. I do not recommend you store the empanadas after cooking, because they will get soggy.

VARIATION

Oil-free: Omit the oil when cooking the onion and use ¼ cup (59 mL) vegetable broth instead.

MUSHROOM MOLE DE OLLA
Mole de Olla de Setas

Don't let the name deceive you: This mole is more of a soup than a traditional mole; the good news is it takes way less time to prepare and is just as good. It is a hearty soup of sweet corn, tender green beans, chayote, potatoes, and carrots simmered in a toasted chile broth. There are many variations; this version is inspired by the state of Tlaxcala, where they make it with dried chipotles instead of ancho and guajillo chiles. It also omits a key ingredient that they use in central Mexico, which is xoconostle, a sour prickly pear. I have added dehydrated mushrooms for a more earthy and meaty texture, but they are not essential. If they are not accessible to you, double the fresh mushrooms instead. Serve with Mexican Red Rice (page 24).

MAKES: **4 to 6 servings**

TOTAL TIME: **40 minutes**

4 dried chipotle meco chiles (28 g), stems and seeds removed

5 medium Roma tomatoes (562 g), cored

¾ large white onion (210 g), finely chopped (about 1⅓ cups), divided

3 garlic cloves (9 g), peeled

1 tablespoon avocado oil

1 pound cremini mushrooms (453 g), sliced

10 cups (2.3 L) vegetable broth

2 ears corn (468 g), shucked and cut into quarters

1 cup assorted dried mushrooms (35 g), rehydrated and sliced

3 epazote sprigs *or* 1 tablespoon dried epazote

2 cups diced red-skin potatoes (296 g)

2 medium carrots (169 g), diced

1 large chayote (316 g), peeled and diced (about ¾ cup)

2 cups green beans (231 g), cut into 1½-inch (4 cm) pieces

2 small Mexican zucchini or green zucchini (294 g), diced (about 2 cups)

1 tablespoon salt

¼ teaspoon freshly ground black pepper

1. Heat a large, heavy-bottomed skillet over medium heat and toast the chiles for 30 seconds on each side. Transfer to a medium pot, cover with water, and add the tomatoes. Bring to a boil over high heat, then reduce the heat to low and simmer for 6 to 8 minutes, until the chiles are soft and pliable.

2. Drain and transfer the chiles and tomatoes to a blender. Add ⅓ cup (65 g) of the onion and the garlic and puree until smooth; you should have about 3 cups (354 mL) of chile puree. Pass through a fine-mesh sieve into a small bowl.

3. Heat the oil in a large pot over medium-high heat. Add the cremini mushrooms and cook until golden brown, stirring occasionally, for 7 to 8 minutes. Reduce the heat to low, add the remaining 1 cup (145 g) onion, and cook until tender, in 3 to 4 minutes. Pour in the chile puree and simmer for 2 to 3 minutes, until it thickens slightly and turns deep red.

4. Add the broth, corn, dried mushrooms, and epazote and simmer for 5 to 6 minutes. Add the potatoes, carrots, and chayote and cook until the potatoes are almost cooked, for 8 to 9 minutes. Finally, add the green beans, zucchini, salt, and pepper and simmer until all the vegetables are tender, for 5 to 6 minutes.

5. Store in an airtight container in the fridge for up to 5 days or in the freezer for up to 6 months.

TIME-SAVING TIP

Cut the green beans, zucchini, carrots, corn, and mushrooms the day before and store in an airtight container in the fridge.

VARIATION

Oil-free: Omit the oil when cooking the mushrooms and use ¼ cup (59 mL) vegetable broth instead.

7

COMIDA CASERA

Home-cooked Mexican meals are the best. The smell of the sopa de arroz (Mexican Red Rice) (page 24), the pot of simmering beans on the stove, the enchiladas carefully rolled and drowning in sauce—I think about it and my heart glows. Home-cooked meals always remind me of my abuelita Dora. She was the orchestrator of the meals made for big family celebrations like Christmas, she made sure there were always beans cooking in a clay pot on the stove, and she made the best albóndiga soup. My mom says that they didn't have a lot of money growing up; their meals consisted of rice, beans, sopita de fideo, tortillas, and maybe a guisado (stew) with some meat, but their door was always open to receive anyone in need of a plate of food. That to me is the heart of Mexican home cooking: At the Mexican table everyone is welcome.

In this chapter I dig into the home-cooked classics. Some of the recipes, like the chiles rellenos, are adapted from the recipes served at our family restaurant; others are my grandmother's recipes, like the pozole, which is made with mushrooms instead of meat; and some are reinventions of my favorites, like the picadillo de lentejas. All these recipes, just like the food my abuelita used to make, come from the heart, and I am 100 percent sure she would give them her seal of approval. Gracias por todo, güeli.

LENTIL PICADILLO

Picadillo de Lentejas

Picadillo is a Mexican home-cooked classic, usually made with beef, potatoes, and carrots simmered in a tomato sauce. For this version, I replace the meat with protein-packed lentils, which absorb all the sweetness of the tomatoes, cumin, and oregano. This is one of those dishes that kids love: I loved it as a kid, and now my kids love it. The recipe changes from family to family and region to region. In central Mexico, they add raisins, olives, capers, cinnamon, cloves, and sometimes even almonds. In southern Mexico, they add vegetables like chayote, green beans, and zucchini. I make it northern Mexico–style, with chipotle chiles, but it can also be made with jalapeños instead. Serve it with a plate of Mexican Red Rice (page 24) and warm corn tortillas, or you can use it to stuff enchiladas, chiles rellenos, and tacos.

MAKES: 4 servings

TOTAL TIME: 35 minutes

LENTILS

8 ounces (227 g) brown lentils, picked over and rinsed (about 1¼ cups)
½ large white onion (152 g)
1 dried bay leaf
1 teaspoon salt

PICADILLO

3 large Roma tomatoes (296 g), cored and cut into quarters
1 chipotle chile in adobo
2 teaspoons avocado oil
½ large white onion (152 g), finely chopped (about 1 cup)
2 garlic cloves (6 g), minced

1 large carrot (103 g), cut into small dice (¾ cup)
3 cups (709 mL) vegetable broth
1 large russet potato (459 g), cut into small dice (about 2½ cups)
½ teaspoon ground cumin
½ teaspoon dried Mexican oregano
1⅛ teaspoons salt
⅛ teaspoon freshly ground black pepper
Mexican Red Rice (page 24), for serving
Corn tortillas, warm, for serving

1. Place the lentils in a medium pot and fill it with enough water to cover them by 2 inches (5 cm). Add the onion, bay leaf, and salt. Bring to a boil over high heat, reduce the heat to low, and simmer for 10 minutes, or until the lentils begin to soften but are not completely cooked. Drain.

2. Place the tomatoes and chipotle in a blender and puree until smooth. You should have about 1½ cups (354 mL) of puree.

3. Heat the oil in a large pot over medium-low heat. Add the onion and cook for 3 to 4 minutes, until it becomes tender and translucent. Add the garlic and cook for 1 minute. Add the lentils and, using a potato masher, mash to break them up a bit, leaving one-quarter of the lentils whole.

4. Add the tomato puree and carrot and simmer for 3 to 4 minutes, until the puree thickens and changes to a deep red color. Add the vegetable broth, potato, cumin, oregano, salt, and pepper. Bring to a boil over high heat, reduce the heat, and simmer until the vegetables are tender, for 20 to 25 minutes. As it cools, the lentils will absorb some of the broth.

5. Serve with rice and warm corn tortillas. Store in an airtight container in the fridge for up to 4 days or in the freezer for up to 3 months.

VARIATIONS

Oil-free: Omit the oil and use ¼ cup (59 mL) vegetable broth to cook the onion.

Central Mexican picadillo: Add 2½ tablespoons raisins, ¼ cup (47 g) chopped Manzanilla olives, 1 tablespoon chopped capers, ¼ teaspoon ground cinnamon, and ⅛ teaspoon ground cloves.

JACKFRUIT POZOLE ROJO

Pozole Rojo de Yaca

Every Christmas for as long as I can remember, my güeli (grandmother) would make the biggest pots of pozole and menudo I have ever seen. As a child, I didn't understand why the adults made such a big deal about it, probably because one time I dared to stir the pot of pozole and was horrified to see half a pig's head and several feet simmering in a red chile broth with hominy. As a teenager, I asked my grandmother to teach me how to make it, and I'm glad I did because now I get to share it with you—without the pig, of course. I make my version with jackfruit, but it will also work with soy curls, mushrooms, or just veggies. There's quite a lot of dried chiles involved in this recipe, but don't let that scare you. If you would like a milder version, just omit the chile de árbol, or increase it for a spicier version.

MAKES: 4 to 6 servings

TOTAL TIME: 50 minutes

2 (20-ounce/565 g) cans young green jackfruit in brine, drained

5 dried guajillo chiles (32 g), stems and seeds removed

2 dried ancho chiles (38 g), stems and seeds removed

5 dried árbol chiles (4 g), stems and seeds removed

6 garlic cloves (18 g), peeled

½ large white onion (152 g), roughly chopped (about 1 cup)

½ teaspoon dried Mexican oregano

10 cups (2.3 L) vegetable broth

3 (15-ounce/425 g) cans white hominy, drained and rinsed

2 teaspoons salt

⅛ teaspoon freshly ground black pepper

1 tablespoon avocado oil

TO SERVE

1 large white onion (232 g), finely chopped (about 1½ cups)

6 small red radishes (60 g), thinly sliced

2 tablespoons dried Mexican oregano

½ small green cabbage (397 g), cored and thinly sliced

4 limes, cut into quarters

1 (11-ounce/312 g) bag corn chips *or* 4 tostadas

1. Place the jackfruit in a colander and rinse with cold water. Cut off the core of the jackfruit (the hard tip of the triangular pieces), remove the seed pods, and shred the jackfruit pieces with your hands. Transfer the jackfruit to a medium pot and add enough water to cover it by 2 inches (5 cm). Bring to a boil over high heat, reduce the heat to low, and simmer for 10 minutes. Drain the jackfruit and let it cool slightly. Using your hands, squeeze all the water out of the jackfruit.

2. To make the chile sauce, place the chiles in a medium pot and add enough water to cover them by 2 inches (5 cm). Bring the water to a boil over high heat, turn the heat off, and let the chiles soak for 15 minutes, or until they are soft and pliable. Drain the chiles, but reserve 1½ cups (354 mL) of the soaking liquid. Transfer the chiles and reserved soaking liquid to a blender, add the garlic, onion, and oregano, and puree until completely smooth. Pass the sauce through a fine-mesh sieve into a small bowl. This should yield about 2¼ cups (532 mL) of sauce.

3. Add the vegetable broth, hominy, salt, and pepper to a large pot and bring to a boil over high heat. Reduce the heat to low. Scoop out 1 cup (293 g) hominy and broth and place it in the blender. Puree until completely smooth, then pour it back into the pot. This will help thicken the soup. Continue to simmer over very low heat while you cook the jackfruit.

4. Heat the oil in a large skillet over medium-high heat. Add the jackfruit and cook for 6 to 7 minutes, until it begins to brown. Reduce the heat to low and pour the chile sauce over the jackfruit, being careful as it may splash. Simmer for 5 to 6 minutes, until the sauce begins to thicken.

5. Add the jackfruit and sauce to the pot with the broth and simmer for 10 to 12 minutes.

6. Serve the pozole very hot with all your garnishes on the table so that every person can add them to their liking. Store the pozole in an airtight container in the fridge for up to 5 days or in the freezer for up to 6 months.

VARIATIONS

Oil-free: Omit the oil and cook the jackfruit in a nonstick pan.

Soy curls: Use 4 ounces (115 g) soy curls instead of the jackfruit. Soak them in hot water for 10 minutes, then drain and squeeze out the excess water with your hands. Cook them as you would the jackfruit.

OYSTER MUSHROOM POZOLE VERDE

Pozole Verde de Setas

A lesser-known cousin of pozole rojo, pozole verde will conquer your heart. I stew oyster mushrooms and hominy in a spicy tomatillo–pumpkin seed broth, then I top the broth with creamy avocado, crisp lettuce, and fresh radishes. This version is inspired by the state of Guerrero, where pozole is an integral part of local cuisine. In Guerrero pozole can be green, red, or white, but in northern Mexico, where I'm from, we eat only red pozole. My grandmother would probably be scandalized by what I'm about to say, but after a visit to Guerrero, this is now the pozole we make every Christmas.

MAKES: **4 to 6 servings**

TOTAL TIME: **40 minutes**

POZOLE BASE

- 1 tablespoon avocado oil
- 1½ pounds (680 g) maitake or oyster mushrooms, pulled into shreds
- ½ medium white onion (125 g), finely chopped (about ¾ cup)
- 6 garlic cloves (18 g), minced
- 8 cups (1.9 L) vegetable broth
- 1 (29-ounce/822 g) can white hominy, drained and rinsed

CHILE SAUCE

- 2 large poblano chiles (205 g)
- 3 to 4 serrano chiles (87 g), stems removed
- 4 medium tomatillos (273 g), husks removed, rinsed
- ½ cup (81 g) raw hulled pumpkin seeds (pepitas)
- 1 cup (175 g) leafy greens, such as spinach, radish greens, or Swiss chard
- 1 epazote sprig *or* 2 teaspoons dried epazote
- ½ cup packed (17 g) fresh cilantro
- ¼ teaspoon ground cumin
- ¼ teaspoon dried Mexican oregano
- ½ cup (118 mL) vegetable broth
- 1 tablespoon avocado oil
- 2½ teaspoons salt
- ¼ teaspoon freshly ground black pepper

TO SERVE

- 1 large avocado (215 g), pitted, peeled, and diced
- 4 red radishes (40 g), sliced
- ½ head romaine or iceberg lettuce (314 g), finely shredded
- 2 limes, cut into quarters
- 1 (11-ounce/312 g) bag corn chips *or* 4 corn tostadas

(CONTINUED)

1. To make the pozole base, heat the oil in a large pot over medium heat. Add the mushrooms and sauté until golden brown, for 6 to 8 minutes, stirring occasionally. Reduce the heat to medium-low, add the onion, and cook until tender and translucent, for 4 to 5 minutes. Stir in the garlic and cook for 1 minute. Pour in the vegetable broth and hominy and bring to a boil over high heat. Reduce the heat to low and let it simmer while you prepare the chile sauce.

2. To make the chile sauce, preheat the broiler to high.

3. Place the poblanos, serranos, and tomatillos on a rimmed baking sheet. Broil for 3 minutes, or until charred. Flip the chiles and tomatillos and broil for 3 more minutes, until they are black and charred all over. Place the poblanos in a heatproof bowl, cover, and let them steam for 5 minutes. Peel the poblanos and remove the stems and seeds. Transfer the poblanos, serranos, and tomatillos to a blender.

4. Toast the pumpkin seeds in a small skillet over medium heat until they pop and turn golden brown, in 3 to 4 minutes. Transfer to the blender, along with the greens, epazote, cilantro, cumin, oregano, and vegetable broth and puree until completely smooth. You should have about 2½ cups (591 mL) of sauce. Pass the sauce through a fine-mesh sieve into a medium bowl.

5. Heat the oil in a medium saucepot over medium-low heat. Pour in the sauce while stirring, being careful as it may splash. Simmer for 2 to 3 minutes, until it slightly thickens and becomes a darker shade of green. Pour the sauce into the pozole base and bring it to a boil over high heat. Add the salt and pepper and stir. Reduce the heat to low and simmer for 10 minutes.

6. Serve the pozole very hot and place all your garnishes on the table so that every person can add them to their liking. Store the pozole in an airtight container in the fridge for up to 5 days or in the freezer for up to 6 months.

VARIATION

Oil-free: Omit the oil when cooking the mushrooms and use ¼ cup (59 mL) broth instead. Simmer the chile sauce without the oil.

MUSHROOM PANCITA

Panseta

When I started researching this recipe, I was immediately overwhelmed by the number of regional variations. Pancita, also known as menudo, is a spicy tripe soup, an adaptation of a dish called mondongo brought to Mexico by the Spanish. I settled on this version from Angélica Martínez (@veganaalamexicana), which is made in the style of Estado de Mexico, where she is from. Two different varieties of mushrooms and potatoes are simmered in a smoky, spicy, and herbal broth to make an amazingly satisfying soup that is sure to cure any hangover. I like to add snow fungus to it, which is a dried mushroom commonly used in Asian cuisine, because it mimics the texture of the tripe. You can find it at your local Asian grocery store or online. If snow mushrooms are not available to you, double the amount of oyster mushrooms. In the notes, I have included the northern Mexico version, which is the version we eat at home.

MAKES: 4 to 6 servings

TOTAL TIME: 45 minutes

---

3 dried guajillo chiles (16 g), stems and seeds removed

1 dried ancho chile (21 g), stems and seeds removed

1 dried pasilla chile (8 g), stems and seeds removed

1 or 2 dried morita chiles (8 g), stems removed

3 medium white potatoes (453 g), cut into medium dice

3 large Roma tomatoes (317 g), cored

½ large white onion (152 g)

2 garlic cloves (6 g)

1 epazote sprig *or* 2 teaspoons dried epazote

1 tablespoon avocado oil

1 pound (453 g) oyster mushrooms, trimmed and shredded into small pieces

1.3 ounces (36 g) dried snow fungus, rehydrated

7 cups (1.6 L) vegetable broth

3 dried bay leaves

2½ teaspoons salt

¼ teaspoon freshly ground black pepper

TO SERVE

⅓ large white onion (91 g), chopped (about ½ cup)

2 tablespoons dried Mexican oregano

2 limes, cut into quarters

(CONTINUED)

1. Place the chiles in a heatproof bowl and pour in enough boiling water to completely cover them. Place a heavy heatproof plate on top to keep the chiles submerged and let them soak for 15 minutes.

2. While the chiles are soaking, place the potatoes in a medium saucepot and fill with enough water to cover them by 2 inches (5 cm). Bring to a boil over high heat, reduce the heat to low, and simmer for 10 minutes, or until they are slightly tender. Drain and transfer to a small bowl.

3. Heat a comal or heavy-bottomed skillet over medium-high heat. Place the tomatoes, onion, and garlic on the hot comal. Let them char until they become soft and have black spots all over, flipping them frequently, for 8 to 9 minutes. The garlic will be done about 2 minutes in; remove and peel it. Transfer everything to a blender.

4. Drain the soaked chiles, but reserve 1½ cups (354 mL) of the soaking liquid. Add the chiles and reserved soaking liquid to the blender. Blend until completely smooth.

5. Heat the oil in a large pot over medium-high heat. Add the oyster mushrooms and cook, stirring occasionally, until they begin to brown, for 4 to 5 minutes. Reduce the heat to low, add the potatoes, and let cook for about 3 minutes. Add the chile sauce, being careful as it may splash, and simmer for 5 minutes, until it slightly thickens and changes to a deep red color.

6. Cut the fibrous stems off the snow mushrooms, then cut into bite-size pieces and add them to the pot. Pour in the vegetable broth, fresh epazote, bay leaves, salt, and pepper and bring to a boil over high heat. Reduce the heat to low and simmer for 25 to 30 minutes.

7. Serve the menudo very hot and place all the garnishes on the table so that every person can add them to their liking. Store in an airtight container in the fridge for up to 5 days or in the freezer for up to 6 months.

VARIATIONS

Oil-free: Omit the oil when cooking the mushrooms and use ¼ cup (59 mL) vegetable broth instead.

Northern Mexico version: Omit the chile pasilla, substitute 1 teaspoon dried Mexican oregano for the epazote, and instead of potatoes use 1 (29-ounce) can white hominy, drained and rinsed. Serve with bolillo or baguette.

Epazote: If you are using dried epazote, add it to the blender with the chiles.

POTATOES AND NOPALES
IN CHILE COLORADO

Guisado de Papas y Nopales en Chile Colorado

This dish is inspired by the northern state of Chihuahua and is simply known as guisado de chile colorado. It is a hearty stew of baby potatoes and nopales simmered in a guajillo and ancho chile sauce spiced with cumin, oregano, bay leaf, and thyme. Sometimes it is also thickened with flour, which I didn't find necessary for this recipe. It is a favorite of mine because of its versatility: You can add any vegetable you like. I often make it with sweet potatoes and chickpeas. I recommend you serve it with Mexican Red Rice (page 24), Refried Pinto Beans (page 20), and warm flour tortillas.

MAKES: **4 servings**

TOTAL TIME: **35 minutes**

1 pound (453 g) nopales, cleaned (see page 17) and cut into small dice (about 3 large paddles)

CHILE SAUCE
5 dried guajillo chiles (33 g), stems and seeds removed
2 dried ancho chiles (35 g), stems and seeds removed
1 large Roma tomato (130 g), cored
5 garlic cloves (15 g), peeled
1 teaspoon dried Mexican oregano
½ teaspoon ground cumin
1 teaspoon salt
⅛ teaspoon freshly ground black pepper

STEW
1 tablespoon avocado oil
½ large white onion (152 g), finely chopped (about 1 cup)
1½ pounds (680 g) baby Yukon Gold potatoes, cut into quarters
2 cups (473 mL) vegetable broth
1 dried bay leaf
1 thyme sprig *or* ½ teaspoon dried thyme
½ teaspoon salt
⅛ teaspoon freshly ground black pepper

1. To cook the nopales, bring a large pot of water to a boil over high heat. Put in the nopales, reduce the heat to medium, cover, and let simmer for 10 minutes. Drain and rinse the nopales very well to remove any excess slime. Transfer to a bowl.

2. To make the chile sauce, heat a large, heavy-bottomed skillet over medium-high heat. Put in the chiles and toast for 30 seconds on each side, until they are slightly darker in color and become fragrant. Place them in a pot, add the tomato, and fill with enough water to cover them by 2 inches (5 cm). Bring the water to a boil, reduce the heat to low, and simmer for 7 to 8 minutes, until the chiles are pliable and the tomato is soft. Drain, but reserve 1½ cups (354 mL) of the cooking liquid. Transfer the tomato, chiles, reserved cooking liquid, garlic, oregano, cumin, salt, and pepper to a blender and puree until smooth. Pass the sauce through a fine-mesh sieve into a small bowl.

3. To make the stew, heat the oil in a large pot over medium-low heat. Add the onion and cook for 4 to 5 minutes, stirring often, until the onion begins to brown. Add the potatoes and let them cook for 5 to 6 minutes, until they begin to soften. Reduce the heat to low, pour in the chile sauce, being careful as it may splash, and simmer for 5 minutes, or until it slightly thickens and becomes a deep red color.

4. Add the vegetable broth, bay leaf, thyme, salt, and pepper. Bring to a boil over high heat, reduce the heat to low, and simmer for 20 to 25 minutes, until the potatoes are tender and the sauce has thickened enough to coat the back of a spoon. If the sauce is too thick and the potatoes are still not cooked, add ½ cup

(118 mL) water and continue cooking until the
potatoes are tender. Add the nopales and stir,
then simmer for 1 more minute to heat the
nopales.

5. Serve hot. Store in an airtight container in the
fridge for up to 4 days or in the freezer for up to
3 months.

VARIATION

Oil-free: Omit the oil when cooking the onion and
use ¼ cup (59 mL) vegetable broth instead.

NOTE

If you can't find nopales, replace them with
1 bunch asparagus, cut into 1-inch (2.5 cm)
pieces. Cook in a pot of boiling water for 1 to
2 minutes, until they start to soften but are still crisp.
Add to the stew in place of the nopales in step 4.

CHILES RELLENOS

A good chile relleno is hard to beat. This one is filled with cashew queso asadero, coated in a thin batter, and fried until golden brown and crisp. I like to serve it on top of a tangy tomato sauce made in the style of Aguascalientes, stewed with chile de árbol and Mexican oregano. The first time I learned how to make chiles rellenos was at the family restaurant, where it is almost a right of passage certifying you as an experienced cook. Back then I was making the nonvegan version, which is a little more complicated than this one, and of course I failed many times before getting it right. The good news is you won't have to struggle as much as teenage me, and these chiles are even better than the ones I used to make. You can also fill them with Almond Queso Fresco (page 31) or Cashew Requesón (page 35). Serve the chiles with Mexican Red Rice (page 24) or Mexican Green Rice (page 27).

MAKES: 4 servings

TOTAL TIME: 40 minutes

TOMATO SAUCE
- 5 large Roma tomatoes (551 g), cored
- 3 to 5 dried árbol chiles, stems and seeds removed
- ¼ large white onion (65 g), roughly chopped (about ⅓ cup)
- 2 garlic cloves (6 g), peeled
- ½ teaspoon dried Mexican oregano
- 1 teaspoon salt
- 2 teaspoons avocado oil

BATTER
- ¼ cup (36 g) all-purpose flour
- ¼ cup (19 g) chickpea flour
- ½ cup (66 g) cornstarch
- ½ teaspoon salt
- ½ cup (118 mL) cold soda water or sparkling water, plus more as needed

CHILES
- 4 large poblano chiles (493 g), roasted (see page 14) and peeled
- 2½ cups (283 g) grated Cashew Queso Asadero (page 32) or vegan mozzarella cheese
- Vegetable oil, for frying
- ½ cup (72 g) all-purpose flour

1. To make the sauce, place the tomatoes and chiles in a medium saucepot and fill with enough water to cover them by 2 inches (5 cm). Bring to a boil over high heat, reduce the heat to low, and simmer for 5 to 6 minutes, until the skins of the tomatoes have burst and the chiles are soft. Drain and transfer them to a blender, add the onion, garlic, oregano, and salt, and puree until completely smooth. You should have about 3 cups (709 mL) of sauce.

2. Heat the oil in a small saucepot over medium-low heat. Reduce the heat to low and pour in the sauce while stirring, being careful as it may splash. Let it simmer for 5 to 6 minutes, until it has thickened slightly and become a deep red color. Remove from the heat.

3. To make the batter, combine the all-purpose flour, chickpea flour, cornstarch, and salt in a large bowl. Pour in the soda water gradually, whisking until the batter reaches the consistency of a thin pancake batter. If your batter is too thick, add an additional ¼ cup (59 mL) soda water and whisk again.

4. Cut a slit from the stem to the tip of each roasted chile. Remove the seeds. Fill each chile with 2 to 3 tablespoons vegan cheese, then close the chile by securing it with two toothpicks. Transfer to a rimmed baking sheet.

5. Heat about 3 inches (7.5 cm) of oil in a large, heavy-bottomed skillet over medium heat to about 350°F (180°C). If you don't have a thermometer, you can test the oil by dropping a small drop of batter into the oil. If it sizzles immediately and starts to brown, then your oil is ready.

(CONTINUED)

6. Put the all-purpose flour on a plate and roll a stuffed chile in the flour so it is lightly coated. Push the chile into the batter, turning it around to completely coat it, but leaving the stem out. (The batter should stick to the chile; if the batter slides off, it means the batter is too thin. If this happens, add 1 tablespoon all-purpose flour to the batter and whisk again.)

7. Place the chile in the hot oil, seam side up; it should immediately start sizzling. Spoon hot oil over the top of the chile while the bottom gets golden brown, in about 2 minutes. Flip the chile and let cook for 1 more minute, or until the chile is golden brown all around. Using a slotted spoon, transfer the chile to a rimmed baking sheet with a rack to drain. Repeat with each chile. Depending on the size of your skillet, you can fry several at a time.

8. Spoon some of the tomato sauce on each plate and place a chile on top. Eat immediately while it is hot and crispy. I do not recommend you store the chiles after frying them. The sauce can be stored in an airtight container in the fridge for up to 5 days or in the freezer for up to 6 months.

TIME-SAVING TIP

The sauce can be made the day before, and the chiles can be roasted and filled.

VARIATION

Oil-free: Omit the oil when simmering the sauce. Place 2 cups (150 g) panko breadcrumbs on a large plate. After coating each chile in batter, drop them in the breadcrumbs and roll to coat completely. Air-fry at 400°F (205°C) for 8 to 10 minutes, until golden brown.

MEATLESS MEATBALLS
IN CHIPOTLE PEANUT SAUCE
Albóndigas sin Carne Encacahuatadas

It was 2016 and I was a new vegan. I was experimenting a lot in the kitchen, trying to make this new way of eating work for me. I had my mind set on making meatballs, but after about six different attempts with rice, beans, mushrooms, tempeh, and everything else you can imagine, my kids begged me to please stop. And so I did, after making these meatballs made with a blend of umami-packed mushrooms and protein-filled tofu, a combination that I first encountered on the vegan blog Connoisseurus Veg. The star of this recipe, however, is without a doubt the sauce. It is a spicy, tangy, and creamy roasted tomato sauce thickened with roasted peanuts and chipotle chiles in adobo. The sauce is also great on top of baked potatoes, as an enchilada sauce, stirred into pasta, or with your favorite veggies. Serve this with white rice or Mexican Red Rice (page 24).

MAKES: **4 servings**

TOTAL TIME: **50 minutes**

MEATBALLS

- 1 (14-ounce/396 g) block extra-firm tofu, drained
- 2 tablespoons ground flaxseed
- 1 small white onion (170 g), grated (about ⅔ cup)
- 8 ounces (226 g) cremini mushrooms, finely chopped (2¾ cups)
- 2 garlic cloves (6 g), finely chopped
- 2 cups (150 g) panko breadcrumbs
- ¼ cup (59 mL) soy sauce
- 1 teaspoon smoked paprika
- 3 mint sprigs, finely chopped (about 1 tablespoon)
- ⅛ teaspoon freshly ground black pepper

PEANUT SAUCE

- 5 large Roma tomatoes (669 g), cored
- ½ large white onion (152 g), chopped (about 1 cup)
- 2 garlic cloves (6 g)
- 1 or 2 chipotle chiles in adobo
- ½ cup (66 g) peanuts, toasted
- ½ cup (118 mL) vegetable broth
- 1 teaspoon salt
- ⅛ teaspoon freshly ground black pepper
- 2 teaspoons avocado oil

(CONTINUED)

1. Preheat the oven to 375°F (190°C). Line a rimmed baking sheet with a silicone mat or parchment paper.

2. To press the tofu, place it between two large plates, and place a heavy object on top. Let it sit for 20 minutes. Discard the liquid that came out of the tofu and crumble the tofu with your hands into a large bowl.

3. In a small bowl, whisk together the flaxseed and 5 tablespoons (75 mL) water. Let it rest for 5 minutes, then pour it into the bowl with the tofu. Place the grated onion on a clean kitchen towel and squeeze out any excess liquid, then add it to the bowl. Add the mushrooms, garlic, breadcrumbs, soy sauce, smoked paprika, mint, and pepper and mix it all together with your hands.

4. Roll into 1½-inch (4 cm) balls; you will get about eighteen of them. Place them on the prepared baking sheet and lightly spray them with cooking spray or brush with oil. Bake for 30 minutes, turning them halfway through.

5. To make the sauce, heat a comal or heavy-bottomed skillet over medium-high heat. Place the tomatoes, onion, and garlic on the hot skillet. Let them char until they become soft and have black spots all over, flipping them frequently, for 8 to 9 minutes. The garlic will be done about 2 minutes in; remove and peel it. Transfer everything to a blender, add the chipotles, peanuts, vegetable broth, salt, and pepper and puree until completely smooth.

6. Heat the oil in a large skillet over medium-low heat. Reduce the heat to low, pour in the sauce while stirring, being careful as it may splash, and simmer for 5 to 6 minutes, until the sauce thickens slightly and becomes a deeper shade of orange. Add the meatballs to the sauce and stir to coat them completely in the sauce. Serve immediately.

7. Store in an airtight container in the fridge for up to 4 days or in the freezer for up to 3 months.

TIME-SAVING TIPS

Chop the mushrooms in the food processor. The sauce can be made the day before. Replace the tomatoes in the sauce with 1 (28-ounce/794 g) can diced roasted tomatoes.

VARIATIONS

Oil-free: Omit the oil when simmering the sauce and baking the meatballs.

Peanut-free: Use almonds instead of peanuts to make the sauce.

LAYERED CHICKPEA ENCHILADAS

Pan de Cazón

Pan de cazón is a traditional Mexican dish from the state of Campeche, which is known for its fishing tradition. Think of it as an enchilada casserole, but way better. In this vegan version, mashed chickpeas stewed in an epazote tomato sauce are layered with homemade corn tortillas, refried black beans, and a spicy habanero-tomato sauce. Epazote is a key ingredient in this dish; if you can't find it fresh, the dried version is a great substitute. The recipe also calls for ground nori seaweed, which you can make by placing two sheets of nori in the blender until they become a powder.

MAKES: 4 servings

TOTAL TIME: 40 minutes

CHICKPEA FILLING

- 4 medium Roma tomatoes (346 g), cut into quarters
- 2 teaspoons avocado oil
- ½ large white onion (152 g), finely chopped (about 1 cup)
- 1 epazote sprig, chopped, *or* 2 teaspoons dried epazote
- 1½ (15-ounce/453 g) cans chickpeas, drained and mashed with a fork (about 2 cups)
- 2 tablespoons ground nori seaweed (see headnote)
- ¾ teaspoon salt
- ⅛ teaspoon freshly ground black pepper

TOMATO-HABANERO SAUCE

- 8 medium Roma tomatoes (700 g), cored

- ¼ large white onion (65 g), roughly chopped (about ⅓ cup)
- 1 epazote sprig, chopped, *or* 2 teaspoons dried epazote
- ½ to 1 habanero chile (6 g), stem and seeds removed
- 1 teaspoon salt
- ⅛ teaspoon freshly ground black pepper
- 2 teaspoons avocado oil

TO SERVE

- 16 corn tortillas
- 2 cups (494 g) Oaxacan Refried Black Beans (page 20), made without avocado leaves
- 4 habanero chiles (68 g), charred on a skillet
- 1 avocado (215 g), pitted, peeled, and sliced

1. To make the chickpea filling, puree the tomatoes in a blender until completely smooth. You should have about 1½ cups (354 mL) of puree. Heat the oil in a large skillet over medium-low heat. Add the onion and epazote and cook until the onion is tender and translucent, for 4 to 5 minutes. Stir in the mashed chickpeas, nori, salt, and pepper and cook for 2 to 3 minutes, until heated through. Reduce the heat to low and pour in the tomato puree while stirring, being careful as it may splash, and simmer for 8 to 9 minutes, until the sauce thickens and becomes a deep red color. Remove from the heat.

2. To make the tomato-habanero sauce, place the tomatoes in a large pot and fill it with enough water to cover them by 2 inches (5 cm). Bring to a boil over high heat, reduce the heat to low, and simmer for 6 to 7 minutes, until the tomatoes soften and the skins burst. Drain and transfer to the blender, add the onion, epazote, habanero, salt, and pepper and puree until completely smooth. You should have about 3¾ cups (887 mL) of sauce.

3. Heat the oil in a large skillet over medium-low heat. Reduce the heat to low and pour in the sauce while stirring, being careful as it may splash. Simmer for 8 to 9 minutes, until the sauce thickens and becomes a deep red color.

4. Preheat a comal or large skillet over medium heat. One by one heat the tortillas for 30 to 40 seconds on each side, or wrap the tortillas in a moistened paper towel and cook them for 1 minute in the microwave, until they are soft and pliable. Then transfer to a tortilla warmer.

(CONTINUED)

181

5. To assemble the pan de cazón, place a dollop of tomato sauce in the middle of a plate, lay a tortilla on top, and spread a thin layer of beans on it. Top with 1½ tablespoons chickpea filling and add 1½ tablespoons sauce on top. Place another tortilla on top and repeat until you have a total of three layers. Place the final tortilla on top and spoon enough sauce on top to cover the tortilla. Garnish with a roasted habanero and three avocado slices. Serve immediately.

6. The filling and sauce can be stored in separate airtight containers in the fridge for up to 3 days or in the freezer for up to 3 months.

NOTE

You can replace the epazote with 1 oregano sprig and 1 cilantro sprig.

TIME-SAVING TIP

The filling and sauce can be made the day before.

VARIATION

Oil-free: Omit the oil when cooking the chickpea filling and instead use ¼ cup (59 mL) vegetable broth. Omit the oil when simmering the tomato-habanero sauce.

MINER'S ENCHILADAS
Enchiladas Mineras

Guanajuato, famous for mining silver in the sixteenth century, is a beautiful city with baroque architecture, deep roots in Mexican history, and the most delicious enchiladas. But forget everything you think you know about enchiladas because these are unlike any version available in the US. A tortilla is dipped in a toasted guajillo chile sauce, pan-fried, filled with queso fresco, then topped with tender carrots and potatoes, lettuce, pickled jalapeños, and more queso fresco. The traditional version uses quite a bit of oil, so I have reduced that a bit and included an oil-free variation in the notes. You can serve them with Mexican Red Rice (page 24) and Refried Pinto Beans (page 20).

MAKES: 4 servings

TOTAL TIME: 45 minutes

VEGETABLE TOPPING
4 teaspoons avocado oil, divided
2 medium carrots (217 g), peeled and cubed (1⅓ cups)
¼ teaspoon + ⅛ teaspoon salt, divided
1 large russet potato (404 g), peeled and cubed (2¼ cups)

ENCHILADA SAUCE
15 dried guajillo chiles (101 g), stems and seeds removed
½ large white onion (152 g), roughly chopped (about 1 cup)
2 garlic cloves (6 g), peeled

½ teaspoon dried Mexican oregano
1 teaspoon salt
⅛ teaspoon freshly ground black pepper

TO ASSEMBLE
4 teaspoons avocado oil, divided
12 corn tortillas
1 recipe Almond Queso Fresco (page 31) or vegan feta
½ head romaine lettuce (313 g), shredded (about 2 cups)
⅓ cup (84 g) pickled jalapeños, sliced

1. To make the vegetable topping, heat 2 teaspoons of the oil in a large skillet over medium-low heat. Add the carrots, cover, and cook, stirring occasionally, for 7 to 8 minutes, until tender but not mushy. Stir in ⅛ teaspoon of the salt and transfer to a plate.

2. Add the remaining 2 teaspoons oil to the skillet. Once the oil is hot, add the potato, cover, and cook, stirring occasionally, for 8 to 10 minutes, until tender but not mushy. Stir in the remaining ¼ teaspoon salt and transfer to the plate with the carrots.

3. To make the enchilada sauce, heat a comal or large, heavy-bottomed skillet over medium heat. Put in the chiles and toast for 30 seconds on each side, or until they are slightly darker in color and become fragrant. Transfer them to a pot and add enough water to cover them by 2 inches (5 cm). Bring the water to a boil, then turn off the heat and let the chiles soak for 15 minutes. Once the chiles are soft and pliable, drain them, but reserve 2 cups (473 mL) of the soaking liquid. Transfer the chiles and reserved soaking liquid to a blender, add the onion, garlic, oregano, salt, and pepper, and blend until completely smooth. You should have about 3½ cups (828 mL) of sauce. Pass it through a fine-mesh sieve into a small bowl.

4. When ready to assemble, preheat the oven to 200°F (95°C).

5. Heat 2 teaspoons of the oil in a large skillet over medium heat. Reduce the heat to low and pour in the sauce while stirring, being careful as it might splash. Simmer the sauce for 5 minutes, or until it slightly thickens. Heat the remaining 2 teaspoons oil in a small skillet on the burner beside the large skillet with the sauce.

(CONTINUED)

COMIDA CASERA

6. Dip a cold tortilla in the hot enchilada sauce until it is completely covered, then immediately transfer it to the small skillet and cook for 10 seconds on each side, then, using a spatula, transfer it to a plate. If you pan-fry the tortilla for too long, it will fall apart, so be careful. Transfer to a plate and fill with 1 tablespoon Almond Queso Fresco and roll it or fold it in half. Keep the assembled tortillas warm in the oven while you continue to pan-fry and fill the rest of the tortillas.

7. To serve, arrange three enchiladas on each plate and top with ½ cup of the potato and carrots, some shredded lettuce, pickled jalapeños, and another sprinkle of queso fresco.

VARIATION

Oil-free: Instead of pan-frying the carrots and potatoes, you can air-fry them at 400°F (205°C) for 10 minutes. Omit the oil when heating up the sauce. One by one heat the tortillas on a comal over medium-high heat for 30 to 40 seconds on each side, or wrap the tortillas in a moistened paper towel and cook them for 1 minute in the microwave, until they are soft and pliable. Dip the warm tortilla in the sauce, transfer to a plate, fill, and fold.

SWISS ENCHILADAS
Enchiladas Suizas

Enchiladas suizas were invented in the famous Mexico City restaurant Sanborns at the beginning of the twentieth century, and they still serve them to this day. One of my favorite dishes before going vegan, they are referred to as Swiss because of the copious amounts of dairy used to make them. While the original enchiladas suizas are filled with chicken, my vegan version is filled with smoky poblano chiles, sweet corn, and chayote, drizzled with a creamy salsa verde, and topped with melty cashew queso asadero. This recipe has been adapted from the original recipe first published in the cookbook *Con Sabor a Sanborns* by Martha Chapa. Serve with Mexican Green Rice (page 27) or Mexican Red Rice (page 24).

MAKES: **4 servings**

TOTAL TIME: **50 minutes**

TOMATILLO SAUCE

10 medium tomatillos (467 g), husks removed, cored and cut into quarters

¼ large white onion (65 g), roughly chopped (about ⅓ cup)

3 garlic cloves (9 g), peeled

1 or 2 serrano chiles (8 g), stems removed

½ bunch cilantro (30 g) (about 1 cup packed leaves)

1 teaspoon salt

⅛ teaspoon freshly ground black pepper

1 tablespoon vegan butter

¾ cup (177 mL) Almond Crema (page 28) or vegan sour cream

FILLING

2 teaspoons avocado oil

½ large white onion (152 g), finely chopped (about 1 cup)

2 garlic cloves (6 g), finely chopped

1 chayote (288 g), peeled, cored, and cut into small dice (1½ cups)

2 ears corn (517 g), shucked, kernels cut off (about 1½ cups corn kernels)

2 poblano chiles (246 g), roasted (see page 14), peeled, and cut into strips

⅓ cup (78 mL) vegetable broth

TO ASSEMBLE

12 corn tortillas

½ recipe Cashew Queso Asadero (page 32), cut into thin slices, or vegan mozzarella

(CONTINUED)

1. To make the tomatillo sauce, place the tomatillos, onion, garlic, serranos, cilantro, ½ cup (118 mL) water, the salt, and pepper in a blender and puree until smooth. Melt the butter in a large skillet over medium-low heat. Reduce the heat to low, pour in the sauce while stirring, being careful as it may splash, and simmer for 10 to 15 minutes, until the sauce thickens enough to coat the back of a spoon and becomes a dull green color. Pour in the Almond Crema and stir to completely incorporate it into the sauce, then simmer for 5 minutes.

2. To make the filling, heat the oil in a large skillet over medium-low heat. Add the onion and cook for 4 to 5 minutes, until it is tender and translucent. Add the garlic and cook for 1 minute. Reduce the heat to low and add the chayote, corn, poblanos, and broth. Cover and continue cooking, stirring occasionally, for 10 to 12 minutes, until the chayote is tender.

3. Preheat the broiler to high.

4. To assemble, pour about ¾ cup (177 mL) of the sauce into a 9 × 13-inch (23 × 33 cm) baking dish. One by one heat the tortillas on a comal over medium-high heat for 30 to 40 seconds on each side, or wrap the tortillas in a moistened paper towel and cook them for 1 minute in the microwave, until they are soft and pliable. Fill each tortilla with 2 tablespoons of the filling and roll, then place them seam side down in the baking dish. Pour the tomatillo sauce on top and cover with the cashew queso asadero. Broil for 3 to 4 minutes to melt and brown the cheese. Serve immediately.

5. Store the filling and sauce in separate airtight containers in the fridge for up to 4 days or in the freezer for up to 3 months.

TIME-SAVING TIP

The sauce and filling can be made the day before and stored in separate airtight containers in the fridge.

VARIATIONS

Oil-free: Omit the oil when cooking the filling, and use ¼ cup (59 mL) vegetable broth to cook the onion instead. Omit the butter when cooking the sauce.

Frozen corn: Substitute 1½ cups (247 g) frozen or drained canned corn for the fresh corn.

8

LA TAMALERÍA

I am going to start by clarifying that in Spanish the singular form of *tamales* is *tamal*, not *tamale*, so I have chosen to use the word *tamal* throughout the book. Multiple tamales are still called *tamales* in either language. Good, now that I got that out of the way, we can continue to talk about the food I am perhaps most passionate about. Tamales are the food of the gods, a ritual and ceremonial food used as an offering to deities in Mesoamerica. There is ample evidence in both the Florentine codex by Fray Bernardino de Sahagún as well as the murals of Bonampak, the most elaborate and well-preserved murals of the Maya civilization, that tamales are one of the oldest pre-Hispanic foods. Even before the existence of tortillas, the Mayans ate tamales, and researchers know this because there is very little evidence of comales (griddles) in the Mayan territory.

Tamales are depicted in codices and murals as an offering, not only for the deities, but also for important rituals such as the Mexica baptism (a ceremony where a newborn was named) and the death of a loved one. Tamales then were not that much different than they are today; the major difference is the absence of fat. With the arrival of the Spanish, tamales lost their symbolic and ritual dimension, but they gained fillings made with beef and pork. Most significantly, lard was added, which made them tender and soft. Today tamales continue to be an important part of major celebrations like Día de Muertos, Christmas, and el Día de la Candelaria, inadvertently continuing the practice of eating them as a ritual food tied to a religious practice. It is estimated that there are more than 300 varieties of tamales, sweet and savory, throughout Mexico; the fillings, shapes, and wrappings change according to the local produce availability in each region. They are sold on carts on the street and at tamalerías, or they are made in people's homes. My recipes are a good mix between the very traditional and vegan versions of meat-filled tamales. I also include some sweet tamales that I am very excited for you to try. If you have never had them before, you are in for a treat!

TAMALES 101: INGREDIENTS

A basic tamal masa (dough) is made up of nixtamalized corn product (masa or flour), fat, liquid, and a leavener. Each one plays a different role in the tamal-making process and is equally important.

Nixtamalized Corn

There are two options when making tamales: You can use either fresh masa or masa harina. Fresh masa is freshly ground nixtamalized corn, and it is how tamales have been made since before the Spanish conquest. Tamales made with fresh masa are tender and have a more intense corn flavor.

Look for masa at your local Mexican market, where sometimes it is referred to as nixtamal, or at a tortillería (a shop that sells tortillas). It can be difficult to find in the US depending on where you live, but I promise it is worth the effort.

When using fresh masa, buy the masa the same day you will be making your tamales. If it is left too long in the refrigerator, it can start to ferment and sour. If you are not able to use the masa within the first two days of purchasing it, freeze it, then thaw it for a couple of hours the day you will be using it.

If fresh masa is not available, you can use masa harina. Masa harina is a very finely ground nixtamalized corn flour. It is easy to use and still makes very good tamales. You can probably find it at your local grocery store. Even though there is a variety of masa harina made specifically for tamales, which is not as finely ground as the one for tortillas, I have chosen to use the one for tortillas in most of the recipes because it is the one most readily available. Unfortunately, masa harina cannot be replaced successfully with cornmeal.

Fat or No Fat?

Pre-Hispanic tamales were made without fat, or at least that is how Fray Bernardino de Sahagún describes them in the *Historia General de la Cosas de la Nueva España*. Lard was added to tamales with the arrival of the Spaniards, and it changed the texture of tamales from dense to tender and fluffy.

There are several fat options you can use instead of lard and even an option to forgo fat entirely and still achieve tender tamales.

Vegetable shortening is the easiest way to replicate the texture of tamales made with lard. Unfortunately, it is neither very tasty nor very healthy. So I don't use it, but if vegetable shortening is the most accessible to you, feel free to use it.

Refined coconut oil makes the tastiest tamales, even savory ones. It doesn't have a coconut flavor, so don't worry—your tamales will not taste like coconut. It also does a great job of mimicking the texture of tamales made with lard. Make sure the coconut oil is stored at room temperature and is solid. If your coconut oil is liquid, place it in the refrigerator for 5 to 10 minutes.

Olive oil or avocado oil also makes very good tamales, but the texture changes significantly: The tamales are slightly denser than the ones made with coconut oil. If you use olive oil, I recommend you use a mild one, as the flavor of extra-virgin oil is too overpowering. Use the oil at room temperature.

Pumpkin puree is a great substitute for fat. I was pleasantly surprised at how well the tamales came out without any fat at all! The consistency of the tamal is definitely denser, but it is not dry. The masa comes out a little bit sweet, but it contrasts well with the spicy fillings in this book. Use canned unsweetened pumpkin puree, the kind you would buy to make pumpkin pie.

Liquid

I use **vegetable broth** to reconstitute the masa harina or adjust the consistency of the fresh masa when making savory tamales. You can find vegetable broth at the grocery store, or you can make it yourself. To ensure that the salt content listed in the recipes is accurate, I recommend using low-sodium vegetable broth. **Water** can be used in place of vegetable broth in a pinch, but the masa won't be as flavorful.

I use **unsweetened almond milk** for the sweet tamales, but any plant milk will work. It is important to remember that the amount of liquid you will need might differ, depending on the humidity where you live, the altitude, the brand of masa harina, and the texture of your fresh masa. Start with the amount listed in each recipe, but adjust the quantity of liquid according to your needs.

Whatever liquid you are using, make sure it is warm when adding it to the masa.

Leavener

Leaveners are used to add small pockets of air into the masa, which improves the texture. In the US, the choice is limited to just baking powder, but in Mexico, tequesquite is also an option. Tequesquite is a mineral salt that combines chloride and sodium carbonate. Baking powder, however, is the only leavener I use for tamales since it is easy to find and use. You can make tamales without it, but they will be denser.

MAKING TAMALES

The Ratio

There is a ratio that I follow when making the masa. It works wonderfully and will give you a solid base that will allow you to play around with different fillings and flavors.

TAMALES MADE WITH MASA HARINA

MAKES: 20 to 24 tamales

FAT	MASA HARINA	BAKING POWDER	SALT	LIQUID
8 ounces (226 g)	1¼ pounds (509 g) or 4¼ cups	1½ teaspoons	1 tablespoon	4 cups (946 mL)

TAMALES MADE WITH FRESH MASA

MAKES: 20 to 24 tamales

FAT	FRESH MASA	BAKING POWDER	SALT	LIQUID
8 ounces (226 g)	2 pounds (907 g) or 3⅔ cups	1½ teaspoons	1 tablespoon	1 cup (236 mL)

Making the Masa

The key to fluffy tamales is the beating of the masa. Traditionally this used to be done by hand, which requires really strong arms! I use an electric stand mixer, but an electric hand mixer will also work. I beat the fat first, then add the masa harina or fresh masa, and then slowly pour in the warm liquid while mixing at low speed. Once everything is incorporated, I beat the masa for 5 minutes at medium speed to beat air into it. The masa should be the consistency of a thick cake batter, but it should still hold its shape when placed on a spoon. There's a trick to know when the masa is done: Pass a spatula through your masa, and if you see small air pockets form, it means it's ready. In Spanish we say, "cuando la masa te hace ojitos," which means "when the masa shows you its eyes," meaning the air pockets.

The Wrapper

The wrapping possibilities for tamales are endless. The most commonly used wrappers are corn husks, banana leaves, and leafy greens. Corn husks are the most well-known. You can use dry or fresh ones. Look for them at your local Mexican market, or your grocery store might carry them. Using dry husks is more convenient, as all you have to do is soak them in hot water for about 1 hour. The fresh ones need to be cut off from the ears of corn and rinsed to remove any dirt, but they do not need to be soaked. The corn husks are not meant to be eaten with the tamales.

Banana leaves are the second-most-used tamal wrapper; they infuse the tamales with an earthy flavor. You can find banana leaves frozen or fresh at your local Mexican market. If you use frozen ones, thaw them the day you are planning to use them. If you use fresh ones, cut them into rectangles, then either pass them over an open flame to soften them or simmer them in water for 20 minutes. The banana leaves are not meant to be eaten with the tamales.

Swiss chard leaves are a very nutritious tamal wrapper. They are big enough to hold a tamal and they are edible. If your Swiss chard leaves are whole, you can remove the fibrous part of the stem and wrap the tamales in them without cooking the leaves first. If your Swiss chard leaves are small or not intact (torn in some parts), it is better to blanch them so you can use more than one to wrap your tamal. To blanch them, boil the leaves in salted water for 5 seconds, then plunge them in ice water to cool them down. Collard greens can also be used in place of Swiss chard, prepared the same way. The Swiss chard leaves and collards are meant to be eaten with the tamales.

Milpa leaves are the long, thin leaves that grow on a corn stalk. They are commonly used in Oaxaca and Michoacán to wrap tamales. You might be able to get some at a local corn farm or farmers' market. All you need to do is rinse them, then use them to wrap the tamal. These are not meant to be eaten.

Parchment paper or aluminum foil can be used successfully if no other wrapper is available.

Corn Husk Wrapper

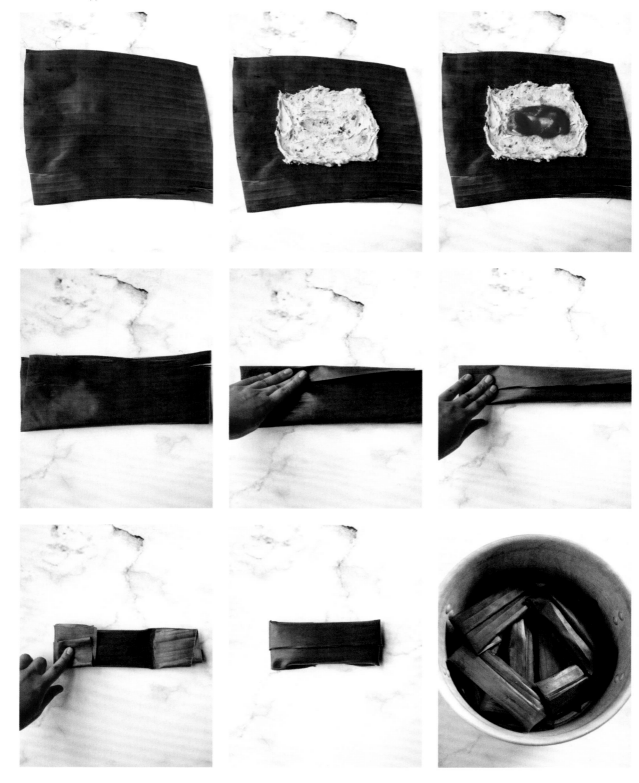

Cooking

The best way to cook tamales is to steam them. There is a common misconception that tamales need to be steamed for 2 hours or more. This results in dry, overcooked tamales. The cooking time for twenty to twenty-four tamales in a medium steamer is 40 to 50 minutes from the time the water in the steamer starts simmering. This time could change depending on the size of your pot and the number and size of your tamales. To check if your tamales are done, remove one from the pot and peel the corn husk (or other wrapper) off the masa. If the corn husk detaches easily, it means the tamales are done. The tamales are going to be really soft, and this will make you doubt their doneness, but they will firm up as they cool.

To cook tamales in an Instant Pot, set up the steamer trivet in the insert of your Instant Pot, add 1 cup (236 mL) water, and arrange the tamales just as you would in the steamer. Cook at high pressure for 25 minutes with a 10-minute natural release.

Setting Up the Steamer

To set-up the steamer for cooking tamales wrapped in corn husks, fill the bottom of the steamer with water, but make sure the water isn't touching the steamer rack. Line the steamer rack and sides of the pot with previously soaked corn husks. Place the tamales in the steamer vertically, leaning against the side of the pot, with the open end on top. Repeat this process until all the tamales are in the steamer. Cover them with a layer of corn husks. If the steamer is not full, fill the empty spaces with more corn husks. Cover the pot and bring the water to a boil.

Serving

Always, always serve tamales with salsa. A tamal without salsa is like a taco without a tortilla. Any salsa will do. Also, serve them right in their wrappers. Guests and family will love to unwrap the tamales themselves.

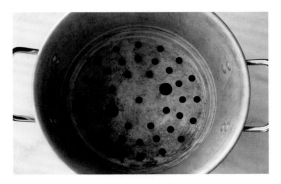

Setting Up the Steamer

Storing

Remove your tamales from the steamer and lay them out on baking sheets. Let them cool completely. Place them in an airtight container, with the wrappers on, and keep them in the refrigerator for up to 5 days or in the freezer for up to 6 months.

Reheating

You can reheat tamales in the microwave, on a griddle or grill, or by steaming them again until warm. The best way is to steam them for 7 to 8 minutes; this prevents them from drying out. To reheat frozen tamales, let them thaw in the refrigerator overnight and then reheat them. My favorite method of reheating corn husk–wrapped tamales is on a griddle or comal. To reheat your tamales on a griddle, heat the griddle to medium heat. Place the tamales, still in their corn husks, on the griddle and cook, rotating every couple of minutes, until the tamales are warm in the center. The corn husks will begin to burn before the tamales are completely warm; this infuses them with a smoky flavor that I really enjoy.

Working Ahead

Making tamales is a time-consuming endeavor, which is why I always recommend you invite friends over to make them; if that is not an option, there are ways you can work ahead. The masa and the filling can be made up 2 days before cooking the tamales; just place them in an airtight container in the refrigerator until you are ready to use them. The wrapped, uncooked tamales can also be stored in an airtight container in the refrigerator 1 day before being cooked. You can also keep a stash of cooked tamales in the freezer and steam them whenever you want. You can have freshly cooked tamales every day!

Tamales in 2 days

Day 1: Make the masa and filling, and store them in the refrigerator overnight.

Day 2: Assemble the tamales and steam them.

Tamales in 3 days

Day 1: Make the masa and filling, and store them in the refrigerator overnight.

Day 2: Assemble the tamales, and store them in the refrigerator overnight.

Day 3: Steam the tamales.

SONORAN RED CHILE TAMALES

Tamales Rojos Sonorenses

These are the tamales that landed me on the news! I made a recipe video on how to make them step-by-step and it went viral, so much so that it got the attention of a local news network. Once you taste them, you will see what all the fuss is about. They are northern Mexico–style red chile tamales, which are easily recognizable by the red-tinted masa and corn husk wrapper. In this recipe, I honor the flavors of Sonora with stewed jackfruit cooked in a spicy chile guajillo and árbol sauce, with bits of potato, carrot, raisins, and olives. My kids adore these tamales and look forward to our annual tamalada, when the whole family gets together to make dozens of tamales. If jackfruit is not readily available to you, you can use 2 pounds (907 g) of your favorite mushrooms instead. The raisins are completely optional, but I enjoy the layers of sweet and salty goodness. Serve with Molcajete Salsa (page 36) or Chile de Árbol Salsa (page 43).

MAKES: 20 to 24 tamales

TOTAL TIME: 2½ hours

---

30 dried corn husks

GUAJILLO CHILE SAUCE

20 dried guajillo chiles (164 g), seeds and stems removed

3 or 4 dried árbol chiles, stems removed

6 garlic cloves (18 g), peeled

½ large white onion (116 g), chopped

1 teaspoon dried Mexican oregano

1 teaspoon salt

¼ teaspoon freshly ground black pepper

JACKFRUIT FILLING

2 (20-ounce/565 g) cans young green jackfruit in brine, drained

1 tablespoon avocado oil

4 garlic cloves (12 g), finely chopped

¾ cup (177 mL) vegetable broth

½ teaspoon salt

⅛ teaspoon freshly ground black pepper

1 medium russet potato (226 g), cut into ¼-inch (6 mm) matchsticks

1 large carrot (141 g), cut into ¼-inch (6 mm) matchsticks

MASA

1 cup (226 g) refined coconut oil, room temperature

1½ teaspoons baking powder

1 tablespoon salt

1½ tablespoons ground cumin

4¼ cups (509 g) masa harina

3 cups (709 mL) low-sodium vegetable broth

TO ASSEMBLE

¾ cup (121 g) pitted Manzanilla olives, sliced in half

½ cup (67 g) raisins

(CONTINUED)

1. **To prepare the corn husks,** place them in your kitchen sink or a large pot and cover them with hot water. Place a heat-resistant plate over the husks to weight them down so they are completely submerged. Soak for at least 1 hour while you prepare the filling.

2. **To make the guajillo chile sauce,** place all the chiles in a medium pot and add enough water to cover them by 2 inches (5 cm). Bring the water to a boil over high heat, turn off the heat, and let them soak for 15 minutes, or until the chiles are soft and pliable. Drain them, but reserve 2 cups (473 mL) of the soaking liquid. Transfer the chiles, reserved soaking liquid, garlic, onion, oregano, salt, and pepper to a blender and puree until completely smooth. Pass the sauce through a fine-mesh sieve. This should yield about 3 cups (709 mL) of sauce.

3. **To make the jackfruit filling,** place the jackfruit in a colander and rinse with cold water. Cut off the core of the jackfruit (the hard tip of the triangle pieces), remove the seed pods, and shred the jackfruit pieces with your hands. Transfer the jackfruit to a medium pot and add enough water to cover it by 2 inches (5 cm). Bring to a boil over high heat, reduce the heat to low, and simmer for 10 minutes. Drain the jackfruit and let it cool slightly. Using your hands, squeeze all the water out of the jackfruit.

4. Heat the oil in a large skillet over medium-high heat. Add the jackfruit and cook for 3 to 4 minutes, until it begins to brown. Reduce the heat to low, add the garlic, and cook for 1 minute, stirring often. Pour in 1½ cups (354 mL) of the chile sauce, the vegetable broth, salt, and pepper and simmer for 6 to 7 minutes, until the sauce thickens. Transfer to a medium bowl and let cool completely in the fridge.

5. Place the potato in a medium saucepot and add enough cold water to cover by 3 inches (7.5 cm). Bring to a boil over high heat, reduce the heat to low, and simmer for 4 minutes. Add the carrot and cook for 8 minutes, or until the carrot and potato are tender. Drain and transfer the carrot and potato to a medium bowl and let cool completely in the fridge.

6. **To make the masa,** beat the coconut oil, baking powder, salt, and cumin in a stand mixer, using the paddle attachment on medium speed, for 1 minute. Add half of the masa harina and beat on low speed for 1 minute, then slowly pour in half of the vegetable broth and continue to beat until the broth is completely incorporated. Add the remaining masa harina and broth and beat until incorporated. Pour in the remaining 1½ cups (354 mL) chile sauce and beat on medium speed until thoroughly mixed, for about 5 minutes. The masa should have the consistency of a thick cake batter, and you should be able to easily pass your spatula through it. If the masa is too thick, add additional vegetable broth or water until you reach the right consistency. The masa should be a little bit salty.

7. **To prepare the steamer,** drain the corn husks and set them on a dry kitchen towel. Reserve the largest husks to wrap the tamales and the small ones to line the steamer. Fill the bottom of the steamer with water, making sure the water does not touch the steamer rack. Line the rack and sides of the steamer pot with corn husks.

8. **To assemble the tamales,** take a husk and pat it dry. Using a spoon, spread 2 to 3 tablespoons of the masa onto the smooth side of the corn husk, about ¼ inch (6 mm) thick. Leave a 3-inch (7.5 cm) border clear of masa at the pointed end of the husk, and 1 inch (2.5 cm) on all the other sides.

9. Place 1 tablespoon of the jackfruit filling in a line down the center of the masa. Add one piece of carrot, one piece of potato, two or three olive halves, and a couple of raisins. Fold over the right side of the husk, surrounding the filling, then continue rolling tightly until there is no overlap left. Fold down the pointy section of the corn husk, leaving one side of the tamal open. Repeat with the rest of the ingredients.

10. To cook the tamales, place each tamal vertically in the steamer, with the folded end leaning against the side of the pot and the open end facing up. Place a layer of corn husks on top of the tamales, cover the pot, and bring the water to a boil over high heat. Once it starts boiling, reduce the heat to medium-low and cook for 40 minutes. Check the tamales: When the husk separates easily from the masa, it means they are done. If they are not done, steam them for 10 more minutes and check again. Remove the steamer from the heat and let the tamales sit, uncovered, for 10 minutes to cool. Don't be alarmed if the tamales seem soft. As they cool, they will firm up.

VARIATIONS

Other fats: Replace the coconut oil with 1 cup plus 2 tablespoons (265 mL) avocado oil or 1¼ cups (295 mL) olive oil.

Oil-free: Use 1¼ cups (226 g) canned unsweetened pumpkin puree to replace the oil.

Fresh masa: Use 2 pounds (907 g) fresh masa instead of the masa harina and decrease the vegetable broth to ¾ cup (177 mL).

LA TAMALERÍA

CREAMY POBLANO AND CORN TAMALES

Tamales de Rajas con Crema

The word *rajas* refers to roasted poblano chiles cut into strips; they're often used to make soups, vegetable sautés like the rajas con papas that fills the itacates (page 118), or even salads. This tamal is filled with smoky rajas, cooked with onion, garlic, corn, and a silky Almond Crema (page 28). This classic rajas con crema filling infuses the masa with a creaminess that makes these tamales a sure crowd-pleaser, which is why I find myself making them over and over again every Christmas. You can also make this recipe with mild Hatch or Anaheim chiles, or if you need more spice in your life, add some jalapeños. Serve with Roasted Tomatillo Salsa (page 39) or Chile de Árbol Salsa (page 43).

MAKES: **20 to 24 tamales**

TOTAL TIME: **2½ hours**

30 dried corn husks
1 cup (226 g) refined coconut oil, room temperature
1½ teaspoons baking powder
1 tablespoon salt
4¼ cups (509 g) masa harina

4 cups (496 mL) low-sodium vegetable broth, warm
1 recipe Rajas con Crema (page 97)

1. **To prepare the corn husks,** place them in your kitchen sink or a large pot and cover them with hot water. Place a heat-resistant plate over the husks to weight them down so they are completely submerged. Soak for at least 1 hour while you prepare the filling.

2. **To make the masa,** beat the coconut oil in a stand mixer, using the paddle attachment on medium speed, for 1 minute. Add the baking powder and salt and beat for 1 minute to incorporate them into the coconut oil. Add half of the masa harina and beat on low speed for 1 minute, then slowly pour in half of the vegetable broth and continue to beat until it is completely incorporated. Add the remaining masa harina and broth and beat on medium speed until thoroughly mixed, for about 5 minutes. The masa should have the consistency of a thick cake batter, and you should be able to easily pass your spatula through it. If the masa is too thick, add additional vegetable broth or water until you reach the right consistency. The masa should be a little bit salty.

3. **To prepare the steamer,** drain the corn husks and set them on a dry kitchen towel. Reserve the largest husks to wrap the tamales and the small ones to line the steamer. Fill the bottom of the steamer with water, making sure the water does not touch the steamer rack. Line the rack and sides of the steamer pot with corn husks.

4. **To assemble the tamales,** take a husk and pat it dry. Using a spoon, spread 2 to 3 tablespoons of the masa onto the smooth side of the corn husk, about ¼ inch (6 mm) thick. Leave a 3-inch (7.5 cm) border clear of masa at the pointed end of the husk, and 1 inch (2.5 cm) on all the other sides.

(CONTINUED)

5. Place 1 heaping tablespoon of the rajas filling in a line down the center of the dough. Fold over the right side of the husk, surrounding the filling, then continue rolling tightly until there is no overlap left. Fold down the pointy section of the corn husk, leaving one side of the tamal open. Repeat with the rest of the ingredients.

6. **To cook the tamales,** place each tamal vertically in the steamer, with the folded end leaning against the side of the pot and the open end facing up. Place a layer of corn husks on top of the tamales, cover the pot, and bring the water to a boil over high heat. Once it starts boiling, reduce the heat to medium-low and cook for 40 minutes. Check the tamales: When the husk separates easily from the masa, it means they are done. If they are not done, steam them for 10 more minutes and check again. Remove the steamer from the heat and let the tamales sit uncovered for 10 minutes to cool. Don't be alarmed if the tamales seem soft. As they cool, they will firm up.

VARIATIONS

Other fats: Replace the coconut oil with 1 cup plus 2 tablespoons (265 mL) avocado oil or 1¼ cups (295 mL) olive oil.

Oil-free: Use 1¼ cups (226 g) canned unsweetened pumpkin puree to replace the oil.

Fresh masa: Use 2 pounds (907 g) fresh masa instead of the masa harina and decrease the vegetable broth to 1 cup (236 mL).

CHICKPEA TUNA TAMALES
Tamales de Atún de Garbanzo

Tamales are a very regional dish in Mexico and are often a reflection of local cuisine and the agricultural practices of the region. In this recipe adapted from the state of Baja California, where seafood is king, I use mashed chickpeas to take the place of tuna in a salad made with tomatoes, onion, jalapeño, and ground nori seaweed. The salad is mixed right into the masa with a chile pasilla salsa. This means this tamal has no filling, but don't let that deter you, as they are easier to wrap and just as enjoyable. The chickpea tuna salad can also be used to make sandwiches, and it is great on tostadas all on its own or with a dollop of vegan mayo. I like to serve this with Chile de Árbol Salsa (page 43).

MAKES: **20 to 24 tamales**

TOTAL TIME: **2 hours**

30 dried corn husks

CHICKPEA TUNA SALAD
1 (15-ounce/425 g) can chickpeas, drained and rinsed (about 1½ cups)
½ large white onion (152 g), finely chopped (about 1 cup)
2 large Roma tomatoes (260 g), diced (about 1½ cups)
1 or 2 jalapeño chiles (26 to 52 g), finely chopped
2 tablespoons (12 g) ground nori seaweed
¼ teaspoon salt

PASILLA CHILE SAUCE
3 dried pasilla chiles (20 g), seeds and stems removed

½ medium white onion (102 g), roughly chopped (about ¾ cup)
2 garlic cloves (6 g), peeled
½ teaspoon dried Mexican oregano

MASA
1¼ cups (295 mL) mild olive oil, room temperature
1½ teaspoons baking powder
1 tablespoon salt
4¼ cups (509 g) masa harina
3 cups (177 mL) low-sodium vegetable broth, warm

1. To prepare the corn husks, place them in your kitchen sink or a large pot and cover them with hot water. Place a heat-resistant plate over the husks to weight them down so they are completely submerged. Soak for at least 1 hour while you prepare the filling.

2. To make the chickpea tuna salad, place the chickpeas in a large bowl and roughly mash with a fork or a potato masher. You don't want them completely pureed. Add the onion, tomatoes, jalapeños, nori powder, and salt and mix. Let the salad sit at room temperature while you prepare the sauce and masa.

3. To make the pasilla chile sauce, place the chiles in a small saucepot and add enough water to cover them by 2 inches (5 cm). Bring the water to a boil over high heat, turn the heat off, and let them sit for 15 minutes. Drain the chiles, but reserve 1 cup (236 mL) of the soaking liquid. Transfer the chiles, reserved soaking liquid, onion, garlic, and oregano to a blender and puree until completely smooth. It should make about 1¼ cups of sauce (295 mL). Pass the sauce through a fine-mesh sieve.

4. To make the masa, beat the olive oil in a stand mixer, using the paddle attachment on medium speed, for 1 minute. Add the baking powder and salt and beat for 1 minute to incorporate them into the olive oil. Add half of the masa harina and beat on low speed for 1 minute. Slowly pour in half of the vegetable broth and the chile puree and continue to beat until completely incorporated, then add the remaining masa harina and broth and beat on medium speed until thoroughly mixed, for about 5 minutes. The masa should have the consistency of a thick cake batter, and you should be able to easily pass

(CONTINUED)

your spatula through it. If the masa is too thick, add additional vegetable broth or water until you reach the right consistency. The masa should be a little bit salty. Add the chickpea tuna salad and mix on low speed until it is completely integrated into the masa, for about 1 minute.

5. **To prepare the steamer,** drain the corn husks and set them on a dry kitchen towel. Reserve the largest husks to wrap the tamales and the small ones to line the steamer. Fill the bottom of the steamer with water, making sure the water does not touch the steamer rack. Line the rack and sides of the steamer pot with corn husks.

6. **To assemble the tamales,** take a husk and pat it dry. Using a spoon, spread 2 to 3 tablespoons of the masa onto the smooth side of the corn husk, about ¼ inch (6 mm) thick. Leave a 3-inch (7.5 cm) border clear of masa at the pointed end of the husk, and 1 inch (2.5 cm) on all the other sides.

7. Fold over the right side of the husk, then continue rolling tightly until there is no overlap left. Fold down the pointy section of the corn husk, leaving one side of the tamal open. Repeat with the rest of the ingredients.

8. **To cook the tamales,** place each tamal vertically in the steamer, with the folded end leaning against the side of the pot and the open end facing up. Place a layer of corn husks on top of the tamales, cover the pot, and bring the water to a boil over high heat. Once it starts boiling, reduce the heat to medium-low and cook for 40 minutes. Check the tamales: When the husk separates easily from the masa, it means they are done. If they are not done, steam them for 10 more minutes and check again. Remove the steamer from the heat and let the tamales sit uncovered for 10 minutes to cool. Don't be alarmed if the tamales seem soft. As they cool, they will firm up.

NOTE

To grind the nori seaweed, place two sheets of seaweed (the kind used to make sushi) in a dry blender container and blend until it becomes a fine powder. Use it in soups, stews, and salads to add a fishy flavor.

VARIATIONS

Other fats: Replace the olive oil with 1 cup (226 g) refined coconut oil or 1 cup plus 2 tablespoons (265 mL) avocado oil.

Oil-free: Use 1¼ cups (226 g) canned unsweetened pumpkin puree to replace the oil.

Fresh masa: Use 2 pounds (907 g) fresh masa instead of the masa harina and decrease the vegetable broth to 1 cup (236 mL).

CHIPILÍN TAMALES

Tamales de Chipilín

Every time I try a new quelite (Mexican wild greens), I am amazed at the subtle differences in their flavors. Chipilín, also known as chepil, is a leafy green found in the southern state of Chiapas. It tastes like a cross between spinach and watercress but with an herbaceous quality to it. It is used in dishes such as soups, to flavor tortillas, and in tamales. The masa for these tamales is studded with these earthy greens and filled with Cashew Queso Asadero (page 32) and a spicy tomato and guajillo chile sauce, wrapped in banana leaves, and steamed until tender. Chipilín is hard to find outside of Mexico, so instead I recommend you use a mixture of spinach and watercress.

MAKES: **20 to 24 tamales**

TOTAL TIME: **2½ hours**

2 (1-pound/454 g) packages fresh or frozen banana leaves

GUAJILLO TOMATO SAUCE

4 dried guajillo chiles (41 g), stems and seeds removed

2 to 4 dried árbol chiles, stems removed

1 garlic clove (3 g), peeled

4 medium Roma tomatoes (500 g), cored

¼ large white onion (65 g), roughly chopped (about ⅓ cup)

½ teaspoon dried Mexican oregano

¾ teaspoon salt

⅛ teaspoon freshly ground black pepper

MASA

1 cup (226 g) refined coconut oil, room temperature

1½ teaspoons baking powder

1 tablespoon salt

4¼ cups (509 g) masa harina

4 cups (946 mL) low-sodium vegetable broth, warm

2 cups (117 g) packed chipilín leaves, roughly chopped, *or* 1 cup watercress + 1 cup spinach

TO ASSEMBLE

1 recipe Cashew Queso Asadero (page 32), thinly sliced, or vegan mozzarella

1. To prepare the fresh banana leaves, unfold them carefully and, using kitchen shears, cut off the stringy edges, then cut them into 10 × 8-inch (25 × 20 cm) rectangles. You will need twenty to twenty-four of them. Stack all the leaves and place them in a large pot, fill the pot with enough water to cover the leaves, and bring to a boil over high heat. Reduce the heat to low and simmer for 20 minutes. Drain the leaves and let them cool. If you are using frozen banana leaves, thaw them, rinse them, and dry them with a clean kitchen towel.

2. To make the sauce, heat a comal or heavy-bottomed skillet over medium-high heat. Toast the chiles for 30 seconds on each side, until they become a deep red color and are fragrant. Be careful not to overtoast them or the sauce will become bitter. Transfer the chiles to a medium saucepot, add the garlic, tomatoes, and onion, and pour in enough water to cover them by 2 inches (5 cm). Bring the water to a boil over high heat, reduce the heat to low, and let them simmer for about 7 minutes, or until the chiles are soft. Drain and transfer everything to a blender, add the oregano, salt, and pepper, and puree until completely smooth. Pass the sauce through a fine-mesh sieve.

3. To make the masa, beat the coconut oil in a stand mixer, using the paddle attachment on medium speed, for 1 minute. Add the baking powder and salt and beat for 1 minute to incorporate them into the coconut oil. Add half of the masa harina and beat on low speed for 1 minute, then slowly pour in half of the vegetable broth and continue to beat until it is completely incorporated. Add the remaining masa harina and broth and beat on medium speed until thoroughly mixed, for about 5 minutes. The

(CONTINUED)

masa should have the consistency of a thick cake batter, and you should be able to easily pass your spatula through it. If the masa is too thick, add additional vegetable broth or water until you reach the right consistency. The masa should be a little bit salty. Mix in the chipilín leaves on low speed until they are evenly distributed throughout the masa, for about 1 minute.

4. To prepare the steamer, fill the bottom with water, making sure the water does not touch the steamer rack, and line the steamer rack with banana leaves.

5. To assemble the tamales, spread 3 generous tablespoons of the masa in the center of a banana leaf, forming a 4 × 3-inch (10 × 8 cm) rectangle. Place one slice of cheese and 1 tablespoon of the sauce in the center of the rectangle. Fold the bottom edge of the banana leaf up and over so that the dough encloses the filling. Fold the top part of the leaf down, then fold the sides to form a pocket. Repeat with the rest of the ingredients.

6. To cook the tamales, place the tamal packets in the steamer horizontally, laying one on top of the other, with the folded part of the packets on the bottom. Place a layer of banana leaf scraps on top of the tamales. Cover the pot and bring the water to a boil over high heat, then reduce the heat to medium-low and simmer for 40 minutes. Check the tamales: When the banana leaves separate easily from the masa, it means the tamales are done. If they are not done, cook for 10 more minutes and check again. Remove the steamer from the heat and let the tamales sit uncovered for 10 minutes. Don't be alarmed if the tamales seem soft. As they cool, they will firm up.

VARIATIONS

Other fats: Replace the coconut oil with 1 cup plus 2 tablespoons (265 mL) avocado oil or 1¼ cups (295 mL) olive oil.

Oil-free: Use 1¼ cups (226 g) canned unsweetened pumpkin puree to replace the oil.

Fresh masa: Use 2 pounds (907 g) fresh masa instead of the masa harina and decrease the vegetable broth to 1 cup (236 mL).

MUSHROOM IN ADOBO TAMALES

Tamales Chanchamitos

These have just become my favorite tamales. A masa infused with achiote surrounds a filling of caramelized oyster mushrooms stewed in a chile ancho and guajillo adobo. They are wrapped almost like candy, tied with a strip of corn husk at both ends. The result is a rounded pocket of goodness bursting with umami. These tamales are from Tabasco, a coastal state known for its lush vegetation, but you can also find variations of them in the state of Veracruz. Wrapping the tamales this way takes a considerable amount of time, so get some help, or you can also wrap them the traditional way. Serve with the spicy tomato habanero sauce and pickled red onions.

MAKES: 24 to 28 small tamales

TOTAL TIME: 3½ hours

---

30 dried corn husks

PICKLED RED ONIONS

½ large red onion, thinly sliced

Juice of 2 limes (about ¼ cup/59 mL)

2 cilantro sprigs, chopped

¼ teaspoon salt

ADOBO SAUCE

3 dried guajillo chiles (25 g), stems and seeds removed

2 dried ancho chiles (23 g), stems and seeds removed

1 teaspoon avocado oil

½ medium white onion (103 g), chopped (about ¾ cup)

½ orange bell pepper (37 g), chopped (about ⅓ cup)

5 garlic cloves (23 g), peeled

3 medium Roma tomatoes (296 g), cored and cut into quarters

1 tablespoon dried epazote

2 whole cloves

½ teaspoon cumin seeds

1 teaspoon dried Mexican oregano

1¼ teaspoons salt

⅛ teaspoon freshly ground black pepper

FILLING

1 tablespoon avocado oil

2 pounds (907 g) oyster mushrooms, trimmed and torn

MASA

2 teaspoons achiote paste

1 cup plus 2 tablespoons (266 mL) avocado oil, room temperature

1½ teaspoons baking powder

1 tablespoon salt

4¼ cups (509 g) masa harina

4 cups (946 mL) low-sodium vegetable broth, warm

HABANERO SALSA

5 medium Roma tomatoes (493 g), cored

¼ large white onion (65 g), roughly chopped (about ⅓ cup)

2 garlic cloves, peeled

1 habanero chile, stem removed

½ teaspoon salt

1 tablespoon avocado oil

(CONTINUED)

1. **To prepare the corn husks,** place them in your kitchen sink or a large pot and cover them with hot water. Place a heat-resistant plate over the husks to weight them down so they are completely submerged. Soak for at least 1 hour while you prepare the filling.

2. **To make the pickled onions,** in a small bowl, combine the onion, lime juice, cilantro, and salt and let marinate in the fridge until you are ready to serve your tamales.

3. **To make the adobo sauce,** place the chiles in a small pot and add enough water to cover them by 2 inches (5 cm). Bring the water to a boil over high heat, turn off the heat, and let them soak for 15 minutes. Once the chiles are soft and pliable, drain them and reserve 1 cup (236 mL) of the soaking liquid. Transfer the chiles and reserved soaking liquid to a blender.

4. Heat the oil in a large skillet over medium-low heat. Add the onion and bell pepper and cook for 4 to 5 minutes, until the onion begins to soften, stirring occasionally. Add the garlic and cook for 1 minute, then add the tomatoes and cook for 4 minutes, or until soft. Transfer to the blender.

5. Heat a small skillet over medium-low heat. Toast the epazote, cloves, cumin, oregano, salt, and pepper for 30 to 40 seconds, until the spices become fragrant. Transfer to the blender and puree until completely smooth. Pass the sauce through a fine-mesh sieve.

6. **To make the filling,** heat the oil in a large skillet over medium heat. Add the mushrooms and cook until they begin to brown, for 8 to 10 minutes. Reduce the heat to low and pour in the adobo sauce, stirring quickly to avoid excess splatter. Simmer until the adobo thickens and becomes a deep red color, for 12 to 14 minutes. Transfer to a heatproof bowl and let cool completely in the fridge.

7. **To make the masa,** in a small bowl, whisk together the achiote paste and 1½ tablespoons water. Beat the avocado oil in a stand mixer, using the paddle attachment on medium speed, for 1 minute. Add the baking powder and salt and beat for 1 minute to incorporate them into the avocado oil. Add half of the masa harina and beat on low speed for 1 minute, then slowly pour in half of the vegetable broth and continue to beat until it is completely incorporated. Add the dissolved achiote paste and the remaining masa harina and broth and beat on medium speed until thoroughly mixed, for about 5 minutes. The masa should have the consistency of a thick cake batter, and you should be able to easily pass your spatula through it. If the masa is too thick, add additional vegetable broth or water until you reach the right consistency. The masa should be a little bit salty.

8. **To prepare the steamer,** drain the corn husks and set them on a dry kitchen towel. Reserve the largest husks to wrap the tamales and the small ones to line the steamer. Fill the bottom of the steamer with water, making sure the water does not touch the steamer rack. Line the rack and sides of the steamer pot with corn husks.

9. **To wrap the tamales,** pull fifty pencil-thin strips off the corn husks; these will function as ribbons. Take a husk and pat it dry. Using a spoon, spread 2 to 3 tablespoons of the masa onto the smooth side of the corn husk, about ¼ inch (6 mm) thick. Leave a 3-inch (7.5 cm) border clear of masa at the pointed end of the husk, and 2 inches (5 cm) on all the other sides.

10. Place 1 tablespoon of the mushroom filling in the center of the dough. Fold over the right side of the husk so the dough surrounds the filling, then continue rolling tightly until there is no overlap left. Pinch the two ends of the husk, pushing the masa to the center. Tie knots on either side, using the husk ribbons and twisting the husk ends just slightly to form a rounded shape in the middle. Cut the ends of the husk so they are 2 inches (5 cm) long.

(CONTINUED)

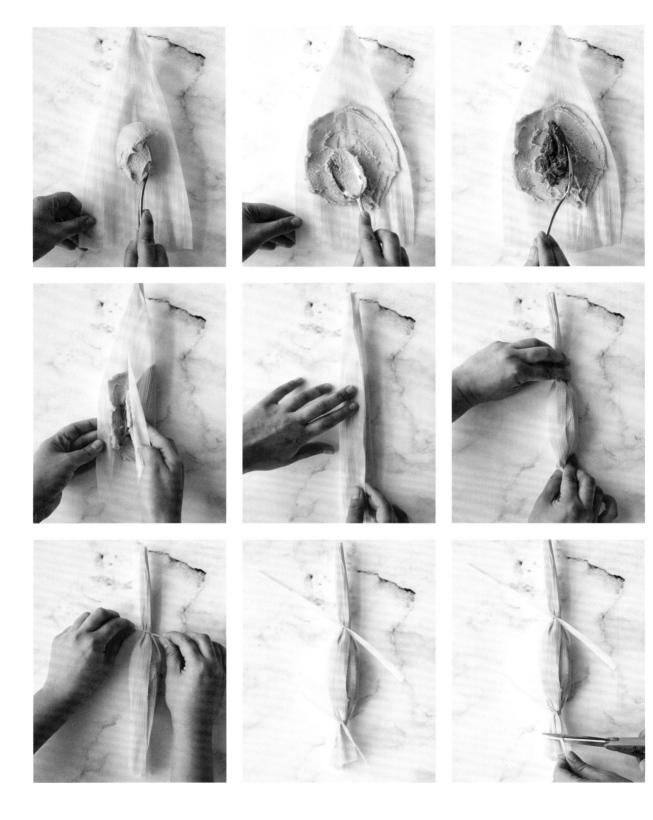

11. **To cook the tamales,** place each tamal horizontally in the steamer along the sides of the pot, stacking them on top of one another. Cover the pot and bring the water to a boil over high heat, reduce the heat to medium-low, and cook for 40 minutes. Check the tamales: When the husk separates easily from the masa, it means they are done. If they are not done, steam them for 10 more minutes and check again. Remove the steamer from the heat and let the tamales sit uncovered for 10 minutes to cool. Don't be alarmed if the tamales seem soft. As they cool, they will firm up.

12. **To make the habanero salsa,** place the tomatoes and onion in a medium pot and add enough water to cover them by 2 inches (5 cm). Bring to a boil over high heat, reduce the heat, and simmer for 10 minutes. Drain and transfer them to a blender. Add the garlic, habanero,

and salt and blend until completely smooth. Heat the oil in a small saucepot over medium heat, reduce the heat to low, and pour in the salsa, stirring constantly and being careful as there will be some splashing. Simmer for 5 to 6 minutes, until the salsa thickens and becomes a deep red color.

VARIATIONS

Other fats: Replace the avocado oil with 1 cup (226 g) refined coconut oil or 1¼ cups (295 mL) olive oil.

Oil-free: Use 1¼ cups (226 g) canned unsweetened pumpkin puree to replace the oil. To make the filling, replace the oil with ¼ cup of water or vegetable broth. To make the adobo sauce, replace the oil with ¼ cup of water or vegetable broth.

Fresh masa: Use 2 pounds (907 g) fresh masa instead of the masa harina and decrease the vegetable broth to 1 cup (236 mL).

BLACK BEAN ZUCCHINI TAMALES

Tamales Púlacles

Tamales púlacles are ceremonial tamales of pre-Hispanic origin from the state of Veracruz. They are filled with black beans and calabacitas (Mexican zucchini), stewed in an hoja santa tomato sauce, then wrapped in banana leaves. They are of special importance to the Indigenous Tototonac people of Veracruz, where they are eaten during Holy Week, Día de Muertos, patron saint days, or the celebration of the planting and harvest. The filling is thickened by toasted ground sesame seeds, which give these tamales a sweet and nutty flavor. To honor these tamales' pre-Hispanic origins, I am using unsweetened pumpkin puree instead of fat. They can also be wrapped in corn husks, and the hoja santa can be replaced with a mixture of basil and fennel leaves or cilantro. Serve with Chile Morita Salsa (page 40).

MAKES: 20 to 24 tamales

TOTAL TIME: 2½ hours

2 (1-pound/454 g) packages fresh or frozen banana leaves

FILLING

4 medium Roma tomatoes (317 g), cored and cut into quarters
1 serrano chile (2 to 4 g), stem removed
½ fresh or dried hoja santa leaf
1 tablespoon avocado oil
½ medium white onion (99 g), finely chopped (about ¾ cup)
3 garlic cloves (9 g), finely chopped
2 medium Mexican zucchini or green zucchini (415 g), diced (about 3¼ cups)

2 cups (333 g) cooked or canned black beans, drained
⅓ cup (39 g) sesame seeds, toasted and ground
2 tablespoons chopped fresh cilantro
½ teaspoon salt
⅛ teaspoon freshly ground black pepper

MASA

1¼ cups (226 g) canned unsweetened pumpkin puree
1½ teaspoons baking powder
1 tablespoon salt
4¼ cups (509 g) masa harina
4 cups (946 mL) low-sodium vegetable broth, warm

1. **To prepare the fresh banana leaves,** unfold them carefully and, using kitchen shears, cut off the stringy edges, then cut them into 10 × 8-inch (25 × 20 cm) rectangles. You will need twenty to twenty-four of them. Stack all the leaves and place them in a large pot, fill the pot with enough water to cover the leaves, and bring to a boil over high heat. Reduce the heat to low and simmer for 20 minutes. Drain the leaves and let them cool. If you are using frozen banana leaves, thaw them, rinse them, and dry them with a clean kitchen towel.

2. **To make the filling,** place the tomatoes, serrano, and hoja santa in a blender and puree until completely smooth. Heat the oil in a large skillet over medium-low heat, add the onion, and cook for 4 to 5 minutes, until it is tender and translucent. Add the garlic and cook for 1 minute. Add the zucchini and cook until almost tender, for 4 to 5 minutes. Reduce the heat to low and add the black beans and tomato puree. Simmer until the tomato puree becomes a deep red color, for about 5 minutes, then stir in the ground sesame seeds, cilantro, salt, and pepper. Let cook for 1 minute, then transfer to a medium bowl and let cool completely in the fridge.

3. **To make the masa,** beat the pumpkin puree in a stand mixer, using the paddle attachment on medium speed, for 1 minute. Add the baking powder and salt and beat for 1 minute to incorporate them into the puree. Add half of the masa harina and beat on low speed for 1 minute, then slowly pour in half of the vegetable broth and continue to beat until it is completely incorporated. Add the remaining masa harina and broth and beat on medium speed until thoroughly mixed, for about 5 minutes. The masa should have the consistency of a thick cake batter, and you should be able to easily pass your

(CONTINUED)

217

spatula through it. If the masa is too thick, add additional vegetable broth or water until you reach the right consistency. The masa should be a little bit salty.

4. **To prepare the steamer,** fill the bottom with water, making sure the water is not touching the steamer rack, and line the steamer rack with banana leaves.

5. **To assemble the tamales,** spread 3 generous tablespoons of the masa in the center of a banana leaf, forming a 4 × 3-inch (10 × 7 cm) rectangle. Place 1 heaping tablespoon of the filling in the center of the rectangle. Fold the bottom edge of the banana leaf up and over so that the dough encloses the filling. Fold the top part of the leaf down, then fold the sides to form a pocket. Repeat with the rest of the ingredients.

6. **To cook the tamales,** place the tamal packets in the steamer horizontally, laying one on top of the other, with the folded part of the packets on the bottom. Place a layer of banana leaf scraps on top of the tamales. Cover the pot and bring the water to a boil over high heat, then reduce the heat to medium-low and simmer

for 40 minutes. Check the tamales: When the banana leaves separate easily from the masa, it means the tamales are done. If they are not done, cook for 10 more minutes and check again. Remove the steamer from the heat and let sit uncovered for 10 minutes. Don't be alarmed if the tamales seem soft. As they cool, they will firm up.

NOTE

Use your blender to grind the toasted sesame seeds if you don't have a spice grinder. If you have leftover filling, make tacos with Molcajete Salsa (page 36).

VARIATIONS

Canned tomatoes: Replace the fresh tomatoes with 1½ (14.5-ounce/411 g) cans diced tomatoes.

Other fats: Replace the pumpkin puree with 1 cup (266 g) refined coconut oil or 1 cup plus 2 tablespoons (265 mL) avocado oil or 1¼ cups (295 mL) olive oil.

Oil-free: Omit the oil when making the filling and use ¼ cup vegetable broth instead.

Fresh masa: Use 2 pounds (907 g) fresh masa instead of the masa harina and decrease the vegetable broth to 1 cup (236 mL).

CLASSIC SWEET TAMALES

Tamales Dulces de Coco y Pasas

Sweet tamales are simply not as well-known in the United States as savory tamales. However, there is recorded evidence of tamales sweetened with honey or fruit as far back as the time of the Mexicas. The best way I can describe them is as an absolute treat. This version, studded with sweet raisins, shredded coconut, and cinnamon, is the one most commonly found today in Mexico, but it is usually dyed a bright neon pink. I didn't learn to love sweet tamales until I was older, but now I find them to be so much fun. In Mexico City the creativity has no bounds—you can even find Oreo tamales! My recipe includes the addition of rice flour, which gives the tamales a soft and fluffy quality. Serve them with warm atole, hot chocolate, or coffee.

MAKES: 20 to 24 tamales

TOTAL TIME: 2 hours

30 dried corn husks

MASA
1 cup (226 g) refined coconut oil, room temperature
⅔ cup (142 g) sugar
1½ teaspoons baking powder
1 teaspoon ground cinnamon
¼ teaspoon salt

2½ cups (287 g) masa harina
2 cups (473 mL) unsweetened almond milk, warm
1¾ cups (255 g) rice flour
1 cup (141 g) raisins
¾ cup (50 g) shredded unsweetened coconut

1. **To prepare the corn husks,** place them in your kitchen sink or a large pot and cover them with hot water. Place a heat-resistant plate over the husks to weight them down so they are completely submerged. Soak for at least 1 hour while you prepare the filling.

2. **To make the masa,** cream the coconut oil and sugar in a stand mixer, using the paddle attachment on medium speed, for about 3 minutes, or until it is light and fluffy. Add the baking powder, cinnamon, and salt and beat for 1 minute to incorporate them into the oil. Add the masa harina and beat on low speed for 1 minute, then slowly pour in the almond milk and continue to beat until it is completely incorporated. Add the rice flour and ¾ cup (177 mL) warm water and beat on medium speed until thoroughly mixed, for about 5 minutes. The masa should have the consistency of a thick cake batter, and you should be able to easily pass your spatula through it. If the masa is too thick, add additional water until you reach the right consistency. Add the raisins and coconut and beat slowly to mix them into the masa, for about 1 minute.

3. **To prepare the steamer,** drain the corn husks and set them on a dry kitchen towel. Reserve the largest husks to wrap the tamales and the small ones to line the steamer. Fill the bottom of the steamer with water, making sure the water does not touch the steamer rack. Line the rack and sides of the steamer pot with corn husks.

4. **To assemble the tamales,** take a husk and pat it dry. Using a spoon, spread 2 to 3 tablespoons of the masa onto the smooth side of the corn husk, about ¼ inch (6 mm) thick. Leave a 3-inch (7.5 cm) border clear of masa at the pointed end of the husk, and 1 inch (2.5 cm) on all the other sides.

(CONTINUED)

5. Fold over the right side of the husk, then continue rolling tightly until there is no overlap left. Fold down the pointy section of the corn husk, leaving one side of the tamal open. Repeat with the rest of the ingredients.

6. To cook the tamales, place each tamal vertically in the steamer, with the folded end leaning against the side of the pot and the open end facing up. Place a layer of corn husks on top of the tamales, cover them, and bring the water to a boil over high heat. Once it starts boiling, reduce the heat to medium-low and cook for 40 minutes. Check the tamales: When the husk separates easily from the masa, it means they are done. If they are not done, steam them for 10 more minutes and check again. Remove the steamer from the heat and let the tamales sit uncovered for 10 minutes to cool. Don't be alarmed if the tamales seem soft. As they cool, they will firm up.

VARIATIONS

Other fats: Replace the coconut oil with 1 cup (226 g) unsalted vegan butter.

Oil-free: Use 1¼ cups (226 g) canned unsweetened pumpkin puree to replace the oil.

Fresh masa: Use 1¼ pounds (544 g) fresh masa instead of the masa harina and decrease the water to ¼ cup (59 mL).

CHOCOLATE AND PECAN TAMALES

Tamales de Chocolate y Nuez

I was flabbergasted to learn that cacao was first cultivated in South America around 5,300 years ago; I have always claimed chocolate as Mexican due to its pre-Hispanic use as a currency and as a key element of ritual offerings. The history of chocolate in Mexico is fascinating, and to this day in the states of Chiapas, Tabasco, and Oaxaca, chocolate is made in the traditional method of grinding cacao beans with sugar and cinnamon on a metate (volcanic rock mealing stone). In Oaxaca, at the very popular Mayordomo chocolate shops, you can request your preferred ratio of cacao beans to sugar and see it ground up on the spot! This tamal honors this history by infusing the masa with artisanal ground Mexican chocolate tablillas and a filling of pecans and chocolate chips. Serve topped with Italian maraschino cherries with their syrup, and pair them with warm atole, hot chocolate, or coffee.

MAKES: 20 to 24 tamales

TOTAL TIME: 1 hour 40 minutes

30 dried corn husks

MASA

3 (3-ounce/85 g) Mexican chocolate tablets

1 cup (226 g) unsalted vegan butter, room temperature

¼ cup (54 g) sugar

1½ teaspoons baking powder

¼ teaspoon salt

½ teaspoon ground cinnamon

4¼ cups (509 g) masa harina

2 cups (473 mL) unsweetened almond milk, warm

FILLING

1¾ cups (283 g) bittersweet chocolate chips

¾ cup (81 g) chopped pecans

TO SERVE

½ cup (154 g) Italian maraschino cherries with syrup

1. **To prepare the corn husks,** place them in your kitchen sink or a large pot and cover them with hot water. Place a heat-resistant plate over the husks to weight them down so they are completely submerged. Soak for at least 1 hour while you prepare the filling.

2. **To make the masa,** chop the Mexican chocolate into small pieces, then grind it to a powder in a food processor. If you don't have a food processor, you can grate the chocolate with a standard kitchen grater. You should end up with 1½ cups (255 g) ground chocolate.

3. Beat the butter and sugar in a stand mixer, using the paddle attachment on medium-high speed, until the butter has doubled in size and is nice and fluffy, for about 3 minutes. Add the baking powder, salt, ground chocolate, and cinnamon and beat for 1 minute to incorporate into the butter. Add half of the masa harina and beat on low speed for 1 minute, then slowly pour in the almond milk and continue to beat until it is completely incorporated. Add the remaining masa harina and 2 cups (463 mL) warm water and beat on medium speed until thoroughly mixed, for about 5 minutes. The masa should have the consistency of a thick cake batter, and you should be able to easily pass your spatula through it. If the masa is too thick, add additional water until you reach the right consistency.

4. **To prepare the steamer,** drain the corn husks and set them on a dry kitchen towel. Reserve the largest husks to wrap the tamales and the small ones to line the steamer. Fill the bottom of the steamer with water, making sure the water does not touch the steamer rack. Line the rack and sides of the steamer pot with corn husks.

(CONTINUED)

223

5. **To assemble the tamales,** take a husk and pat it dry. Using a spoon, spread 2 to 3 tablespoons of the masa onto the smooth side of the corn husk, about ¼ inch (6 mm) thick. Leave a 3-inch (7.5 cm) border clear of masa at the pointed end of the husk, and 1 inch (2.5 cm) on all the other sides.

6. Place five to ten chocolate chips and a sprinkle of chopped pecans in the center of the masa. Fold over the right side of the husk, surrounding the filling, then continue rolling tightly until there is no overlap left. Fold down the pointy section of the corn husk, leaving one side of the tamal open. Repeat with the rest of the ingredients.

7. **To cook the tamales,** place each tamal vertically in the steamer, with the folded end leaning against the side of the pot and the open end facing up. Place a layer of corn husks on top of the tamales, cover them, and bring the water to a boil over high heat. Once it starts boiling, reduce the heat to medium-low and cook for 40 minutes. Check the tamales: When the husk separates easily from the masa, it means they are done. If they are not done, steam them for 10 more minutes and check again. Remove the steamer from the heat and let the tamales sit uncovered for 10 minutes to cool. Don't be alarmed if the tamales seem soft. As they cool, they will firm up. Serve topped with Italian maraschino cherries with their syrup.

VARIATIONS

Other fats: Replace the vegan butter with 1 cup (226 g) refined coconut oil.

Oil-free: Use 1¼ cups (226 g) canned unsweetened pumpkin puree to replace the vegan butter.

Fresh masa: Use 2 pounds (907 g) fresh masa instead of the masa harina and omit the water.

APPLE CINNAMON TAMALES

Tamales de Manzana con Canela

The state of Chihuahua is Mexico's largest producer of apples, growing varieties like Red and Golden Delicious, Fuji, and Granny Smith, which are used to make flaky apple pies and tarts, pecan and apple salads, sticky caramel-covered apples, and these apple cinnamon tamales. I was inspired by a friend from Chihuahua who told me his aunt used to fill tamales with a sort of apple butter, and I knew just what I had to do. These tender tamales are reminiscent of a sweet apple pie, filled with chunky apple and walnut butter spiced with cinnamon and cloves, and wrapped in a corn husk. I use Granny Smith apples, but you can also use Fuji or Golden Delicious. Serve these tamales with a drizzle of cajeta and pair with warm atole, hot chocolate, or coffee.

MAKES: 28 tamales

TOTAL TIME: 2 hours

30 corn husks

FILLING

6 medium Granny Smith apples (907 g), cored, peeled, and cubed
⅓ cup (67 g) sugar
⅓ cup (78 mL) apple cider
1 teaspoon ground cinnamon
Pinch ground cloves
¼ cup (24 g) chopped walnuts

MASA

1 cup (228 g) unsalted vegan butter, room temperature
½ cup (100 g) sugar
1½ teaspoons baking powder
¼ teaspoon salt
4¼ cups (509 g) masa harina
4 cups (946 mL) unsweetened almond milk, warm

TO SERVE

½ cup (118 mL) Boozy Mexican Caramel (page 284)

1. To prepare the corn husks, place them in your kitchen sink or a large pot and cover them with hot water. Place a heat-resistant plate over the husks to weight them down so they are completely submerged. Soak for at least 1 hour while you prepare the filling.

2. To make the filling, place the apples in a large saucepot, along with the sugar, apple cider, cinnamon, and cloves. Cook over low heat, stirring occasionally, for 25 minutes, or until the apples are soft and falling apart. If all your liquid has evaporated and the apples are still not soft, add ¼ cup (59 mL) water. Using a potato masher, press down on the apples to form a chunky apple puree. Mix in the walnuts, transfer to a bowl, and let cool completely in the fridge.

3. To make the masa, beat the butter and sugar with an electric mixer, using the paddle attachment on medium-high speed, until the butter has doubled in size and is nice and fluffy, for about 3 minutes. Add the baking powder and salt and beat for 1 minute to incorporate into the butter. Add half of the masa harina and beat on low speed for 1 minute, then slowly pour in half of the almond milk and continue to beat until it is completely incorporated. Add the remaining masa harina and almond milk and beat on medium speed until thoroughly mixed, for about 5 minutes. The masa should have the consistency of a thick cake batter, and you should be able to easily pass your spatula through it. If the masa is too thick, add additional water until you reach the right consistency.

(CONTINUED)

4. **To prepare the steamer,** drain the corn husks and set them on a dry kitchen towel. Reserve the largest husks to wrap the tamales and the small ones to line the steamer. Fill the bottom of the steamer with water, making sure the water does not touch the steamer rack. Line the rack and sides of the steamer pot with corn husks.

5. **To assemble the tamales,** take a husk and pat it dry. Using a spoon, spread 2 to 3 tablespoons of the masa onto the smooth side of the corn husk, about ¼ inch (6 mm) thick. Leave a 3-inch (7.5 cm) border clear of masa at the pointed end of the husk, and 1 inch (2.5 cm) on all the other sides.

6. Place 1½ to 2 tablespoons of the apple filling in a line down the center of the masa. Fold over the right side of the husk, surrounding the filling, then continue rolling tightly until there is no overlap left. Fold down the pointy section of the corn husk, leaving one side of the tamal open. Repeat with the rest of the ingredients.

7. **To cook the tamales,** place each tamal vertically in the steamer, with the folded end leaning against the side of the pot and the open end facing up. Place a layer of corn husks on top of the tamales, cover them, and bring the water to a boil over high heat. Once it starts boiling, reduce the heat to medium-low and cook for 40 minutes. Check the tamales: When the husk separates easily from the masa, it means they are done. If they are not done, steam them for 10 more minutes and check again. Remove the steamer from the heat and let the tamales sit uncovered for 10 minutes to cool. Don't be alarmed if the tamales seem soft. As they cool, they will firm up. Serve drizzled with cajeta.

VARIATIONS

Other fats: Replace the vegan butter with 1 cup (226 g) refined coconut oil.

Oil-free: Use 1¼ cups (226 g) canned unsweetened pumpkin puree to replace the vegan butter.

Fresh masa: Use 2 pounds (907 g) fresh masa instead of the masa harina and decrease the almond milk to 1 cup (236 mL).

STRAWBERRY TAMALES

Tamales de Fresa

Strawberries are the star of this tamal. A puree of fresh strawberries is mixed with the nixtamalized corn masa, then filled with a sweet strawberry jam. The combination of corn and strawberry might sound strange, but I'm pretty sure you may have tried it already, especially if you like breakfast cereal. Think strawberry cornflakes or berry-flavored Cap'n Crunch. Traditionally these tamales are not filled with jam, but instead raisins are added, and they are dyed a bright pink color. I usually skip the food coloring and live for the jammy center of this warm tamal. Serve them warm with atole, hot chocolate, or coffee.

MAKES: 20 to 24 tamales

TOTAL TIME: 1 hour 40 minutes

---

30 dried corn husks

MASA

2 cups (282 g) strawberries, hulled and chopped, divided

2 cups (473 mL) unsweetened almond milk, warm

1 cup (226 g) unsalted vegan butter, room temperature

½ cup (100 g) sugar

1½ teaspoons baking powder

¼ teaspoon salt

4¼ cups (509 g) masa harina

3 drops red gel food coloring (optional)

FILLING

1 cup (261 g) strawberry jam

1. **To prepare the corn husks,** place them in your kitchen sink or a large pot and cover them with hot water. Place a heat-resistant plate over the husks to weight them down so they are completely submerged. Soak for at least 1 hour while you prepare the filling.

2. **To make the masa,** in a blender, combine half of the chopped strawberries and the almond milk and puree until smooth.

3. Beat the butter and sugar in a stand mixer, using the paddle attachment on medium-high speed, until the butter has doubled in size and is nice and fluffy, for about 3 minutes. Add the baking powder and salt and beat for 1 minute to incorporate into the butter. Add half of the masa harina and beat on low speed for 1 minute, then slowly pour in the strawberry almond milk and continue to beat until it is completely incorporated. Add the remaining masa harina, 1 cup (236 mL) warm water, and food coloring (if using) and beat on medium speed until thoroughly mixed, for about 5 minutes. The masa should have the consistency of a thick cake batter, and you should be able to easily pass your spatula through it. If the masa is too thick, add additional water until you reach the right consistency. Add the remaining chopped strawberries and beat slowly to mix them into the masa, for about 1 minute.

4. **To prepare the steamer,** drain the corn husks and set them on a dry kitchen towel. Reserve the largest husks to wrap the tamales and the small ones to line the steamer. Fill the bottom of the steamer with water, making sure the water does not touch the steamer rack. Line the rack and sides of the steamer pot with corn husks.

5. **To assemble the tamales,** take a husk and pat it dry. Using a spoon, spread 2 to 3 tablespoons of the masa onto the smooth side of the corn

husk, about ¼ inch (6 mm) thick. Leave a 3-inch (7.5 cm) border clear of masa at the pointed end of the husk, and 1 inch (2.5 cm) on all the other sides.

6. Place 1½ teaspoons of the jam in a line down the center of the masa. Fold over the right side of the husk, surrounding the filling, then continue rolling tightly until there is no overlap left. Fold down the pointy section of the corn husk, leaving one side of the tamal open. Repeat with the rest of the ingredients.

7. To cook the tamales, place each tamal vertically in the steamer, with the folded end leaning against the side of the pot and the open end facing up. Place a layer of corn husks on top of the tamales, cover them, and bring the water to a boil over high heat. Once it starts boiling, reduce the heat to medium-low and cook for 40 minutes. Check the tamales: When the husk separates easily from the masa, it means they are done. If they are not done, steam them for 10 more minutes and check again. Remove the steamer from the heat and let the tamales sit uncovered for 10 minutes to cool. Don't be alarmed if the tamales seem soft. As they cool, they will firm up.

VARIATIONS

Other fats: Replace the vegan butter with 1 cup (226 g) refined coconut oil.

Oil-free: Use 1¼ cups (226 g) canned unsweetened pumpkin puree to replace the vegan butter.

Fresh masa: Use 2 pounds (907 g) fresh masa instead of masa harina and omit the water.

9

MODERN MEXICO

When I graduated from culinary school, I tried to get a job at Topolobampo, Rick Bayless's fine-dining restaurant in Chicago. I desperately wanted to apply everything I had learned in school to my own cuisine, and I thought this was the place to do it. Sadly I didn't get the job, but this began a quest to eat at as many fine-dining and modern Mexican restaurants as I could. Over the years I have seen the food at these restaurants evolve into something beautiful, and more than authentic. A true evolution of the cuisine is happening at restaurants like Elena Reygadas's Rosetta and Gabriela Ruiz Lugo's Carmela & Sal in Mexico City. But it wasn't always like this.

For years, Mexican food was simply not part of the fine-dining scene, even in Mexico. In the United States it was often stereotyped as cheap food—just burritos and tacos—and in Mexico, French and European-style restaurants dominated. All this changed with the influence of chefs Gabriela Cámara and Enrique Olvera, who opened fine-dining Mexican restaurants showcasing Mexican ingredients, while using new and old techniques to create a cuisine that went beyond the taco but still stayed true to its Mexican roots. In culinary school one of our class projects was to create our own fictional restaurant, complete with a menu; my restaurant was called Centli (which means "corn" in Nahuatl) and it was a fine-dining restaurant serving modern Mexican cuisine, not unlike the ones that exist today. I never got to open my restaurant, so these recipes are an expression of the kind of food I would've served at Centli. I draw upon my years of experience in professional kitchens to combine modern cooking techniques with traditional Mexican flavors and ingredients, and some influences from the cuisines of other cultures. The recipes are more elaborate, but the detailed step-by-step instructions make them doable. ¡Buen provecho!

PICKLED CHAYOTE AND QUELITE SALAD

Ensalada de Chayote Curtido y Quelites

There had to be at least one salad recipe in this book; otherwise can I really call myself vegan? There are a lot of bad salads out there, but for me, a good salad is one that is crunchy, creamy, and full of robust greens. This salad uses chayote, which adds a crisp, fresh pear and cucumber flavor. The chayote is charred and pickled in rice vinegar, and then tossed with radishes, quelites (greens), and a creamy and spicy raw tomatillo and avocado dressing. It is topped with popped amaranth, which adds some crunch. You can buy amaranth already popped or you can pop it yourself. I include the instructions to do so in the notes below.

MAKES: **4 servings**

TOTAL TIME: **20 minutes**

PICKLED CHAYOTE
2 teaspoons avocado oil
1 chayote (316 g),
   peeled and sliced
   ¼ inch (6 mm) thick
¼ cup (59 mL) rice
   vinegar

TOMATILLO AVOCADO DRESSING
2 medium tomatillos
   (151 g), husks
   removed, chopped
1 large avocado (386 g),
   pitted, peeled, and
   flesh scooped out
½ cup (16 g) packed
   fresh cilantro
¼ large white onion
   (49 g), chopped
1 garlic clove (3 g),
   peeled

2 tablespoons fresh lime
   juice
Pinch sugar
1 teaspoon salt
⅛ teaspoon freshly
   ground black pepper

SALAD
4 small purple daikon
   radishes (63 g), thinly
   sliced
¾ cup (15 g) arugula
¾ cup (15 g) mâche
   greens
¾ cup (25 g) watercress
1 tablespoon olive oil
⅛ teaspoon salt
⅛ teaspoon freshly
   ground black pepper
½ cup (17 g) popped
   amaranth

1. To make the pickled chayote, heat the oil in a large skillet over medium-high heat. Add the chayote and cook for 1 to 2 minutes, until the edges char. Only do this on one side of the chayote. Transfer to a small bowl and pour the rice vinegar over it. Let it sit in the fridge while you prepare the rest of the salad.

2. To make the dressing, place the tomatillos, avocado, cilantro, onion, garlic, lime juice, ½ cup (118 mL) water, sugar, salt, and pepper in the blender and puree until smooth. Transfer to an airtight container and place in the fridge until ready to use.

3. To assemble, drain the chayote and cut it into thin strips. Transfer it to a large bowl and add the radishes, arugula, mâche, and watercress. Add the olive oil, salt, and pepper and toss to combine. Spread 2 to 3 tablespoons of the dressing in a circle on each plate and add the tossed greens. Sprinkle with the popped amaranth.

4. The salad doesn't store well after it has been assembled, but the dressing and pickled chayote can be stored in separate airtight containers in the fridge for up to 2 days. Store the popped amaranth in an airtight container at room temperature for up to 3 days.

NOTE

To pop your own amaranth, you will need ½ cup (97 g) amaranth seeds. Heat a small skillet over medium heat and add half of the amaranth. Cover the skillet and shake it back and forth while securing the lid. You will begin to hear the amaranth pop like popcorn. Once the popping slows down, in 2 to 3 minutes, remove from the heat and transfer the amaranth to a small bowl. Repeat with the remaining amaranth.

VARIATION

Oil-free: Omit the oil when tossing the greens. To char the chayote, omit the oil, and cook directly on the skillet.

WATERMELON TARTARE
WITH MEZCAL CHILE PONZU
Tartar de Sandía con Vinagreta de Mezcal

I was living in Washington, DC, right after culinary school, and my boyfriend at the time was working at Charlie Palmer Steak. They used to have a tuna tartare that I would beg him to bring me almost every day. I never learned how to make it, but lucky for me, the recipe is in Palmer's *The Art of Aureole* cookbook, which I have used as inspiration for this recipe. I use watermelon as a substitute for tuna. I know it's hard to believe watermelon is the best option here, but I tried a lot of different options, and this really is the best one. The watermelon is marinated in a ponzu sauce and then baked, which gives it a very tuna-like texture; the taste, however, does lean toward the sweet side. To give it a Mexican twist, I make the ponzu sauce with mezcal, soy sauce, lime juice, ginger, and jalapeño, and serve it with sliced avocado and Toasted Amaranth Sesame Crisps (page 236).

MAKES: **4 servings**

TOTAL TIME: **1 hour 30 minutes + 3 hours marinating time**

PONZU SAUCE
1½ teaspoons mezcal
1 tablespoon toasted sesame oil
⅓ cup (78 mL) soy sauce
⅓ cup (78 mL) lime juice
2 tablespoons rice vinegar
1 (1-inch/2.5 cm) piece ginger, peeled and grated (about 1 teaspoon)
1 or 2 jalapeños (32 g), thinly sliced
1 piece kombu seaweed (4 g)

SALAD
½ large watermelon (3 kg), peeled and cut into 1-inch (2.5 cm) cubes
2 avocados (306 g), halved, pitted, and peeled
¼ cup (8 g) fresh cilantro leaves
1 recipe Toasted Amaranth Sesame Crisps (page 236) or corn chips

1. To make the ponzu sauce, combine the mezcal, sesame oil, soy sauce, lime juice, ⅓ cup (78 mL) water, rice vinegar, ginger, jalapeño, and kombu in a medium saucepot and bring to a simmer over high heat. Once it simmers, remove from the heat and let it steep for 10 minutes. Discard the kombu. Transfer to a small bowl and let cool completely in the fridge. Reserve ½ cup (118 mL) for assembling the tartare.

2. Place the watermelon in a reusable silicone bag or a zip-top bag and pour in the rest of the ponzu sauce, seal it, and lay it flat in the fridge. Let it marinate for at least 3 hours, flipping it halfway through.

3. Preheat the oven to 350°F (175°C). Line a rimmed baking sheet with a silicone mat or parchment paper.

4. Drain the watermelon and place it on the prepared baking sheet, making sure it is evenly distributed, and bake for 1½ hours. Stir occasionally to prevent it from getting brown. Remove from the oven, transfer it to a large bowl, and place it in the fridge to cool completely.

5. To assemble, add the reserved ponzu sauce to the watermelon, stir to combine, and let it marinate for 10 minutes. Lay one-half of the avocado cut side down and slice thinly widthwise. Fan out the avocado slices to form a long line with the slices overlapping each other. Curl the avocado slices to form a ring. Repeat this with the remaining avocado halves. Place the avocado rings on the plates. Remove the watermelon from the sauce with a slotted spoon, reserving the sauce, and divide it among the plates. Top with the cilantro leaves, a drizzle

of the remaining sauce, and some of the thinly sliced jalapeños from the sauce. Serve with the sesame crisps or corn chips.

6. Store the watermelon tartare in an airtight container in the fridge for up to 3 days. The avocado will not store well after being sliced.

TIME-SAVING TIP

The watermelon can be marinated and baked the day before, then placed in the fridge to cool for the next day. Make the sesame crisps the day before or use store-bought sesame flatbread crackers or corn chips.

VARIATION

Oil-free: Omit the oil in the ponzu sauce.

TOASTED AMARANTH SESAME CRISPS

Galletas Saladas de Amaranto y Ajonjolí

Amaranth is a plant that has been cultivated in Mexico for over 7,000 years. The seeds of the amaranth plant were used to make atole or ground into flour for tamales. They have a mild, nutty flavor with hints of earthiness. Today, much as in pre-Hispanic times, amaranth is still used to make atoles and tamales, and it is puffed to make a candy called alegría (joy). The leaves of the amaranth plant are known as quintoniles and are used in soups, stews, or salads. I toast and grind amaranth seeds to make flour, which is then mixed with all-purpose flour to make the dough for these sesame crisps. I use a pasta machine to roll out the dough, but if you don't have one, you can use a rolling pin.

MAKES: **4 servings**

TOTAL TIME: **1½ hours + resting time**

½ cup (97 g) amaranth seeds
1 tablespoon olive oil
2 tablespoons toasted sesame oil
1 teaspoon sugar
1½ teaspoons active dry yeast
¾ cup (104 g) all-purpose flour

½ teaspoon salt
½ teaspoon white sesame seeds
½ teaspoon ground ginger
2 tablespoons unsweetened almond milk
¼ cup (40 g) black sesame seeds

1. To make the amaranth flour, place the amaranth seeds in a small skillet over medium heat. Toast, stirring frequently, for about 5 minutes, or until the amaranth becomes golden brown but before it begins to pop. Transfer to a small bowl and let it cool for 10 minutes. Transfer to a blender and pulse to grind it into flour.

2. In a small bowl, combine 6 tablespoons (88 mL) warm water, the olive oil, sesame oil, sugar, and yeast and stir. Let it rest for 5 minutes. In a large bowl, combine the all-purpose flour, ¼ cup (31.5 g) of the toasted amaranth flour, the salt, white sesame seeds, and ground ginger.

3. Make a well in the center of the flour and pour in the yeast mixture. Using your hand, mix everything together to form a shaggy ball of dough. Transfer it to a lightly floured surface and knead for 5 minutes, or until the dough has a smooth texture. Place in an airtight container and let it rest in the fridge overnight.

4. Preheat the oven to 325°F (160°C). Line a rimmed baking sheet with a silicone mat or parchment paper.

5. To roll out the dough, lightly flour your kitchen counter. Cut the dough in half. Flatten one piece with the heel of your hand. Set the roller of your pasta machine to the widest setting and pass the dough through. Fold the edges of the dough inward to form a rectangle roughly the width of the pasta machine and pass the dough through again. The goal is to get a smooth rectangle. Roll the dough once through each setting, adding flour as needed so it doesn't stick, until the dough is about ¼ inch (6 mm) thick. Cut into triangles or rectangles and place on the prepared baking sheet. Repeat this process with the other half of the dough. (Alternatively, you can use a rolling pin.)

6. Brush the cut dough with the almond milk and sprinkle the black sesame seeds on top. Bake for 12 to 15 minutes, until the crisps are golden brown. Let them cool, then store in an airtight container at room temperature for up to 3 days. The unbaked dough can be frozen for up to 3 months; thaw before rolling it out.

TIME-SAVING TIP

Use store-bought amaranth flour.

VARIATION

Oil-free: Omit the olive and sesame oils and add 3 additional tablespoons water.

KING OYSTER MUSHROOM AGUACHILE

Aguachile de Setas de Cardo

Aguachile is a ceviche-style type of preparation popular in coastal states like Sinaloa and Nayarit. This version is prepared as in Nayarit, but I use sous-vide oyster mushrooms instead of shrimp. Sous-vide is a method of cooking in a temperature-controlled water bath. This allows the food to cook evenly and precisely to the desired temperature. It is a lot of fun to play with but does require a device called a circulator that keeps the water at the right temperature. If you don't want to sous-vide, you'll find variations below. If you can't find oyster mushrooms, thinly sliced cremini or shiitake mushrooms will also work.

MAKES: 4 servings

TOTAL TIME: 2 hours

**SOUS-VIDE
MUSHROOMS**
1½ cups (354 mL)
   vegetable broth
1 piece kombu seaweed
   (4 g)
¼ teaspoon salt
4 medium king oyster
   mushrooms (900 g)

MARINADE
½ large cucumber
   (184 g), peeled
1 tablespoon olive oil
1 or 2 serrano chiles
   (49 g)
1 garlic clove (3 g),
   peeled
¾ cup (177 mL) fresh
   lime juice

¼ cup (59 mL) fresh
   mandarin juice or
   orange juice
1 cup (32 g) packed
   fresh cilantro
1 teaspoon salt
⅛ teaspoon freshly
   ground black pepper
½ large red onion (88 g),
   thinly sliced

TO ASSEMBLE
¼ cup (8 g) packed fresh
   cilantro leaves
1 avocado (153 g),
   halved, pitted, peeled,
   and thinly sliced
2 mandarin oranges
   (152 g), peeled and
   divided into segments
4 corn tostadas

1. To prepare the mushrooms, combine the vegetable broth, kombu, and salt in a small saucepot and bring to a boil over high heat. Remove from the heat, cover, and let steep for 10 minutes. Transfer to a small bowl and let sit in the fridge until it is completely cool. Discard the kombu.

2. Preheat a water bath to 185°F (85°C).

3. Slice the mushrooms ¼ inch (6 mm) thick lengthwise and place them in three reusable sous-vide bags. Distribute the cold broth equally among the bags and seal them. Drop them in the water bath and cook for 30 minutes. Transfer the bags to a bowl full of ice water to cool down.

4. To make the marinade, cut the cucumber in half lengthwise and scoop the seeds and inner soft flesh into a blender. Cut the cucumber into thin half-moons and transfer to a large bowl. To the blender, add the olive oil, serranos, garlic, lime juice, mandarin juice, cilantro, salt, and pepper and puree until smooth, then transfer to the bowl with the cucumber.

5. Open the sous-vide bags, drain the mushrooms, discard the broth, and add the mushrooms to the bowl. Add the onion and stir to combine. Let marinate in the fridge for at least 1 hour.

6. To assemble, arrange the mushrooms on a plate and garnish with the cilantro leaves, the onion and cucumber from the marinade, the avocado slices, and mandarin segments. Serve with the corn tostadas. The aguachile will keep in an airtight container in the fridge for up to 1 day.

TIME-SAVING TIP

The mushrooms can be cooked sous-vide the day before and kept in the fridge.

VARIATIONS

Oil-free: Omit the oil in the marinade.

Stovetop instructions: Instead of steps 1 through 3, thinly slice the mushrooms and steam them for 10 minutes. Drop the mushrooms into an ice water bath, drain, and add to the bowl with the marinade in step 4.

Coconut aguachile: Replace the mushrooms with the flesh of 1 fresh young coconut (627 g), cut the same way as for the Coconut and Caramelized Pineapple Atole (page 262), then toss it with the spicy cucumber cilantro marinade.

HUITLACOCHE CREPES

Crepas de Huitlacoche

Savory crepes make an excellent brunch or light dinner. These crepes are infused with fresh epazote, then filled with stewed huitlacoche (corn smut), served with a smoky roasted poblano cream sauce, and topped with a zucchini blossom and herb salad. The marriage of huitlacoche, poblano chiles, and zucchini blossoms is a classic combination reminiscent of the milpa and it really shines with these crepes. Fresh huitlacoche can be found at farmers' markets or Mexican grocery stores, but you can also find it canned.

MAKES: 4 servings

TOTAL TIME: 2 hours + soaking time

CORN CREPES
- ½ cup (118 mL) unsweetened almond milk
- 1½ tablespoons avocado oil
- 1½ teaspoons ground flaxseed
- ½ cup (73 g) all-purpose flour
- ¼ cup (30 g) masa harina
- Pinch salt
- ¼ cup (8 g) chopped fresh epazote or cilantro

POBLANO CREAM SAUCE
- ¾ cup (85 g) blanched slivered almonds, soaked in water overnight and drained
- ¼ cup (59 mL) unsweetened almond milk
- 1 garlic clove (3 g), peeled
- ½ cup (16 g) packed fresh cilantro
- 1 tablespoon fresh lemon juice
- 4 poblano chiles (600 g), roasted (see page 14), peeled, and seeded
- ½ teaspoon salt

SALAD
- 1 tablespoon fresh lemon juice
- 2 tablespoons olive oil
- ⅛ teaspoon salt
- ⅛ teaspoon freshly ground black pepper
- 4 zucchini blossoms (18 g), stems and pistils removed
- 1 epazote sprig
- 1 cilantro sprig

TO ASSEMBLE
- 2 tablespoons vegan butter, divided
- 1 recipe huitlacoche filling from Huitlacoche and Zucchini Blossom Quesadillas (page 126), warmed

1. To make the crepe batter, in a small bowl, combine the almond milk, ¾ cup (177 mL) water, avocado oil, and flaxseed and let sit for 5 minutes. In a large bowl, combine the flour, masa harina, and salt. Add the wet mixture to the dry ingredients and whisk to incorporate the batter. Add the herbs and let the batter rest in the fridge for 1 hour.

2. To make the poblano cream sauce, in a blender, combine the almonds, almond milk, garlic, cilantro, lemon juice, ¾ cup (177 mL) water, poblanos, and salt and puree until smooth, for about 2 minutes. If you don't have a high-speed blender, I recommend you pass the sauce through a fine-mesh sieve.

3. To make the dressing for the salad, put the lemon juice in a small bowl. Slowly pour in the olive oil while whisking until it incorporates, forming an emulsion, then add the salt and pepper. Place in the fridge until ready to assemble the crepes.

4. Cut the zucchini blossoms into strips and place them in a small bowl. Using your fingers, tear the epazote leaves into ½-inch (1.25 cm) pieces and add them to the bowl. Pick the cilantro leaves off the stem and add them to the bowl. Place in the fridge until you are ready to assemble the crepes.

5. To cook the crepes, heat 1 teaspoon of the butter in a medium nonstick pan over medium heat. Add ¼ cup (59 mL) of the crepe batter and tilt the pan in a circular motion to spread the batter evenly. Cook for 2 minutes, until the edges begin to separate from the pan, flip and cook for 1 minute, then flip once more and cook for 1 more minute. The crepe should be soft and have brown spots throughout. Transfer it to a tortilla warmer. Repeat this process with the rest of the batter. You should have about 6 crepes.

6. To assemble, heat the poblano cream sauce in a medium skillet over medium-low heat for 5 minutes. Toss the zucchini blossom salad with the dressing. Place a crepe on a cutting board and spread 1 tablespoon of the poblano cream sauce on the circumference of the crepe. Place about 3 tablespoons of the huitlacoche filling in the bottom right corner of the crepe. Fold the top half over the filling, then fold the left side over, forming a triangle. Pour ¼ cup (59 mL) of the sauce on a plate and place the filled crepe in the center of the sauce. Top the crepe with 2 tablespoons of the salad. Repeat this process with the rest of the crepes.

7. The crepes, sauce, and filling can all be stored separately. To store the crepes, let them cool completely, then store in an airtight container in the fridge for up to 4 days or in the freezer for up to 3 months. The filling and sauce can be stored in separate airtight containers in the fridge for up to 5 days or in the freezer for up to 3 months.

VARIATIONS

Oil-free: Omit the oil in the crepe batter. Omit the oil for the salad and sprinkle it with lemon juice, salt, and pepper. To cook the crepes, omit the oil and use a nonstick skillet.

Zucchini blossom filling: Use the zucchini blossom filling from the Huitlacoche and Zucchini Blossom Quesadillas (page 126) to fill the crepes.

Mushroom filling: Use the mushroom filling from the Fava Bean and Mushroom Stuffed Blue Corn Cakes (page 123) to fill the crepes.

HERBED MEXICAN RICOTTA AGNOLOTTI

Agnolotti Relleno de Requesón a las Finas Hierbas

I first encountered fresh pasta in culinary school, but I really learned how to make it at 2941 Restaurant in Falls Church, Virginia, where I did my externship. This was my first time working in a fine-dining kitchen and it was so stressful; the chef at the time was an old-school yell-at-you kind of chef, which put me on the verge of a nervous breakdown all the time. Making pasta was the best part of my day or, as one of the cooks called it, my Zen moment. Making vegan pasta isn't much different from making pasta with egg—in fact, most dried pasta available in grocery stores doesn't have any egg at all. Agnolotti is a small pocket shape that I have filled here with cashew requesón mixed with hoja santa, and served on a tangy and spicy roasted tomato morita chile sauce. To make the pasta, I use 00 flour, a very finely ground Italian flour, because it provides elasticity to the dough and results in delicate pasta. You can find it at specialty food stores.

MAKES: **4 servings**

TOTAL TIME: 1½ **hours**

PASTA DOUGH

1⅓ cups (225 g) semolina flour
½ cup (75 g) 00 flour
⅛ teaspoon salt
1 tablespoon extra-virgin olive oil

FILLING

1 recipe Cashew Requesón (page 35) or vegan ricotta
1 fresh hoja santa leaf, chopped, *or* ¼ cup chopped fresh cilantro or epazote

SAUCE

1½ pounds (680 g) cherry tomatoes
2 tablespoons extra-virgin olive oil, divided
1 medium onion (242 g), thinly sliced
3 garlic cloves (9 g), finely chopped
1 fresh or dried hoja santa leaf, chopped
½ cup (118 mL) Pinot Grigio
2 cups (473 mL) vegetable broth
1 dried morita chile, stem removed, chopped
1 basil sprig
1 teaspoon salt
⅛ teaspoon freshly ground black pepper
1 tablespoon avocado oil

TO SERVE

¼ cup (22 g) sun-dried tomatoes, thinly sliced
1 fresh hoja santa leaf, thinly sliced

(CONTINUED)

1. To make the pasta dough, in a large bowl, combine the semolina and 00 flours, salt, and olive oil. Make a well in the center of the flour and pour in ⅔ cup (157 mL) room-temperature water while whisking with a fork. The dough will begin to come together to form a shaggy ball. Using your hand, form the dough into a ball and knead for 10 minutes, until it is smooth and bounces back when you make an indentation with your finger. Let it rest at room temperature in an airtight container for a minimum of 30 minutes.

2. To make the filling, place the Cashew Requesón in a medium bowl and mix in the hoja santa. Transfer to a piping bag.

3. To roll out the pasta, lightly dust a rimmed baking sheet with semolina flour. Cut the dough into 4 equal pieces and flatten one piece with the heel of your hand. Set the roller of your pasta machine to the widest setting and pass the dough through. Fold the edges of the dough inward to form a rectangle roughly the width of the pasta machine, then pass the dough through again. The goal is to get a smooth rectangle. Roll the dough once through each setting until it is about ¼ inch (6 mm) thick, adding flour as needed so the dough doesn't stick to the pasta machine. Once you get to this stage, start rolling the dough twice through each setting until the dough is 1/16 inch (2 mm) thick. (Alternatively, you can do this with a rolling pin.)

4. To fill the pasta, lay a pasta sheet on a floured surface. Pipe a line of ½-teaspoon dots of filling 1 inch (2.5 cm) apart. Carefully fold the pasta over the filling and push it down to seal. Using a knife or pasta roller, trim away the excess pasta. You should end up with something that looks like a tube. Use your fingers to pinch between the filling to seal and create pockets. Cut in between the pockets to separate and seal the ends. Transfer them to the prepared baking sheet and repeat this process with the rest of the dough.

5. Preheat the oven to 425°F (220°C). Place a wire rack on a rimmed baking sheet.

6. To make the sauce, place the tomatoes in a large bowl and toss them with 1 tablespoon of the olive oil. Place them on the prepared rack and bake for 25 to 30 minutes, until they soften, the skin wrinkles, and there are brown spots on them. Transfer the tomatoes to a small bowl.

7. Heat the remaining 1 tablespoon olive oil in a large skillet over medium-low heat. Add the onion and cook until it is tender and translucent, for 5 to 6 minutes. Add the garlic and hoja santa and cook for 3 minutes, stirring occasionally. Pour in the wine and cook until it almost evaporates, in about 4 minutes. Add the tomatoes, broth, chile, basil, salt, and pepper and bring to a simmer over medium-low heat. Let it simmer for 10 minutes, or until the chile completely softens. Transfer to a blender and puree until completely smooth, then transfer to a medium bowl.

8. To assemble, heat the avocado oil in a medium saucepot over medium-low heat. Pour in the sauce and simmer, while stirring, for 5 minutes. Bring a large pot of salted water to a boil. Add the agnolotti and simmer for about 2 minutes, or until they float to the top. Drain and add the agnolotti to the sauce. Transfer to plates and garnish with the sun-dried tomatoes and hoja santa.

TIME-SAVING TIPS

The agnolotti can be made the day before and frozen until ready to cook. The sauce can also be made the day before.

VARIATION

Oil-free: Replace the oil in the pasta dough with 1 tablespoon water. Omit the oil when roasting the cherry tomatoes, and replace the oil for cooking the onion with ¼ cup (59 mL) vegetable broth. Omit the oil when simmering the sauce.

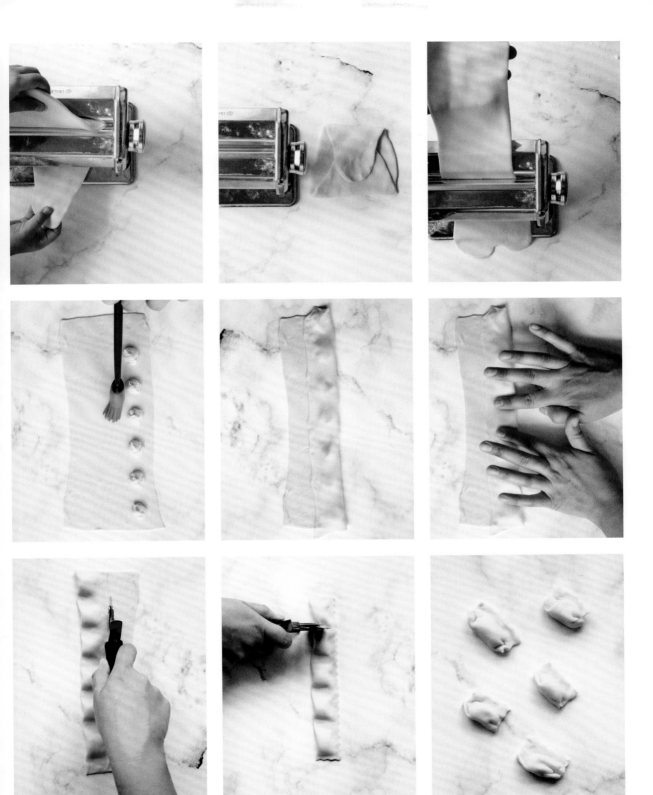

ONION TARTE TATIN IN PINK MOLE

Tarta Tatin de Cebolla en Mole Rosa

This dish is a study in pink that blurs the line between sweet and savory. A tarte tatin is a French dessert of caramelized apples baked in puff pastry, but for this savory version I use onions cooked in beet juice, butter, and thyme and brushed with pomegranate molasses. It is inspired by an endive tarte tatin that I learned how to make when I was working at the Four Seasons Hotel in Washington, DC, with Chef Dominique Filoni a long time ago. My tarte tatin is served with a creamy mole rosa, pomegranate seeds, pink pine nuts, and pink peppercorns. Pink pine nuts are rose-colored pine nuts endemic to the forests of the state of Hidalgo. They have a mildly sweet flavor and creamy texture, and are a traditional ingredient in the pink mole from Guerrero. They are difficult to find outside of Mexico, so if you can't find them, you can use regular white pine nuts.

MAKES: 4 servings

TOTAL TIME: 40 minutes

1 medium beet (156 g), peeled and roughly chopped

2 tablespoons vegan butter, divided

1 thyme sprig

¼ teaspoon salt

1 large red onion (352 g), cut crosswise into 4 (½-inch/1.25 cm thick) slices, keeping the rings together

1 (8.65-ounce/245 g) sheet puff pastry, thawed

2 tablespoons pomegranate molasses

TO ASSEMBLE

½ recipe Pink Mole (page 151), warm

2 tablespoons pomegranate seeds

2 tablespoons pink pine nuts

1 teaspoon pink peppercorns

¼ cup (9 g) micro salad greens (broccoli, kale, mustard greens)

1. Place the beet in a blender, add 1 cup (236 mL) water, and puree until smooth. Pass through a fine-mesh sieve into a small bowl. Melt 1 tablespoon of the butter in a medium saucepot over medium-low heat. Add the beet puree, thyme, and salt. Lay the onion slices in the saucepot, keeping the rings of each slice together. Simmer the onion for 5 minutes, only on one side. Use a slotted spoon to transfer the onions to a plate and let them cool in the fridge. Discard the leftover cooking liquid.

2. Preheat the oven to 400°F (205°C).

3. To make the tart, using a 4-inch (10 cm) round cookie cutter, cut 4 circles out of the puff pastry. Grease 4 (4-ounce/118 mL) ramekins with the remaining 1 tablespoon butter and brush the bottom with the pomegranate molasses. Place an onion slice cooked side down in the center of each ramekin. Lay a puff pastry circle over each onion and use a small offset spatula to press the excess pastry down inside the ramekin. Use a fork to poke a couple of holes in the pastry. This will help the steam release from the pastry while it cooks and prevents your pastry from getting soggy.

4. Place the ramekins on a rimmed baking sheet and bake for 20 to 25 minutes, until the pastry is golden brown. Remove from the oven and let cool for 5 minutes. Run a knife along the edges of the ramekins to loosen the tarts, then invert onto a plate.

5. To assemble, spread 2 tablespoons of the mole rosa in a teardrop shape on each plate. Place the tarte tatin on the tail of the teardrop and garnish the mole with pomegranate seeds, pink pine nuts, pink peppercorns, and micro greens.

6. The tarts don't store well, so serve right away.

TIME-SAVING TIP

The onions can be cooked up to 3 days before and stored in an airtight container in the fridge.

VARIATION

Oil-free: You can't make the puff pastry fat-free, but you can omit the butter when cooking the onion and when greasing the ramekins.

NIXTAMALIZED BUTTERNUT SQUASH
IN ALMOND PIPIÁN

Calabaza Nixtamalizada en Pipián Rojo de Almendra

Nixtamalization is a pre-Hispanic cooking method that transforms a grain, usually corn, from a dry kernel to a nutrient-filled nourishing ingredient. The Indigenous civilizations of Mesoamerica—the Mayans, Toltecs, Mexicas, and Zapotecs—all used this technique to transform corn into masa for tortillas and tamales. It consists of cooking the corn in powdered slaked lime (calcium hydroxide) diluted in water, then letting it soak, and finally grinding it. This cooking method can also be applied to starchy vegetables such as sweet potato and butternut squash, as we do in this recipe. The result is a squash with a firm exterior and a soft, almost custard-like interior. I serve it with almond pipián and a multicolored black bean tetela, a triangular corn cake filled with Oaxacan refried beans.

MAKES: 4 servings

TOTAL TIME: 7 hours

NIXTAMALIZED SQUASH

- 1 medium butternut squash (1.1 kg), peeled, seeded, and cut into 2.5-inch (6.5 cm) cubes
- ½ ounce (15 g) food-grade slaked lime (calcium hydroxide)
- Kosher salt, for spreading
- 4 garlic cloves (12 g), peeled and smashed
- 1 thyme sprig
- 1 oregano sprig

TETELAS

- 1 cup (121 g) white masa harina
- 1 cup (142 g) blue corn masa harina
- ¼ teaspoon salt, divided
- ½ recipe Oaxacan Refried Black Beans (page 20)

QUELITES

- 2 teaspoons avocado oil
- 1½ pounds (680 g) fresh greens (Swiss chard, purslane, lamb's quarters)
- 1 garlic clove (3 g), minced
- ½ teaspoon salt
- ⅛ teaspoon freshly ground black pepper

TO ASSEMBLE

- ½ recipe Red Almond Mole (page 148), warm
- ¼ cup (27 g) chopped toasted almonds
- ½ cup (58 g) Almond Queso Fresco (page 31) or vegan feta cheese
- 2 small radishes, cut into thin strips

(CONTINUED)

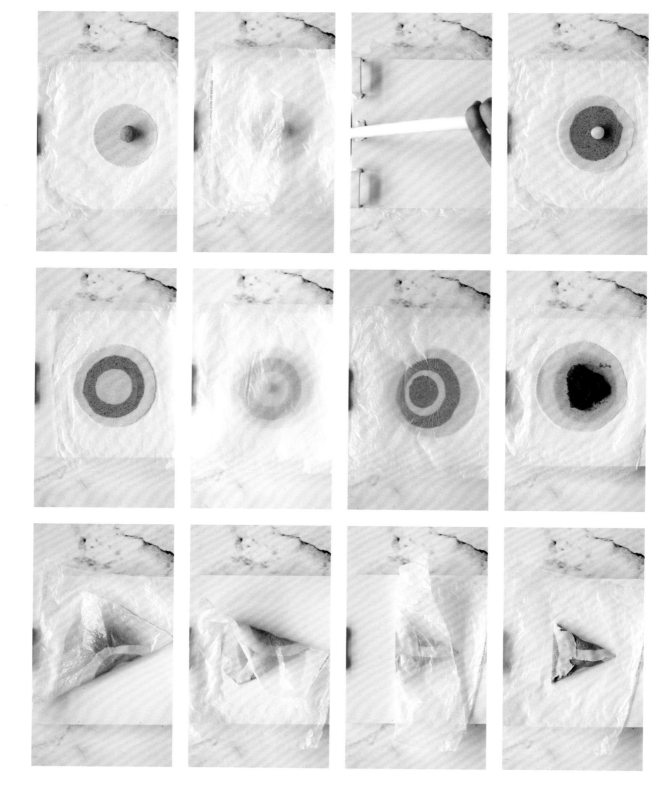

1. To nixtamalize the squash, place 4¼ cups (1 L) water and the squash in a nonreactive pot. Add the slaked lime (use gloves for this part), stir, and let sit for 4 hours, stirring occasionally. Drain and rinse the squash really well.

2. Preheat the oven to 400°F (205°C).

3. Place a ¼-inch (6 mm) layer of kosher salt in a 9 × 13-inch (13 × 23 cm) baking dish. Arrange the butternut squash cubes on top of the salt and surround them with the garlic and herb sprigs. Cover and bake for 1½ hours, or until the squash is soft.

4. To make the tetelas, place the white masa harina and blue masa harina in separate bowls. Gradually pour ¾ cup (177 mL) water and ⅛ teaspoon salt into each bowl while mixing it with your hand. Knead for 5 minutes, or until there are no dry spots in the masa and it is soft like Play-Doh, pliable but not sticky. To test if the masa is too dry, roll a small piece into a ball and lightly press it; if the edges crack, the dough is too dry. Add an additional ¼ cup (59 mL) water and knead again.

5. Preheat a comal or heavy-bottomed skillet over medium heat. To shape each tetela, lay a plastic liner (I like to cut squares out of grocery bags) on the bottom of a tortilla press. If you don't have a tortilla press, you can do this with two heavy flat objects, like books. Place a ball of white masa a little smaller than a Ping-Pong ball in the center of the liner and lay a second liner on top of the ball. Use your fingers to lightly press down on the masa ball and close the press, pushing down the lever to apply pressure. Remove the top liner. Now roll a ball of blue masa about ¼ inch (6 mm) smaller than the previous ball and place it on top of the already pressed tortilla. Press the liner on top and push the lever down.

6. Do this two more times, alternating masa colors to form a tortilla with multicolored rings. Flip the tortilla while still in the liners, so the rings are on the bottom side. Remove the top liner and place 1 tablespoon of the refried beans in the center. Using the plastic liner, fold down one side of the tortilla over the filling, then fold down the other side, forming the top of a triangle. Fold up the bottom side, sealing the triangle.

7. Reduce the heat to medium-low and place the tetelas on the comal. Let them cook for 3 to 4 minutes on each side, until they are browned in spots. Remove from the heat and let sit for 5 minutes.

8. To cook the quelites, heat the oil in a large skillet over medium-high heat. Add the greens and cook, stirring often, for about 1 minute. Once the greens begin to wilt, add the garlic, salt, and pepper. Cook for 1 minute, until the greens are completely wilted.

9. To assemble, remove the squash from the oven and, using a culinary blowtorch, char the top of the squash. (Alternatively, you can do this under your oven broiler set to high for 1 minute.) Spread about ½ cup (118 mL) of the pipián on one side of the plate, place ½ cup (100 g) of the sautéed quelites on the center of the pipián, and place the squash on top. Sprinkle the pipián with the toasted almonds. On the other side of the plate, place a dollop of the beans, place the tetela on top, and sprinkle with queso fresco and sliced radishes.

10. The squash and tetelas can be stored in separate airtight containers in the fridge for up to 3 days. To reheat the tetelas, splash a little bit of water on them and cook them in a skillet over medium heat.

NOTE

If you can't find blue corn masa harina, use double the amount of white masa harina, and don't make the layers.

TIME-SAVING TIP

The tetelas and the pipián can be made up to 3 days before.

VARIATION

Oil-free: Omit the oil when cooking the quelites.

BELUGA LENTIL CHILES EN NOGADA

Chiles en Nogada con Lenteja Caviar

Chiles en nogada is one of the dishes that best illustrates the beauty and complexity of Mexican cuisine. A roasted chile poblano is stuffed with a picadillo of beluga lentils (the traditional version is filled with pork), fruit, nuts, olives, and capers, then bathed in a walnut cream sauce (nogada), and topped with parsley and pomegranate seeds. Legend says it was created in 1821 in the Convent of Santa Monica in Puebla to celebrate Mexico's independence from Spain, with this dish representing the colors of the Mexican flag. Unfortunately, it is not well known outside of Mexico, probably because it is a very laborious dish. The original recipe calls for acitrón, which is a candied fruit originally made with biznaga cactus. The biznaga cactus is now in danger of extinction, so instead of cactus, I use candied jicama. For this modern interpretation, instead of leaving the chiles whole, I fill them and roll them like tortillas, almost like an enchilada.

MAKES: 4 servings

TOTAL TIME: 45 minutes + soaking time

CANDIED JICAMA
- ½ jicama (325 g), peeled and cut into small cubes
- ¾ cup (150 g) sugar

LENTILS
- 1½ cups (313 g) beluga lentils
- ½ large white onion (152 g)
- 2 garlic cloves (6 g), peeled and smashed
- ½ teaspoon salt

SAUCE
- 1½ cups (181 g) walnuts, soaked in boiling water overnight and drained
- 1½ cups (64 g) cubed crustless baguette or bolillo
- 1½ cups (354 mL) unsweetened almond milk
- 2 teaspoons sugar or sweetener of choice
- 1 tablespoon sweet sherry wine
- ½ teaspoon salt

LENTIL PICADILLO
- 6 poblano chiles (715 g)
- 3 Roma tomatoes (241 g), cored
- 1 tablespoon avocado oil
- ½ large white onion (152 g), sliced (about 1 cup)
- 3 garlic cloves (9 g), finely chopped
- 2½ tablespoons raisins
- ½ ripe plantain (113 g), peeled and cut into small cubes (about ½ cup)
- ¼ Bosc pear (56 g), cored and diced (about ¼ cup)
- ¼ Honeycrisp apple (35 g), cored and diced (about ¼ cup)
- 2 tablespoons pine nuts
- 2 tablespoons slivered almonds
- 2 tablespoons quartered pitted Manzanilla olives
- 1 tablespoon chopped capers
- ⅛ teaspoon ground cloves
- ¼ teaspoon ground cinnamon
- ⅛ teaspoon dried thyme
- ⅛ teaspoon dried oregano
- 1 teaspoon salt
- ⅛ teaspoon freshly ground black pepper
- 1½ cups (354 mL) vegetable broth

TO ASSEMBLE
- 1 pomegranate (282 g), seeds removed and reserved
- ⅓ cup (10 g) packed fresh parsley, finely chopped

(CONTINUED)

1. To make the candied jicama, place the jicama in a medium saucepot and pour in enough water to cover it by 3 inches (7.5 cm). Bring to a boil over high heat, reduce the heat to low, and simmer for 20 minutes. Drain, discard the water, and return the jicama to the pot. Add 2 cups (473 mL) water and the sugar and bring to a boil over high heat. Reduce the heat to low and simmer for 40 minutes, or until the liquid has a light syrup consistency. Remove from the heat and let it cool to room temperature. Drain the jicama and transfer it to a small bowl.

2. To cook the lentils, place the lentils, onion, garlic, and salt in a medium saucepot and fill with enough water to cover the lentils by 3 inches (7.5 cm). Bring to a boil over high heat, reduce the heat to low, and simmer for 10 minutes. Drain and discard the onion and garlic.

3. To make the sauce, use a paring knife to scrape off the papery skin from the drained walnuts. Transfer to a blender. Combine the bread and milk in a small bowl and let sit for 5 minutes, then transfer to the blender. Add the sugar, sherry, and salt and puree until smooth, for 2 to 3 minutes. If you don't have a high-powered blender, pass through a fine-mesh sieve into a small bowl.

4. Preheat the broiler to high.

5. Place the poblanos and tomatoes on a rimmed baking sheet and broil for 2 minutes on each side, or until they begin to soften and have black spots all over. Transfer the chiles to a heatproof bowl, cover, and let rest for 5 minutes. Transfer the tomatoes to the blender and puree until smooth, then transfer to a small bowl. Peel the chiles and cut off the stems. Make a 3-inch slit lengthwise from the top of the chile to the bottom, open the chile completely, and remove the seeds. Transfer to a small bowl.

6. Heat the oil in a large skillet over medium heat. Add the onion and cook, stirring occasionally, for 5 to 6 minutes, until the onion is soft and translucent. Add the garlic and cook for 1 minute, or until fragrant. Add the cooked lentils, mix well, and pour in the tomato puree. Let cook for 4 to 5 minutes, until the puree begins to bubble and becomes a dark red color. Add the raisins, 3 tablespoons of the candied jicama, and the plantain and bring to a simmer. Stir in the pear, apple, pine nuts, almonds, olives, capers, cloves, cinnamon, thyme, oregano, salt, and pepper. Add the vegetable broth and simmer for 15 to 18 minutes, until the plantain is cooked through and the lentils are tender.

7. To assemble, lay a chile on a cutting board and cut it in half lengthwise. Turn the two pieces horizontally and place 2 tablespoons of the picadillo in the center of each piece. Roll like you would an enchilada. Transfer to a serving plate, seam side down, and repeat this process with the rest of the chiles. Each plate should have 3 rolls. Pour the walnut sauce over them and sprinkle with the pomegranate seeds and chopped parsley. Serve immediately. You can store the chiles and the filling in separate airtight containers in the fridge for up to 3 days or in the freezer for up to 3 months.

TIME-SAVING TIPS

The filling and walnut sauce can be made up to 3 days before. If you want to save time, omit peeling the walnuts; the sauce will still be delicious, but it won't be as white. Instead of rolling the chiles like an enchilada, stuff them as if you were making chiles rellenos.

VARIATION

Oil-free: Replace the oil with ¼ cup (59 mL) vegetable broth when cooking the onion.

Jugos y Licuados
"EL COCHITO"

- Perejil/ Parsley
- Espinaca/ Spinach
- Piña/ Pineapple
- Nopal/ Prickly pe...
- Apio/ Celery
- Naranja/ Orange
- Miel/ Honey (Al g...

AGUA DE FRUTAS
- Limón
- Papaya
- Melón
- Naranja
- Piña
- Pepino
- Mango
- Fresa

PARA MI
- Fresa/ Strawberry
- Papaya/ Papaya
- Naranja/ Orange

VAMPIRO
- Zanahoria/ Carro...
- Apio/ Celery
- Betabel/ Beet
- Naranja/ Orang...

RECUERDAME
- Fresa/ Strawberry
- Piña/ Pneapple
- Naranja/ Orange
- Miel/ Honey (Al gusto)

JUGO HAWAIANO
- Apio/ Celery
- Piña/ Pineapple
- Naranja/ Orange
- Miel/ Honey (Al gusto)

CRUDA
- Alka-Seltzer
- Limón/ Lemon
- Sal/ Salt
- Agua Mineral

DISCOVERY:
- hocomilk
- ompope
- atano
- che

JUGO FIBRAS:
- Granola
- Avena
- Nuez
- Almendra
- Linaza

Rompe Viento:
- Platano
- Avena
- Rompope
- Miel
- Leche

Platanazo:
Platano
Cho...
Hielo • Vainilla
Miel • Carnation

Fiesta
- Papaya
- Manzana
- Platano
- Avena
- Miel

Leche

Rompe Hielo
- Fresa
- Papaya
- Avena
- Nuez-almendra
- Yoghurt
- Miel

10

¡SALUD!

¡Salud! is how we say "Cheers!" in Mexico, so let's raise a glass and enjoy the colorful and refreshing abundance of drinks Mexico has to offer. In the summer I cool down with aguas frescas, which is a name for a refreshing cold, alcohol-free beverage made with fresh fruit, sugar, and water. You can find them at markets being sold in big glass jars (vitroleros) and on stands on the side of the road, but I like to make them at home to enjoy with my lunch. With aguas frescas the possibilities are endless—there's watermelon, cantaloupe, lime, banana, tamarind, hibiscus, and strawberry. Practically any fruit can be made into an agua fresca. There are also aguas frescas thickened with grains, seeds, or nuts, and these are called horchatas.

In the winter, I prefer atoles. Atoles are warm drinks thickened with corn masa; they can be fruit, nut, vegetable, or grain based. They are a pre-Hispanic food, one consumed daily by the Indigenous civilizations of Mexico. Just like tamales, atole was used as an offering to deities in rituals and religious ceremonies. And also like tamales, atole is still very much present in today's Mexico; in the winter it is sold alongside tamales in carts outside office buildings or churches, and consumed at religious celebrations like Día de Muertos, Christmas, and el Día de la Candelaria. It is also used for medicinal purposes to relieve digestive problems or to increase milk supply in breastfeeding mothers. There are so many atoles, and they all change according to the regional availability of fruits, nuts, seeds, and grains. There's plantain atole in Oaxaca, blackberry atole in Mexico City, almond atole in Coahuila, quince atole in Michoacán—the list could go on and on. There's even atole made with chile (chileatole) in Puebla! ¡Salud!

GUAVA ATOLE

Atole de Guayaba

I moved to the US in 2004 to go to culinary school, and at the time I was confident that I wasn't going to have a problem adapting to the language. My whole life I lived right on the border of Texas and Mexico, I traveled into the US almost every day, and I was fluent in English. What I didn't know is that I wasn't fluent in slang, movie references, or people's mispronunciations of Spanish words, and that what I knew as a guayaba is actually called a guava here. Guayaba is one of my favorite fruits. It can have a fleshy exterior that is yellow or pink and a center of sweet pulp with many seeds. It is sweet and tangy, with notes of pineapple, pear, and melon. Atole de guayaba is popular in Mexico City, Guanajuato, and Michoacán. This version is inspired by the state of Guanajuato, where the guayabas are blended and added to water or milk, then thickened with masa. This is my preferred version because the flavor of the guayaba really stands out.

To make sure your guavas are ripe, check that they are completely yellow all over and soft to the touch, and you should be able to perceive their sweet scent. If your guavas are not ripe, your atole will be bitter.

MAKES: 4 servings

TOTAL TIME: 15 minutes

8 small yellow ripe Mexican guavas (453 g), halved
2 cups (473 mL) unsweetened oat milk
½ cup (55 g) sugar
1 (3-inch/7.5 cm) Ceylon cinnamon stick *or* ½ teaspoon ground cinnamon
⅓ cup (40 g) masa harina *or* 1½ tablespoons cornstarch

1. Place the guavas and 1 cup (236 mL) water in a blender and puree until smooth. Pass through a fine-mesh sieve into a small bowl.

2. Combine the milk, sugar, and cinnamon in a medium saucepot and bring to a simmer over medium-low heat. While the milk is heating, place 1 cup (236 mL) water in a small bowl and slowly pour in the masa harina while whisking to dissolve it. Whisk until all the lumps have disappeared. Pour this into the pot with the milk and simmer while stirring for 5 to 6 minutes, until the atole thickens enough to coat the back of a spoon. It is important to thicken the milk with the masa harina before you add the guava puree; otherwise the atole may curdle. Add the guava puree and simmer for 2 to 3 minutes. Serve immediately.

3. Store in an airtight container in the fridge for up to 2 days. To reheat it, place in a medium saucepot and bring to a simmer over medium-low heat. If it is too thick, add enough water to get it back to the desired consistency.

VARIATION

Fresh masa: To make this with fresh masa, dissolve ½ cup (124 g) fresh masa in 1 cup (236 mL) water, then pass through a fine-mesh sieve.

STRAWBERRY ATOLE

Atole de Fresa

Strawberry is one of the most popular flavors of atole. They even sell it in little packets at the grocery store. It is especially popular in Mexico City, where it is thickened with cornstarch, which results in a super-smooth and comforting atole. I prefer to make mine with masa or masa harina, because I love the combination of sweet strawberries and corn, just like in the Strawberry Tamales (page 228). Michoacán, Baja California, and Guanajuato are Mexico's largest producers of strawberries, so strawberry atole is also popular there. If you want to try the classic pairing of atole and tamales, I recommend you try this with the Chocolate and Pecan Tamales (page 223).

MAKES: **4 servings**

TOTAL TIME: **15 minutes**

2¾ cups (340 g) fresh or thawed frozen strawberries, hulled and halved

2 cups (473 mL) unsweetened oat milk

¼ cup (55 g) sugar

1 teaspoon vanilla extract

⅓ cup masa harina (40 g) *or* 1½ tablespoons cornstarch

1. Place the strawberries in the blender and puree until completely smooth.

2. Combine the milk, sugar, and vanilla in a medium saucepot and bring to a simmer over medium-low heat. While the milk is heating, place 1 cup (236 mL) water in a small bowl and slowly pour in the masa harina while whisking to dissolve it. Whisk until all the lumps have disappeared. Pour this into the pot with the milk and simmer while stirring for 5 to 6 minutes, until the atole thickens enough to coat the back of a spoon.

3. Add the strawberry puree to the pan and simmer for 2 to 3 more minutes, stirring occasionally. Serve immediately. If your atole is too thick, add ½ to 1 cup (120 to 237 mL) water until you reach the desired consistency.

4. Store in an airtight container in the fridge for up to 2 days. To reheat it, place it in a medium saucepot and bring it to a simmer over medium-low heat. If it is too thick, add enough water to get it back to your desired consistency.

VARIATION

Fresh masa: To make this with fresh masa, dissolve ½ cup (124 g) fresh masa in 1 cup (236 mL) water, then pass through a fine-mesh sieve.

COCONUT AND CARAMELIZED PINEAPPLE ATOLE

Atole de Coco y Piña Caramelizada

This irresistible atole is inspired by the state of Colima, Mexico's second-largest producer of coconut, where it is used to make coconut oil, flour, candies, coconut cream, and atole. Coconut atole is often drunk at festivities or street fairs, and sometimes pineapple is added to it. I like to caramelize the pineapple in a little bit of piloncillo, which mellows out the sharpness of the pineapple. I use fresh young coconut to make this, which I can find at my local grocery store, but I have included in the notes a version made with dried unsweetened coconut.

MAKES: 4 servings

TOTAL TIME: 20 minutes

1 fresh young coconut (624 g)
¼ cup (54 g) grated piloncillo
½ cup (96 g) fresh pineapple chunks
1 cup (236 mL) unsweetened coconut milk
¼ cup (55 g) sugar
1 (3-inch/7.5 cm) Ceylon cinnamon stick
¼ cup (30 g) masa harina

VARIATIONS

Dried coconut: Place ½ cup (50 g) dried unsweetened coconut and 1½ cups (354 mL) coconut water in a blender and puree until smooth, then proceed to step 2. Increase the masa harina to ⅓ cup (40 g).

Fresh masa: To make this with fresh masa, dissolve ½ cup (124 g) fresh masa in 1 cup (236 mL) coconut milk, then pass through a fine-mesh sieve.

1. To open the coconut, press the hilt of your knife into it, forming a small circle at the top to make a sort of lid. Wedge the knife and use it as a lever to remove the lid. Pour the coconut water into a blender, then use a spoon to scrape the flesh of the coconut into the blender.

2. Heat the piloncillo and ¼ cup (59 mL) water in a small saucepot over medium-low heat. Stir until the piloncillo dissolves, then add the pineapple and cook for 5 minutes, or until the pineapple softens and the piloncillo resembles a syrup. Transfer to the blender and puree until smooth.

3. Combine the milk, sugar, and cinnamon in a medium saucepot and bring to a simmer over medium-low heat. While the milk is heating, place 1 cup (236 mL) water in a small bowl and slowly pour in the masa harina while whisking to dissolve it. Whisk until all the lumps have disappeared. Pour this into the pot with the milk and simmer while stirring for 5 to 6 minutes, until the atole thickens enough to coat the back of a spoon. It is important to thicken the milk with the masa harina before you add the coconut-pineapple puree; otherwise the atole may curdle. Pour in the pineapple-coconut puree and simmer for 2 to 3 minutes. Serve immediately.

4. Store in an airtight container in the fridge for up to 2 days. To reheat it, place in a medium saucepot and bring to a simmer over medium-low heat. If it is too thick, add enough water to get it back to your desired consistency.

CORN-THICKENED MEXICAN HOT CHOCOLATE

Champurrado

As soon as it starts to get cold, I immediately crave a steaming-hot cup of champurrado. I like to make mine at home, but in the winter months in Mexico, it is sold on the streets along with tamales. It is a celebratory and ritual drink drunk throughout Mexico but is most commonly made for special occasions like the Feast of Our Lady of Guadalupe or Día de Muertos (Day of the Dead). The masa gives this hot chocolate a special kind of thickness, one that sticks to your ribs and fills your belly. But what really makes it unique is the Mexican chocolate, which is made by grinding toasted cacao beans with sugar and cinnamon. It doesn't contain any additives or milk solids, which lets the flavor of the cacao shine through. Go to the Resources (page 309) to see my recommendations for Mexican chocolate.

MAKES: 4 servings

TOTAL TIME: 15 minutes

1 (3-inch/7.5 cm) Ceylon cinnamon stick
⅓ cup (99 g) chopped piloncillo
2 (3-ounce/85 g) Mexican chocolate tablets
⅓ cup (40 g) masa harina

1. In a medium saucepot, combine the cinnamon, piloncillo, and 2 cups (473 mL) water. Bring to a simmer over medium-low heat and stir to make sure the piloncillo dissolves, for about 5 minutes. Add the chocolate and continue to simmer, stirring occasionally, until it dissolves, for about 5 minutes.

2. Add 1 cup (236 mL) water to a small bowl and slowly pour in the masa harina while whisking. Whisk until all the lumps have disappeared. Pour this into the pot and simmer while stirring for 5 to 6 minutes, until the hot chocolate thickens.

3. Serve immediately or use a molinillo (wooden frother) to froth your champurrado until it foams. This can also be done with an immersion blender.

4. Store in an airtight container in the fridge for up to 2 days. To reheat it, place it in a medium saucepot and bring it to a simmer over medium-low heat. If it is too thick, add enough water to get it back to your desired consistency.

VARIATION

Fresh masa: To make this with fresh masa, dissolve ½ cup (124 g) fresh masa in 1 cup (236 mL) water, then pass through a fine-mesh sieve.

PAPAYA AND STRAWBERRY SHAKE

Licuado de Papaya y Fresa

Mexico was doing fresh fruit juices and smoothies way before green juice became a thing in the US. Just like there are panaderías (bakeshops) and paleterías (ice cream shops), there are juguerías (juice shops). Like Jugos Maria Cristina, the oldest juice shop in the Centro Histórico of Mexico City, which has been run by four generations of the same family since 1938. Juguerías sell freshly squeezed fruit juices, licuados (smoothies), aguas frescas, and light breakfasts or lunches. They are mostly health focused, promoting the benefits of eating fresh fruit and vegetables. Licuados are different from American smoothies, as they consist of fresh fruit, juice or milk, and ice, resulting in a lighter, less sweet version of its American counterpart. This licuado includes papaya, which is native to Mexico and known for being rich in vitamins C and A and an enzyme that aids in digestion.

MAKES: 2 servings

TOTAL TIME: 10 minutes

1 banana (168 g)
¾ cup (133 g) hulled strawberries (about 6 strawberries)
1 cup (148 g) papaya chunks
1 cup (236 mL) unsweetened almond milk
1 cup ice

1. Place all the ingredients in a blender and puree until smooth. Serve immediately. If you have some left over, freeze it to make ice pops.

ORANGE AND BEET AGUA FRESCA

Agua Fresca de Naranja con Betabel

Beet and orange is a classic combination; in the 2000s it was all the rage at fancy restaurants as a salad, but as an agua fresca it is delicious, refreshing, and easy to make. I know beets are a contentious vegetable—either you love them or you hate them—but I love their sweetness, texture, and earthiness. The fresh orange juice adds a bright, citrusy sweetness that helps balance the earthiness of the beets. Plus beets are rich in antioxidants and high in fiber and potassium. This recipe is an easy way to get your beets in, and it can be found all throughout Mexico. I also love a version made in Guanajuato called Lágrimas de la Virgen (Virgin's Tears), which adds bananas, apples, peanuts, orange segments, and lettuce to it. It is drunk on Good Friday as a commemoration of the day Jesus died on the cross. The bright red color represents the tears of Our Sorrowful Lady. I have included a recipe for this version in the notes.

MAKES: **4 servings**

TOTAL TIME: **5 minutes**

2 cups (473 mL) fresh orange juice (about 8 large oranges)
2 medium beets (312 g), cooked and peeled, *or* **1 (15-ounce/425 g) can beets, drained**

½ cup (118 mL) light agave syrup or your favorite sweetener

1. Place the orange juice and cooked beets in a blender and puree until smooth. Add 2½ cups (591 mL) water and the agave syrup and puree once more. Pass through a fine-mesh sieve into a pitcher.

2. Let it chill in the fridge until you are ready to serve it. Serve over ice. Store it in the fridge for up to 2 days. If you have some left over, freeze it to make ice pops.

VARIATION

Lágrimas de la Virgen: Before serving, add 1 banana, sliced into rounds (123 g); 1 red apple, cored and diced (130 g); ¼ cup peanuts (44 g); ¼ head (134 g) iceberg lettuce, thinly sliced; and 1 orange (154 g), peeled and separated into segments.

BANANA AGUA FRESCA
Agua de Plátano

In my hometown of Acuña, Mexico, there is an agua fresca vendor called Aguas Kon Chabelo, where you can find fresh fruit aguas frescas being poured from large garrafas (glass tumblers). It is a local favorite, and during the summer months, the line at the stand wraps around the sidewalk, because there is nothing better than sipping on a banana agua fresca from Aguas Kon Chabelo on a scorching-hot summer day. Their version is not vegan, so I re-created it at home and spiced it with vanilla and cinnamon. If your bananas are ripe enough, you might not even need to add the agave syrup, because the bananas will be perfectly sweet. Food coloring is often added to make it bright yellow, but I don't find this necessary. Serve it over ice and enjoy a little piece of my hometown.

MAKES: **4 servings**

TOTAL TIME: **5 minutes**

2½ cups (591 mL) unsweetened almond milk
3 ripe bananas (369 g)
½ cup (118 mL) light agave syrup or your favorite sweetener

1 teaspoon vanilla extract
⅛ teaspoon ground cinnamon

1. In a blender, combine the milk, bananas, 2 cups (473 mL) water, the agave syrup, vanilla, and cinnamon and puree until smooth. Pour into a pitcher and let it chill in the fridge until you are ready to serve it. Serve over ice.

2. I don't recommend you store this agua fresca for more than a day because the bananas oxidize and turn the whole thing a muddy brown color. If you have some left over, freeze it to make ice pops.

VARIATION

Real vanilla bean: Instead of vanilla extract, scrape the seeds of a vanilla bean into the blender.

CANTALOUPE SEED HORCHATA

Horchata de Semillas de Melón

Horchata is a type of agua fresca traditionally made with soaked rice, milk, and cinnamon. However, rice is not the only grain used in Mexico; you can also find it made with oatmeal, almonds, and even cantaloupe seeds. Cantaloupe seed horchata is popular in the states of Chiapas, Veracruz, and Oaxaca. The addition of the seeds makes the agua fresca super creamy, without having to add any kind of milk to it. This version reminds me of a creamy honeydew ice pop that my mother-in-law, Kihong Stone, would buy me every time we visited the Korean grocery store. I became obsessed with them during my pregnancy, and she made sure we always had them in the house.

MAKES: **4 servings**

TOTAL TIME: **15 minutes**

½ cup (128 g) cantaloupe seeds
½ teaspoon vanilla extract

½ cup (101 g) diced cantaloupe
½ cup (118 mL) light agave syrup or your favorite sweetener

1. Add the cantaloupe seeds and 2 cups (473 mL) water to a blender and puree until smooth. Pass through a fine-mesh sieve into a large bowl, but do not discard the seed paste. Add the paste to the blender with another 2½ cups (591 mL) water, the vanilla, cantaloupe, and agave syrup and puree until smooth. Pass through the sieve into the bowl, then discard the solids.

2. Pour into a pitcher and let it chill in the fridge until you are ready to serve it. Serve over ice. Store it in the fridge for up to 2 days. If you have some left over, freeze it to make ice pops.

CUCUMBER AND LIME AGUA FRESCA

Agua de Pepino con Limón

This is a refreshing agua fresca that is very easy to make and very popular at juguerías (juice shops) across Mexico. I have added mint to it, which is not traditional but makes it very refreshing. Enjoy it on a blistering-hot day and cool down in an instant!

MAKES: **4 servings**

TOTAL TIME: **10 minutes**

2 medium cucumbers (556 g)
½ cup (118 mL) light agave syrup or your favorite sweetener
½ cup (118 mL) fresh lime juice
Leaves of 1 mint sprig

1. Cut the ends off the cucumbers and partially peel them, leaving half of the peel on. Cut into large pieces and transfer to a blender. Add the agave syrup, lime juice, 5 cups (1.1 L) water, and mint and puree until smooth.

2. Pass through a fine-mesh sieve into a pitcher and let it chill in the fridge until you are ready to serve it. Serve over ice. Store it in the fridge for up to 2 days. If you have some left over, freeze it to make ice pops.

TAMARIND AGUA FRESCA

Agua de Tamarindo

Tamarind is a tropical fruit from a leguminous tree native to Africa and Asia. It arrived in Mexico with the Spaniards and took so well to the tropical climate of the southern states that it flourished all along the Pacific Coast. It is tangy, tart, and sweet, with a flavor combination reminiscent of citrus and dates. It is immensely popular in Mexico as a candy and as a refreshing agua fresca. Tamarind is available at your local Mexican market, but you can also find it fresh or in paste form at Asian or Indian markets.

MAKES: **4 servings**

TOTAL TIME: **25 minutes + 1 hour resting time**

5 ounces (141 g) fresh tamarind pods (about 7 pods)

½ cup (118 mL) light agave syrup or your favorite sweetener

1. Peel the shells off the tamarind pods and remove the strings that are attached. Transfer the pods to a medium saucepot and add 3 cups (709 mL) water. Bring to a boil over high heat. Reduce the heat to low and simmer for 7 to 8 minutes, until the pods begin to soften.

2. Turn off the heat and let cool completely at room temperature. Use your hands to squeeze the pods to separate the tamarind flesh from the seeds. Pass the tamarind water through a fine-mesh sieve into a blender and use a spoon to push against the sieve to extract as much of the liquid from the flesh as you can. Add the agave syrup and puree until smooth.

3. Pour the tamarind water into a pitcher, add another 3 cups (709 mL) water, and stir. Serve over ice. Store in the fridge for up to 2 days. If you have some left over, freeze it to make ice pops.

VARIATION

Tamarind paste: If you can't find fresh tamarind, you can use ⅓ cup (84 g) tamarind paste instead.

11

LA PANADERÍA
AND LA PALETERÍA

When you walk in, the aroma of freshly baked bread surrounds you, and the rows upon rows of colorful sugar-dusted buns, buttery cookies, and crisp pies will captivate your senses. La panadería is a Mexican bakery that makes fresh bread daily; there's savory bread like bolillos and teleras, pan dulce (sweet bread) like conchas, marranitos, mantecadas, and besos, and cake. Mexican pan dulce is not as sweet as American pastries and is meant to be enjoyed with a nice hot mug of Mexican hot chocolate or café de olla. Panaderías do not only exist in Mexico; wherever there is a Mexican community, there is a panadería, especially if you live in Texas or California. Most panaderías are not exclusively vegan, but some of the classic pan dulce is made with vegetable shortening to cut costs, so ask at your local panadería and you might be surprised at the accidentally vegan options.

I must confess that bread is my weakness—my children lovingly call me a bread monster, and they're not wrong. But I also love paletas (ice pops); in the hot Mexican summers it's impossible for me not to stop by the colorful paleterías for a mango con chile paleta or a scoop of lime nieve de agua (water-based ice cream). The thing that makes Mexican paletas so unique and refreshing is that they are made with chunks of fresh seasonal fruit. Paleterías have tons of vegan options; paletas are easy to re-create at home too—all you need is fresh fruit, water, and sugar. Paleterías are also known for their unique flavors like avocado, corn, and cheese ice cream. My favorite unique flavor is Sweet Corn Ice Cream (page 300), which is best made in the summer when corn is in season.

VANILLA FLAN

Flan de Vainilla

When I told my parents I wanted to go to culinary school, they were in shock. Never once had I expressed an interest in the kitchen, and in an effort to dissuade me or test my mettle, they had me work at the family restaurant. Flan was one of the first things I made; I still remember the interminable cracking of eggs, and that the cook I was shadowing wouldn't let me do the caramel part for fear I would burn myself and get her in trouble. When I became vegan I thought I would never eat flan again. But after some extensive testing, I came up with a version of flan that makes my heart happy and takes me back to the many family meals at the restaurant. I use agar-agar, a plant-based gelatin derived from seaweed, to give the flan a custard-like texture. If you can't find agar-agar, you can use cornstarch instead as they do in Puerto Rico to make tembleque (see the variation below). The chickpea flour gives the flan an eggy taste, but if you can't find it, you can omit it without a problem.

MAKES: **4 servings**

TOTAL TIME: **30 minutes + chilling time**

CARAMEL
⅔ cup (130 g) sugar

FLAN BASE
1 cup (236 mL) unsweetened oat milk
¼ cup (54 g) sugar
1 teaspoon chickpea flour

1 teaspoon vanilla extract
1 (13.6-ounce/403 mL) can full-fat coconut milk
1¼ teaspoons agar-agar powder

VARIATION

If you don't have access to agar-agar, you can use ⅓ cup + 1 tablespoon (54 g) cornstarch instead. Dissolve the cornstarch in the oat milk, then add it to the blender with the sugar, vanilla, and chickpea flour. Then add that mixture to the coconut milk mixture on the stove and simmer for 5 minutes while whisking vigorously, until it has the consistency of pudding. If you would like the flan to be yellow, you can add a couple drops of food coloring.

1. To make the caramel, pour the sugar into a medium saucepot and heat it over medium-low heat. Let the sugar dissolve, gently stirring, until it turns a deep golden color, for 8 to 9 minutes. Immediately remove the pot from the heat and pour 1 to 2 tablespoons of the caramel into each of four (4-ounce/118 mL) ramekins. Gently lift and tilt the ramekins to coat the bottom with caramel. You must do this quickly, because the caramel will harden almost instantly when it hits the bottom of the ramekin.

2. To make the flan base, place the oat milk, sugar, chickpea flour, and vanilla in a blender and puree until smooth. In a medium saucepot, whisk together the coconut milk and agar-agar and bring to a simmer over medium-low heat, then pour in the contents of the blender. Simmer for 5 minutes, while whisking, until it thickens slightly. The flan will thicken and set as it cools. Remove the pot from the heat and let cool for 10 minutes.

3. Pour the flan base into the ramekins and let them chill in the fridge for a minimum of 8 hours or up to 3 days. The caramel will dissolve as it sits, so the longer it's in the fridge, the easier it will be to unmold.

4. To unmold, slide a knife around the edges of the flan and invert it onto a plate, then shake the ramekin gently to release the flan. If the flan doesn't release, place the bottom of the ramekins in a warm water bath for 1 to 2 minutes to melt the caramel.

5. Store the flan in the ramekins in the fridge, covered, for up to 3 days.

STRAWBERRY MOSTACHON

Mostachón de Fresa

There's a very special bakeshop in my hometown of Acuña, called Pastelería D'Letty. One of our favorite cakes there is Letty's mostachón de fresa, a glazed strawberry-topped cake with a cookie-like base, made with meringue, nuts, crackers, and a whipped cream cheese filling. It is very popular in Coahuila and the neighboring state of Nuevo León. I was doubtful at first that I could make a comparable vegan version, but it was actually quite easy: instead of egg whites I used aquafaba (the liquid in a can of chickpeas) to make the meringue, and a cashew yogurt whipped cream replaced the cream cheese. To give the strawberries the appearance of a glaze, I used thawed orange juice concentrate, which adds a vibrant citrus flavor to the strawberries as well as a glossy shine. I am very happy with the results and I know you will be too.

MAKES: 6 servings

TOTAL TIME: 35 minutes + soaking and chilling time

CASHEW CREAM
1½ cups (256 g) cashews, soaked in water overnight and drained
¾ cup (183 g) unsweetened plant-based yogurt
3 tablespoons light agave syrup
¼ cup (59 mL) refined coconut oil, melted
1 teaspoon vanilla extract

COOKIE BASE
¾ cup (177 mL) aquafaba (liquid from a can of low-sodium chickpeas), room temperature
¼ teaspoon cream of tartar
½ cup (100 g) sugar
1 teaspoon vanilla extract
1 cup (113 g) pecans, roughly chopped
2 sleeves (203 g) Ritz crackers, roughly crushed

STRAWBERRY TOPPING
1 pound (453 g) strawberries, hulled and diced
1 tablespoon thawed orange juice concentrate *or* 1 tablespoon sugar + ½ teaspoon grated orange zest

1. Preheat the oven to 350°F (175°C). Grease an 8-inch (20 cm) springform pan with vegetable oil spray.

2. To make the cashew cream, combine the drained cashews, yogurt, agave syrup, coconut oil, and vanilla in a blender and blend until smooth. Place in the refrigerator for at least 1 hour so it thickens and firms up.

3. Meanwhile, to make the cookie base, combine the aquafaba and cream of tartar in the bowl of a stand mixer fitted with the whisk attachment and whip on medium-high speed until soft peaks form, for about 4 minutes. Add the sugar and vanilla and beat for 1 minute. Using a spatula, gently fold in the pecans and crushed crackers without overmixing.

4. Pour the cookie base into the springform pan and bake for 20 to 25 minutes, until the edges become golden brown. Remove from the oven and let cool completely at room temperature, then remove it from the pan.

5. To make the glazed strawberry topping, in a large bowl, combine the strawberries and orange juice concentrate and let sit at room temperature for 10 minutes.

6. To assemble, place the cookie base on a plate, spread the cashew cream on the cookie base, and top with the glazed strawberries.

TIME-SAVING TIP

The cookie base and cashew whipped cream can be made the day before. Use a food processor to chop the nuts and crush the cookies.

VARIATION

Mostachón de mango: Instead of strawberries, use 1 pound (453 g) diced fresh mango to top the cake.

BOOZY MEXICAN CARAMEL

Cajeta Envinada

Cajeta is traditionally a goat's milk caramel from Celaya, Guanajuato, where it is sold in markets and candy stores in small round wooden boxes called cajetes, thus the name. It is flavored with vanilla, cinnamon, or rum. For this vegan version I use soy milk, but any plant-based milk will do, and flavor it with bourbon for a sweet treat that you can use to top everything from churros, crepes, and ice cream to Chocoflan (page 286) and Apple Cinnamon Tamales (page 225).

MAKES: 1 cup (236 mL)

TOTAL TIME: 1 hour 35 minutes

4¼ cups (1 L) unsweetened soy milk

1⅓ cups (284 g) turbinado or brown sugar

¼ cup (59 mL) light agave syrup

1 teaspoon vanilla extract

¼ teaspoon baking soda

1 to 2 tablespoons bourbon

1. In a large, heavy-bottomed pot, combine the soy milk, sugar, agave syrup, vanilla, and baking soda. Bring to a simmer over medium heat. Reduce the heat to low and simmer for 1 hour 15 minutes, stirring frequently to prevent sticking and burning. As it simmers, it will thicken and turn a dark caramel color.

2. Add the bourbon and simmer for 15 minutes, or until the cajeta has reached the consistency of thick maple syrup. If you feel it is too thin, you can continue to simmer it, but keep in mind that it will thicken as it cools.

3. Let cool at room temperature and store in an airtight container in the fridge for up to 2 weeks or in the freezer for up to 1 year.

CHOCOFLAN

Pastel Imposible

This cake is known in Mexico as the impossible cake, a feat that seems unsurmountable: a rich chocolate cake is topped with a creamy vanilla flan, all baked in the same pan! But how? In the traditional version, the cake batter is poured into the pan and then the flan base on top; in the oven the difference in density makes the cake rise to the top, leaving the flan on the bottom of the pan. For this vegan version, I had to make some adjustments to get the same effect, but the result is equally as good, and when you drizzle the vegan caramel and chopped pecans on top, you will wonder why you would ever need eggs and milk to make this in the first place.

MAKES: 8 servings

TOTAL TIME: 1 hour 5 minutes + 4 hours chilling time

FLAN BASE

1 cup (236 mL) unsweetened oat milk
⅓ cup (66 g) sugar
1 teaspoon chickpea flour
1 teaspoon vanilla extract
⅓ cup + 1 tablespoon (51 g) cornstarch
1 (13.6-ounce/403 mL) can full-fat coconut milk
1 or 2 drops yellow food coloring (optional)

CHOCOLATE CAKE

1 cup (135 g) all-purpose flour
½ cup (60 g) whole wheat flour
¼ cup (20 g) cocoa powder
½ cup (100 g) sugar
1 teaspoon baking soda
¼ teaspoon salt
⅓ cup (78 mL) vegetable oil
1 teaspoon vanilla extract
1 teaspoon distilled white vinegar

TO SERVE

½ cup (78 mL) Boozy Mexican Caramel (page 284) or vegan caramel sauce
⅓ cup (41 g) pecans, chopped

1. Preheat the oven to 350°F (175°C). Grease a Bundt pan with vegetable oil spray and spread it with a pastry brush to make sure all the folds in the pan are coated.

2. To make the flan base, place the oat milk, sugar, chickpea flour, vanilla, and cornstarch in a blender and puree until smooth. Heat the coconut milk in a medium saucepot over medium-low heat until it begins to simmer, then pour in the contents of the blender and the food coloring (if using). Simmer for 5 minutes while whisking vigorously, or until the flan base thickens and has the texture of a thick pudding. Transfer to the prepared Bundt pan and give it a little shake to evenly distribute it in the bottom of the pan. Let it cool at room temperature while you prepare the cake batter.

3. To make the cake, sift the all-purpose flour, whole wheat flour, cocoa powder, sugar, baking soda, and salt into a large bowl and whisk to combine. Make a well in the center and add the oil, vanilla, vinegar, and 1 cup (236 mL) water. Whisk until smooth. Pour the cake batter on top of the flan mixture.

4. Place a large baking pan on the center rack of the oven and add about 1 inch (2.5 cm) water. Place the Bundt pan in the center of the large pan and bake for 40 to 45 minutes, until a toothpick inserted into the cake comes out clean. Be careful not to insert the toothpick all the way to the bottom of the Bundt pan, as we want to test just the cake, not the flan.

5. Remove the cake from the oven and let it cool. Place it in the fridge for at least 4 hours or until it is completely chilled; when you touch the pan, it should feel cold. Pass a butter knife around the edges of the pan only at the cake level. Place the bottom of the pan in a warm water bath

for 2 minutes so the flan releases from the pan. Flip the Bundt pan over onto a plate and give it a shake. The cake should slide out. If it doesn't, place the cake back in the water bath and try again. Garnish with cajeta and pecans.

6. Store the cake in the fridge for up to 3 days.

TIME-SAVING TIP

Make the cajeta the day before or use store-bought vegan caramel.

VARIATION

Oil-free: Replace the oil in the cake with ⅓ cup (83 g) unsweetened applesauce and decrease the baking time to 35 to 40 minutes.

TRES LECHES CAKE

Pastel de Tres Leches

We have a family friend, Maria Elena de León, who makes the most deliciously sweet and moist tres leches cake. Every year I would request it for my birthday, and it quickly became a centerpiece of all my birthday celebrations. One particular memory stands out vividly in my mind: As the familiar "Happy Birthday" song filled the room, Maria Elena carefully carried the cake toward the table. Suddenly she tripped, causing the cake to soar through the air and land on the floor with a resounding smack. The room went completely silent, but the silence was quickly shattered by Maria Elena's infectious laughter, and soon the entire room was laughing too. That day we rescued what we could of the cake from the floor and happily ate it. The traditional tres leches cake is a sponge cake soaked with three different milks: condensed milk, evaporated milk, and half-and-half, then topped with whipped cream and fresh fruit. For this vegan version I make a milk syrup with three plant-based milks and a sponge cake with aquafaba, resulting in a cake worthy of Maria Elena.

MAKES: **6 to 8 servings**

TOTAL TIME: **45 minutes + soaking time**

CAKE

- 1¼ cups (295 mL) unsweetened soy milk
- 2 teaspoons apple cider vinegar
- 1¾ cups (279 g) all-purpose flour
- ½ cup (100 g) sugar
- 2 teaspoons baking powder
- ½ teaspoon baking soda
- ¼ cup (59 mL) vegetable oil
- 2 teaspoons vanilla extract
- 6 tablespoons (88 mL) aquafaba (liquid from a can of low-sodium chickpeas)
- ⅛ teaspoon cream of tartar

MILK SYRUP

- 1 cup (236 mL) unsweetened oat milk
- 1 cup (236 mL) unsweetened macadamia nut milk or soy milk
- 1 cup (236 mL) unsweetened almond milk
- ½ cup (100 g) sugar

TO ASSEMBLE

- 1 (10-ounce/283 g) tub vegan whipped topping
- 8 ounces (226 g) strawberries, thinly sliced
- ½ cup (60 g) raspberries
- ½ cup (74 g) blueberries

(CONTINUED)

1. Preheat the oven to 350°F (175°C). Line a 9 × 13-inch (20 × 33 cm) baking pan with parchment paper.

2. To make the cake, in a small bowl, whisk together the soy milk and apple cider vinegar and let it sit for 5 minutes. In a medium bowl, combine the flour, sugar, baking powder, and baking soda. Pour the milk-vinegar mixture into the dry ingredients, add the oil and vanilla, and whisk to combine.

3. Add the aquafaba and cream of tartar to the bowl of a stand mixer fitted with the whisk attachment (or a large bowl if using a handheld mixer) and whip on medium-high speed until soft peaks form, in about 4 minutes.

4. Fold the whipped aquafaba into the cake batter with a spatula. Be careful not to overmix or the cake will not rise as intended. Pour the batter into the prepared baking pan and bake on the middle rack for 25 to 30 minutes, until a toothpick inserted in the center comes out clean.

5. Remove from the oven. Let the cake cool for 10 minutes, then unmold onto a wire rack. Peel off the parchment paper and let the cake cool completely.

6. To make the milk syrup, in a medium saucepot, combine the oat milk, macadamia nut milk, almond milk, and sugar and bring to a simmer over medium-low heat. Reduce the heat to low and simmer for 25 to 30 minutes, until the milk slightly thickens. Transfer to a heatproof bowl and place in the fridge until completely cold. You should have about 2 cups (473 mL) of milk syrup.

7. To assemble, using a serrated knife, gently cut off the top of the cake. This will make it easier for the cake to absorb the milk. Place the cake back in the same pan it was baked in and poke the cake all over with a fork. Be sure to press the fork all the way down through the cake.

8. Pour the milk syrup over the cake, starting from the center. Continue pouring until the cake is soaked all over. There might be some liquid that hasn't been absorbed on the sides of the cake, but that's OK. Cover, place in the fridge, and let the cake soak for a minimum of 4 hours, or up to overnight.

9. When you're ready to serve, spread the whipped topping evenly over the cake with a spatula. Arrange the fresh berries on top and serve. The assembled cake will hold in the fridge for up to 1 day.

TIME-SAVING TIP

The cake and milk syrup can be made the day before.

VARIATION

Oil-free: When mixing the cake batter, replace the oil with ¼ cup (62 g) unsweetened applesauce. Instead of vegan whipped topping, you can make coconut whipped cream: Place 1 (13.6-ounce/403 mL) can full-fat coconut milk in the fridge overnight. Avoid shaking the can. When you open the can, you will see that the thickened coconut cream has risen to the top. Scoop it out and place it in a bowl, then add about 1 tablespoon powdered sugar and ½ teaspoon vanilla extract. Beat for 30 seconds with an electric mixer.

WHOLE WHEAT CONCHAS
Conchas Integrales

This is the most iconic pan dulce (sweet bread) of them all: a soft, pillowy bread topped with a crunchy, almost cookie-like topping shaped like a seashell (concha). You can find them at any panadería in white, neon pink, or chocolate colors. In the cold winter months, I like to dip them in Mexican hot chocolate. This is one of my most tested recipes; I struggled a lot to find an egg substitute that would provide just the right amount of moisture and leavening for a soft roll. I tried everything you can imagine, and then discovered that potatoes work beautifully. Potato starch holds more water than wheat starch, which increases the moisture content, resulting in light and airy bread. I use sweet potato for this recipe, but you can also use Yukon Gold or russet potato. To make the topping I use granulated sugar, which makes it a little bit more difficult to work with than powdered sugar, but results in a crunchy topping. The dough is left to rise overnight in the refrigerator, but if you want to make them the same day, I have included instructions in the notes.

MAKES: **6 servings (10 small conchas)**

TOTAL TIME: **45 minutes + resting time**

DOUGH
2 teaspoons active dry yeast
½ cup + 2 tablespoons (150 mL) unsweetened soy milk, warm
⅓ cup (85 g) cooked and mashed sweet potato
1¾ cups (231 g) bread flour
½ cup + 1 tablespoon (77 g) whole wheat flour
¼ cup (50 g) sugar
½ teaspoon salt
⅓ cup + 1 tablespoon (77 g) unsalted vegan butter, cut into cubes, room temperature

TOPPING
⅓ cup (66 g) sugar
⅓ cup (76 g) unsalted vegan butter, room temperature
½ cup (60 g) all-purpose flour
½ teaspoon vanilla extract
½ teaspoon ground cinnamon (optional)

1. In a small bowl, whisk together the yeast and soy milk. Let it rest for 5 minutes. Add the mashed sweet potato and whisk until there are no lumps. If it is too lumpy, I like to use my immersion blender to get it super smooth.

2. In the bowl of a stand mixer fitted with the dough hook, combine the bread flour, whole wheat flour, sugar, and salt. Add the yeast mixture and mix on low speed until a shaggy dough begins to form, in about 3 minutes. Add the softened butter little by little and increase the speed to medium. Mix for 13 to 15 minutes, until the dough pulls away from the sides of the bowl and is smooth and stretchy but not sticky. If the dough is too sticky, add a little more flour (2 to 3 tablespoons) around the sides of the bowl. If you don't have a stand mixer, you can knead by hand for 25 minutes.

3. Place the dough in a large oiled bowl, cover it with a towel, and let it rise for 1½ hours, or until doubled in size. Punch down the dough, fold the sides over onto each other, and flip. Cover the bowl with plastic wrap and refrigerate overnight. The next day, take the dough out of the fridge, remove the plastic wrap, and cover it with a towel. Let rise in a warm place (70 to 75°F/20 to 25°C) until the dough comes to room temperature, for about 1½ hours.

4. To prepare the topping, cream the sugar and butter with a whisk or hand mixer. Add the flour, vanilla, and cinnamon (if using) and mix well. Knead lightly to fully incorporate. It should have the consistency of a soft Play-Doh. If it's too sticky, add flour in small amounts until you've reached the right consistency. Divide the topping into ten equal balls.

(CONTINUED)

5. For the shaping, line a rimmed baking sheet with a silicone mat or parchment paper. Divide the dough into ten equal pieces. Roll each piece tightly into a round and place them on the prepared baking sheet 2 inches (5 cm) apart. Lay down a piece of plastic wrap, place a topping ball in the center, and place another piece of plastic on top (almost like you're making tortillas). Press down with your hand until it is ⅓ inch (8 mm) thick and 3 inches (7.5 cm) wide. Peel one side of the plastic off, then take the piece of plastic wrap with the topping on it and place it on a dough round. Slowly peel off the plastic. Using a concha cutter dusted with flour, press down on the topping and the concha to make the seashell design. Don't be afraid to press down hard and flatten the concha a little. (If you don't have a concha cutter, you can use a paring knife to make the seashell design.) Repeat these steps with the rest of the dough and topping. Let the conchas rise until they double in size, about 1½ hours.

6. Preheat the oven to 350°F (175°C).

7. Bake the conchas on the middle rack for 18 to 20 minutes, until the bottom of the conchas are golden brown. Remove from the oven and let them cool completely before eating. This step is very important, as the conchas continue to cook as they cool, and if you eat them warm, they will be gummy.

8. Store in an airtight container at room temperature for up to 2 days.

VARIATION

Same day: If you want to make these on the same day you serve them, after kneading the dough, let it rise for 1½ hours, punch the dough down, then shape it, and let it rise for 1½ more hours, or until doubled in size.

DATE PECAN LOAF

Panqué de Dátil y Nuez

On my first visit to the sunny Baja California Sur town of La Paz, I discovered that dates are inexpensive, readily available, and an important element in Baja Californian cuisine. Come to find out, date-producing palms are abundant there because they were introduced by Jesuit missionaries between 1697 and 1768. Dates are used to make candies, sauces, pies, and empanadas. One of the most popular ways of using dates there is by baking them in this melt-in-your-mouth date pecan loaf. There is enough natural sugar in the dates to sweeten the whole loaf, so I didn't need to add any processed sugar. I like to toast it and spread some vegan butter on it to eat with my morning chamomile anise tea.

MAKES: **6 servings (1 loaf)**

TOTAL TIME: **1 hour 20 minutes**

1½ cups (260 g) Medjool dates, pitted and chopped into small pieces
1 teaspoon vanilla extract
⅓ cup (96 g) unsweetened plant-based yogurt
½ cup (118 mL) unsweetened almond milk
¼ cup (59 mL) vegetable oil

1 cup (147 g) all-purpose flour
1 cup (130 g) whole wheat flour
2 teaspoons baking powder
½ teaspoon baking soda
⅛ teaspoon salt
1 cup (97 g) pecans, chopped

1. Preheat the oven to 350°F (175°C). Grease an 8½ × 4½-inch (22 × 11 cm) loaf pan with vegetable oil spray.

2. Place the dates in a small heatproof bowl, pour in 1 cup (236 mL) hot water and let sit for 5 minutes. Stir in the vanilla, yogurt, almond milk, and oil.

3. In a large bowl, combine the all-purpose flour, whole wheat flour, baking powder, baking soda, and salt. Pour the wet ingredients into the dry ingredients and stir to combine. Fold in the chopped pecans, then transfer the batter to the prepared loaf pan.

4. Bake for 45 to 50 minutes, until a toothpick inserted in the center comes out clean. Let cool in the pan for 15 minutes, then unmold onto a wire rack and let cool completely before cutting.

5. Store in an airtight container at room temperature for up to 3 days or in the freezer for up to 6 months.

VARIATIONS

Oil-free: Instead of oil, use ¼ cup (62 g) unsweetened applesauce.

Spiced cake: Add 1 teaspoon ground cinnamon and ⅛ teaspoon ground cloves.

COCONUT AND CHOCOLATE STONES

Piedras de Coco con Chocolate

This pan dulce (sweet bread) is one of my favorites! The name literally translates to *rock*, supposedly because you bake it until it is as hard as a rock. It was invented in panaderías (bakeshops) as a way to use leftover bread from the night before. The leftover bread is ground into breadcrumbs and used as the base for the dough. It is a wonderful way to use any leftover stale bread or finally give a purpose to the lonely bread butts from your sandwich bread.

MAKES: **6 servings**

TOTAL TIME: **40 minutes**

- 8 ounces (250 g) dry stale bread, cut into large chunks
- ¼ cup (57 g) packed grated piloncillo or light brown sugar
- 1 teaspoon baking powder
- 1 teaspoon ground cinnamon
- ½ cup (30 g) grated unsweetened coconut
- 4 tablespoons (55 g) vegan butter, room temperature
- ½ cup (123 g) unsweetened plain vegan yogurt
- 1 teaspoon vanilla
- ¾ cup (90 g) all-purpose flour
- ½ cup (118 mL) unsweetened almond milk
- 1 cup (157 g) semi-sweet chocolate chips

1. Preheat the oven to 375°F (190°C). Line a rimmed baking sheet with a silicone mat or parchment paper.

2. Place the bread in a food processor and pulse until it turns into coarse breadcrumbs, then transfer them to a large bowl. You may have to do this in two batches depending on the size of your food processor. You should end up with about 1¾ cups (153 g) breadcrumbs.

3. Add the piloncillo, baking powder, cinnamon, and coconut to the bowl and mix with a wooden spoon. Add the butter, yogurt, and vanilla and mix until a dough begins to form. Add the flour and incorporate it into the dough with your hands. At this point it will be a bit too dry. Slowly pour in the almond milk and continue to mix with your hands until the dough is the consistency of cookie dough.

4. Divide the dough into six equal pieces, a little smaller than your palm. Plop the dough pieces onto the prepared baking sheet and use your fingers to give them a ball-like shape. The edges should be uneven and scraggly so when they bake they look like rocks.

5. Bake for 25 to 30 minutes, until the edges and the bottom are golden brown. Remove from the oven and let cool on a wire rack.

6. Place the chocolate in a heatproof bowl. Microwave for three 30-second intervals, stirring between each, until the chocolate is smooth, shiny, and completely melted. Dip the top of each piedra in the chocolate and return it to the wire rack. You can eat them as is or let the chocolate set at room temperature.

VARIATION

Oil-free: Replace the vegan butter with ¼ cup (62 g) applesauce.

CRUMBLY CORN COOKIES

Pemoles

Pemoles are sweet and crumbly corn cookies, similar to shortbread cookies, found throughout the Huasteca region, which encompasses northern Veracruz, southern Tamaulipas, parts of San Luis Potosí, Querétato, Hidalgo, and Puebla. This version is inspired by the state of Tamaulipas, where they sometimes add coffee to them. Traditionally they are made with lard and nixtamalized corn flour, then baked in a clay wood-burning oven, but for this version, I used vegan butter instead. They are easy to make and very versatile—you can use piloncillo instead of sugar or add ground cinnamon or even sesame seeds. They are meant to be eaten with coffee or hot chocolate.

MAKES: **12 cookies**

TOTAL TIME: **35 minutes**

1 tablespoon ground flaxseed
2 teaspoons instant coffee
½ cup + 1 tablespoon (125 g) unsalted vegan butter

¼ cup (50 g) sugar
1 cup (121 g) masa harina
2 tablespoons (16 g) all-purpose flour

1. Preheat the oven to 400°F (205°C). Line a rimmed baking sheet with a silicone mat or parchment paper.

2. To make the flax egg, in a small bowl, combine the flaxseed, instant coffee, and 3 tablespoons hot water and whisk to dissolve the coffee. Let it sit while you prepare the cookie dough.

3. In a large bowl, beat together the butter and sugar with a handheld mixer on medium speed for 3 to 4 minutes, until it is light and fluffy. Add the flaxseed mixture and whisk for 1 minute. Using a spatula, scrape down the sides of the bowl, and with the mixer on low, slowly add the masa harina and all-purpose flour.

4. Once the dough comes together, knead it with your hands to make sure the masa harina is completely incorporated. The dough should have the consistency of soft Play-Doh; if it is too wet, add an additional tablespoon of all-purpose flour.

5. To shape the cookies, roll the dough into balls a little larger than a golf ball. Working with one ball at a time, roll the dough into a rope 4 to 5 inches (10 to 13 cm) long. Using your fingers, flatten the ends of the rope, press them together to form a doughnut shape, and transfer to the prepared baking sheet. Repeat this process with the rest of the dough.

6. Place the baking sheet in the oven and reduce the temperature to 325°F (160°C). Bake for 15 to 20 minutes, until the bottom of the cookies are golden brown. Remove the cookies from the oven and let them cool on the baking sheet.

7. Store in an airtight container at room temperature for up to 3 days.

TIME-SAVING TIP

Make the dough the day before and store in the fridge. You can also freeze the dough for up to 3 months and defrost it when you're ready to use.

SWEET CORN ICE CREAM

Helado de Elote

Mexico is the king of what some would consider weird—or rather, unexpected—ice cream flavors. There is avocado, corn, cheese, and even mole ice cream. I first tried corn ice cream in Sahuayo, Michoacán, when I was eighteen years old, and I was immediately put off by the chunks of corn in my ice cream. Now it is one of my favorite flavors, but I prefer it nice and smooth, with no corn chunks. This recipe is made with American sweet corn, but if you are using the starchier Mexican corn, you will have to increase the sugar to 1 cup (200 g). The vodka is optional, but because vodka doesn't freeze, it helps prevent large ice crystals from forming, resulting in a creamier ice cream.

MAKES: **4 servings (1 quart/1 L)**

TOTAL TIME: **45 minutes + chilling time**

4 ears corn (1.2 kg), shucked, kernels cut off and cobs reserved (about 3 cups kernels)
3 cups (709 mL) unsweetened oat milk
½ cup (100 g) sugar
2 tablespoons vodka (optional)
Pinch salt
Boozy Mexican Caramel (page 284), for serving (optional)

1. Combine the corn kernels, cobs, milk, and sugar in a medium saucepot. Bring to a simmer over medium heat, then reduce the heat to low and simmer for 15 minutes. Remove from the heat and let sit for 30 minutes at room temperature. Transfer to a heatproof bowl and place in the fridge until completely cold, for about 3 hours.

2. Remove and discard the cobs. Transfer the corn and milk mixture to a blender, add the vodka (if using) and salt, and puree until smooth.

3. Spin in an ice cream machine according to the manufacturer's instructions. Transfer to an airtight container and freeze for 5 hours.

4. Remove the ice cream from the freezer 5 to 6 minutes before serving to allow it to soften. Serve in cups or cones or drizzle some caramel on it.

VARIATION

Canned or frozen corn: Use 3 cups (495 g) canned or frozen corn and add 2 tablespoons cornstarch to the milk mixture.

LIME SORBET

Nieve de Garrafa de Limón

Tlaquepaque, a town on the outskirts of Guadalajara, is famous for their nieve de garrafa, a sorbet made in a metal tin inserted into a wooden barrel surrounded by salted ice. The sorbet base (usually known as nieve de agua) is poured into the tin and then stirred constantly until it solidifies, forming a sweet and icy treat typically made with regional seasonal fruit. The most famous ice cream store in Tlaquepaque is Nieves de Garrafa Chapalita, where there is always a line and you can see the endless rows of metal tins with a rainbow of flavors being scooped into cups or cones. This is an easy version of one of the most popular flavors; I spin it in an ice cream maker, and it almost tastes like I'm in Tlaquepaque. You can serve it as is or top it with chamoy sauce (a fruity chile sauce) and chile powder.

MAKES: 4 servings (1 quart/1 L)

TOTAL TIME: 15 minutes + chilling time

½ cup (100 g) sugar
1 teaspoon grated lime zest
½ cup (118 mL) fresh Key lime juice (about 10 limes)
2 teaspoons vodka (optional)

TO SERVE
¼ cup (50 g) chile powder for fruits
½ cup (118 mL) chamoy sauce

1. In a large bowl, combine 4¼ cups (1 L) room-temperature water and the sugar and stir to dissolve the sugar. Add the lime zest, lime juice, and vodka (if using). Transfer to the fridge and let it chill, covered, for at least 4 hours, or until completely cold.

2. Spin in your ice cream machine according to the manufacturer's instructions. Transfer it to an airtight container and freeze for at least 4 hours.

3. Serve in cups and top with chile powder and chamoy to taste.

STRAWBERRIES AND CREAM PALETAS

Paletas de Fresas con Crema

Fresas con crema is a classic Mexican dessert that consists of fresh strawberries bathed in a thick and slightly sour cream. It is sold in ice cream shops all over the country, but it is not Mexican at all; it is our version of the British strawberries and cream. Strawberries were introduced into Mexico in 1849 during the Frenchification of Mexico under President Porfirio Díaz's dictatorship, and they immediately took off. Now Mexico is the world's third-largest producer of strawberries, with the states of Michoacán, Baja California, and Guanajuato leading the way. These paletas are inspired by the traditional fresas con crema with the addition of orange liqueur and agave syrup for a touch of sweetness.

MAKES: 10 paletas

TOTAL TIME: 20 minutes + chilling time

ICE CREAM BASE
- 1½ cups (354 mL) unsweetened soy milk or full-fat coconut milk, divided
- 3 tablespoons cornstarch
- 1½ cups (354 mL) unsweetened almond milk
- 1 teaspoon vanilla extract
- ½ cup (118 mL) light agave syrup

STRAWBERRIES
- 2 cups (286 g) strawberries, hulled and cut into small dice
- 2 tablespoons orange liqueur (optional)
- 1 tablespoon sugar
- ½ teaspoon fresh lemon juice

1. To make the ice cream base, in a small bowl, whisk together ½ cup (118 mL) of the soy milk and the cornstarch until the cornstarch is completely dissolved.

2. In a medium saucepot, combine the remaining 1 cup (236 mL) soy milk, the almond milk, vanilla extract, and agave syrup. Bring to a simmer over medium-low heat, then pour in the cornstarch-milk mixture while stirring. Continue to simmer for 5 minutes, stirring constantly to prevent the cornstarch from sticking to the bottom of the pot, until the milk thickens enough to coat the back of a spoon. Remove from the heat and pass through a fine-mesh sieve into a heatproof bowl. Let it chill in the fridge for at least 4 hours, or until completely cold.

3. In a medium bowl, combine the strawberries, orange liqueur (if using), sugar, and lemon juice. Place them in the fridge to macerate. Once the ice cream base is cold, fold in the strawberries. Pour the base into ice pop molds, add the lid and sticks, and freeze for at least 5 hours.

4. You can store the paletas in reusable silicone bags or zip-top bags in the freezer for up to 1 month.

VARIATION

Fresas con crema ice cream: Follow steps 1 and 2, and the macerating of the strawberries in step 3. Spin the ice cream base in an ice cream machine according to the manufacturer's instructions; 5 minutes before the ice cream is done spinning, add the strawberries. Transfer to an airtight container and freeze for 5 hours. Remove the ice cream from the freezer 5 minutes before serving to allow it to soften.

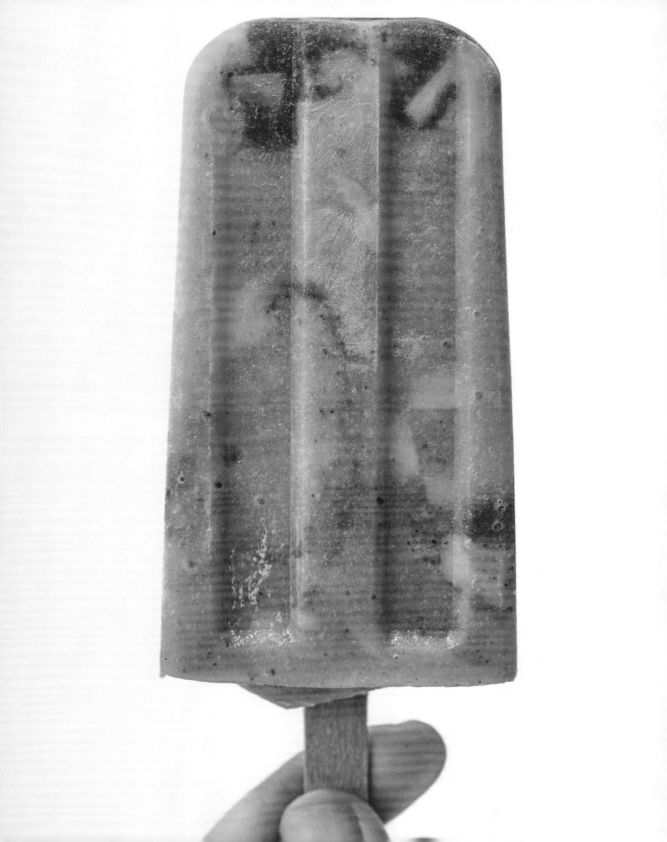

MANGO AND CHILE ICE POPS
Paleta de Mango con Chile

This is a classic flavor in all the paleterías and a favorite in my family, especially in the summer months, when mango is in season. The combination of sweet fruit and chile is a common one in Mexico; kids learn from an early age to enjoy spicy candy, sprinkle chile on their watermelon, or dip their orange slices in chile powder. You can find this flavor combination in many forms, sold as mango on a stick, as a shaved treat (mangonada), or as a mango lollipop covered in a layer of chile powder. You could say mango without chile is almost a crime. However you like to eat it, you can't deny it is a combination worth repeating. My local paletería, Helados Aguirre, adds cucumber to their paleta de mango con chile; I love the combination of flavors, so I use cucumber here as well. The recipe calls for Ataulfo mangoes, but any mango will work, as well as frozen mango.

MAKES: 10 paletas

TOTAL TIME: 20 minutes + chilling time

---

6 large Ataulfo mangoes (1.1 kg), peeled, pitted, and diced (about 3½ cups), divided
½ cucumber (81 g), peeled
1 tablespoon fresh lime juice
¼ cup (59 mL) light agave syrup
1 tablespoon chile powder for fruits
¼ cup (59 mL) chamoy

1. Place 2½ cups (423 g) of the diced mango, the cucumber, ½ cup (118 mL) water, the lime juice, agave syrup, and chile powder in a blender and puree until smooth.

2. Pour 1 teaspoon chamoy into each ice pop mold, fill them halfway with mango puree, then add 1 tablespoon of the remaining diced mango. Pour the rest of the mango puree into the molds, add the lid and sticks, and freeze for at least 5 hours.

3. You can store the paletas in reusable silicone bags or zip-top bags in the freezer for up to 1 month.

RESOURCES

WHERE TO FIND INGREDIENTS LOCALLY

Asian market: Asian markets are my go-to for tofu and affordable mushrooms.

Farmers' market: Check your local farmers' market to see what farmers in your area are producing. Produce like zucchini blossoms might not be sold at the market, but you can talk to a farmer and see if they are willing to sell you some. If they have zucchini, they have blossoms.

Mexican market: Mexican markets come in all sizes. The larger markets tend to have a greater variety of produce, so visit those first. They will also have canned items, dried chiles, and spices.

Tortillería: Check to see if there is a tortillería in your town. You might be able to purchase fresh masa from them.

WHERE TO FIND INGREDIENTS AND EQUIPMENT ONLINE

Agar-agar:
Living Jin (LivingJin.com)

Avocado leaf, white olotillo heirloom corn, hibiscus, masa harina, and tortilla press:
Masienda (Masienda.com)

Beans (ayocote beans, Chiapas black beans), herbs and spices (hibiscus, cinnamon, dried Mexican oregano), and xoconostle:
Rancho Gordo (RanchoGordo.com)

Calcium hydroxide (slaked lime), kappa carrageenan:
Modernist Pantry (ModernistPantry.com)

Chamomile anise tea, cinnamon, oregano, cumin, coriander, allspice, bay leaf, pepitas, chile pequin:
Tadin Herb & Tea (Tadin.com)

Chiles (árbol, ancho, guajillo, meco, morta, mulato, pasilla), cinnamon, dried epazote, hibiscus, Mexican oregano:
1400s Spices (1400sSpices.com)

Chile chilhuacle rojo and chile chilhuacle negro:
Spice Trekkers (SpiceTrekkers.com)

Dried hoja santa:
Evergreen Herbs (EGHerbs.com)

Epazote, fresh fava beans, jicama, nopales, tomatillos, and tamarind:
Melissa's Produce (Melissas.com)

Mexican clay pot, Mexican hot chocolate, molcajete, comal, and molinillo:
Hernán (HernanMexico.com)

Soy curls:
Butler Foods (ButlerFoods.com)

BIBLIOGRAPHY

Alvarez, Linda. *Food Is Power. Food Empowerment Project.* https://foodispower.org/our-food-choices/colonization-food-and-the-practice-of-eating/.

Cocina Prehispánica Recetario. Revista Arqueología Mexicana 12. Editorial Raices, S.A. de C.V. 2002.

Cortés, Hernán. *Second Letter of Hernan Cortes, 1485–1547.* World Digital Library.

Escuela de Gastronomía Mexicana. *Diplomado de Historia de la Gastronomía Mexicana.* January 2022. https://www.cocinaidentidad.com.mx/diplomado-historia-gastronomia-mexicana.

Gavira, Jorge. *Masa.* Chronicle Books. 2022.

Gerson, Fany. *My Sweet Mexico.* Ten Speed Press. 2010.

Gironella De'Angeli, Alicia, and Jorge De'Angeli. *Gran Larousse de la Cocina Mexicana.* Ediciones Larousse S.A. de C.V. 1994.

López Sanchez, Cecilia Ofir. *México, Tierra de Hongos.* Instituto Nacional de Los Pueblos Indígenas. 2022.

Los Tamales en Mexico Panorama Visual. Revista Arqueología Mexicana 76. Editorial Raices, S.A. de C.V. 2017.

Muñoz Zurita, Ricardo. *Larousse Diccionario Enciclopédico de la Gastronomía Mexicana.* Ediciones Larousse S.A. de C.V. 2012.

Neruda, Pablo. *Memoirs.* Penguin Group. 1978.

Sahagún, Fray Bernardino de. *General History of the Things of New Spain.* 1577.

Soustelle, Jacques. *La Vida Cotidiana de los Aztecas en Visperas de la Conquista.* Fondo de la Cultura Económica. 1997.

Sterling, David, and Mario Canul. *Recipes from the Markets of Mexico.* University of Texas Press, Austin. 2019.

Zizumbo-Villarreal, D., A. Flores-Silva, and P. Colunga-GarcíaMarí. "The Food System During the Formative Period in West Mesoamerica." *Economic Botany* 68, no. 1: 67–84. 2014.

THANK YOU!

This book is for you, the readers of Dora's Table! It was only possible because you have been making my recipes, watching my videos, and showing me your unending support since 2015. I hope I can make you proud.

To Thomas Stone. Thank you for your support, encouragement, and trust, and for putting a stop to my self-doubt and perfectionism when I needed it the most.

To my beautiful children, Tomasito, Karina, and Pio. Thank you for always being my source of inspiration, my reason for being, and for eating all of my food, even when you didn't want to. (At one point they asked me to please stop making tamales, because just the thought of eating another one was too much to bear.) A special thank-you to Tomasito, who was my official dishwasher throughout this process.

To my family, my mom, dad, sisters, nieces, and nephews, who cheered me on through this whole process, and never let me forget that I am a chingona and I can do anything. A special thank-you to my sister Alejandra Ramirez and Darryl Galman, who watched my kids countless times while I cooked and traveled. Mamá y papá, gracias por todo el amor incondicional, todo el apoyo, y por enseñarme que todo se puede cogida de la mano de Dios.

To Christie Phillips, my California friend who hounded me until I watched the documentary *Forks Over Knives*, which led me to veganism. To Jackie Sobon from the blog Vegan Yack Attack for introducing me to my agent, Marilyn Allen.

To my agent, Marilyn Allen, who took a chance on me almost immediately. Thank you for making this possible. To my wonderful editor, Renee Sedliar, thank you for believing in me from the start and helping me stay true to my vision. To the team at Balance and the talented design team, Cisca Schreefel, Karen Wise, Amanda Kain, and Shubhani Sarkar, for bringing my vision to life.

To Felipe Barrera and Amy Rushing at the UTSA Special Collections Library, for granting me access to the beautiful collection of Mexican cookbooks so I could do my research, and for your unending support. To the Escuela de Gastronomía Mexicana in Mexico City for always being willing to share their knowledge with me.

To Liliana Palma Santos, Florinda Vásquez Palma, Evangelina Aquino Luis, Francisca Maurilio Godinez, Isabel Lazo Chavez, Ariadna Pinacho Cruz, Silvia Diaz, and Bruno Cocom, the cocinero and cocineras tradicionales who were generous with their time and shared their ancestral knowledge to bring the Indigenous kitchen into our homes.

311

This book would not be possible without the army of recipe testers spanning from Costa Rica all the way to Australia, who scoured the internet and their towns for dried chiles, herbs, and spices. Thank you for all your hard work—you made this book 100 times better! A special thanks to Tasenka Kushner, Joanne McNeal, Barbara Ann Romano, Natalia Vanegas, and Vanessa Andrade, who between them tested more than thirty recipes each.

To Dianne Jacob: Dianne, I did it! Thank you for asking all the hard questions and helping me structure my vision into an excellent proposal. To Toni Okamoto, thank you for being my mentor throughout this process and taking the time to help me and answer all my questions.

To my culinary mentors: Temple Turner, who was the first woman chef I ever worked for and showed me that being a woman in the kitchen was my strength, not my weakness. Dominique Filoni, who told me as a young cook that I needed to find the thing that was truly mine and go for it. It took me a while, Dom, but I found it!

Gracias, Virgencita, por nunca dejarme sola y gracias a ti, Señor, por tu fidelidad y tu amor.

COMIDA CASERA RECIPE TESTERS

Abigail Evans
Allan Churchmack
Allison Reed
Amelia Villa
Angela Moreno
Angela Ramsammy
Angelica Macklin
Angilique Falcon
Barbara Ann Romano
Bariann Gonzales
Brenda Quezada
Candice Cadena
Carlene Van Patten
Christina Gary
Cindy Uthus
Dan Randall
Dawn Waibel
Debra Wendell-Evans
Diana Campos
Dr. Diane Martin
Emily Walker
Enrique Edward Lozano
Ericka Perez
Erin Nixon
Gayle Dickerson
Genesis Villalobos
Grace Arce
Hannah Layland
Helen Sewell
Hilda Pena-Alfaro
Holly Tomren
Jackeline Martinez
Jackie Tatelman
Janna Kay Whitley
Jen Panhorst
Jennie Speegle
Jennifer D. Legate
Jennifer Spivey
Jimmy Warrick
Joanna Ramirez
Joanne McNeal
Julie Willis
Karen L. Maas
Karina Contreras

Arellano
Kate Siemens
Katelynn Jensen
Kelly McLaughlin
Laura Patton
Laura Posner
Lisa Zepeda
Lora Liebich
Lorena Natividad
Lori Henson
Lupe Díaz Lara
Mackenzie Morison
Marian Villaseñor
Maya Acosta
Megan King
Melissa Johnson
Michelle Green
Monica Dejesus
Natalia Vanegas
Natalie Weston
Nicole Boney Sharpe
Paige Truax
Rebecca Amabisca
Rebecca Bolduc
Rebecca L. Kirsch
Ruth A. Rehak
Ruth Leach-Stevens
Sandra Maskell
Savannah Devinee Lomeli
Stephanie Cadena
Stephanie Pone
Susannah Dickman
Suzanne Watson
Tammy Sanchez McCormick
Tasenka Kushner
Terri-Gayl Hoshell
Tiffany Wilkerson
Traci Savage Gunn
Valerie Carrillo
Valerie Corry
Vanessa Andrade
Victoria Maloney

INDEX